PRISON GROWTH AND ECONOMIC IMPACT

LAW, CRIME AND LAW ENFORCEMENT

Additional books in this series can be found on Nova's website
under the Series tab.

Additional E-books in this series can be found on Nova's website
under the E-book tab.

LAW, CRIME AND LAW ENFORCEMENT

PRISON GROWTH AND ECONOMIC IMPACT

LEWIS C. SAWYER
EDITOR

Nova Science Publishers, Inc.
New York

LIBRARY OF CONGRESS CATALOGING-IN-PUBLICATION DATA

Prison growth and economic impact / editor, Lewis C. Sawyer.
     p. cm.
  Includes index.
  ISBN 978-1-61728-864-7 (hbk.)
  1. Imprisonment--Economic aspects--United States. 2. Prisons--Economic aspects--United States. 3. Corrections--Economic aspects--United States. 4. Criminal justice, Administration of--Economic aspects--United States. I. Sawyer, Lewis C.
  HV9471.P745 2009
  338.4'7365973--dc22

                                                                                2010025444

Published by Nova Science Publishers, Inc. † *New York*

CONTENTS

Preface   vii

Chapter 1   Economic Impacts of Prison Growth   1
Suzanne M. Kirchhoff

Chapter 2   Prisoners in 2008: Bureau of Justice Statistics   35
United States Department of Justice

Chapter 3   Prison Construction: Clear Communication on the Accuracy of Cost
Estimates and Project Changes is Needed   85
United States Government Accountability Office

Chapter 4   Cost of Prisons: Bureau of Prisons Needs Better Data to Assess
Alternatives for Acquiring Low and Minimum Security Facilities   107
United States Government Accountability Office

Chapter 5   Cost, Performance Studies Look at Prison Privatization   133
Gerry Gaes

Index   139

PREFACE

The U.S. prison system has exploded in size and economic importance during the past three decades, due to a variety of factors including mandatory sentencing laws and tougher drug enforcement efforts. At the end of 2008, more than 2.3 million adults were in local, state, or federal custody, according to the U.S. Department of Justice. More than 5 million more were on probation or parole. Overall, one in every 31 adults was under the authority of the correctional system in 2007. The record U.S. prison population is creating pressures on the federal and state governments as spending on corrections claims a larger share of tax dollars, potentially crowding public investment in other areas. This book explores U.S. prison growth and its economic impacts.

Chapter 1 - The U.S. corrections system has gone through an unprecedented expansion during the last few decades, with a more than 400% jump in the prison population and a corresponding boom in prison construction. At the end of 2008, 2.3 million adults were in state, local, or federal custody, with another 5.1 million on probation or parole. Of that total, 9% were in federal custody. Globally, the United States has 5% of the world's population but 25% of its prisoners. Prison growth has been fueled by tough drug enforcement, stringent sentencing laws, and high rates of recidivism—the re-arrest, re-conviction, or re-incarceration of an ex-offender.

The historic, sustained rise in incarceration has broad implications, not just for the criminal justice system, but for the larger economy. About 770,000 people worked in the corrections sector in 2008. The U.S. Labor Department expects the number of guards, supervisors, and other staff to grow by 9% between 2008 and 2018, while the number of probation and parole officers is to increase by 16%. In addition to those working directly in institutions, many more jobs are tied to a multi-billion dollar private industry that constructs, finances, equips, and provides health care, education, food, rehabilitation and other services to prisons and jails. By comparison, in 2008 there were 880,000 workers in the entire U.S. auto manufacturing sector. Private prison companies have bounced back from financial troubles in the late 1 990s, buoyed in part by growing federal contracts. Nearly all new U.S. prisons opened from 2000-2005 were private. Private prisons housed 8% of U.S. inmates in 2008, including more than 16% of federal prisoners.

The growth of the corrections sector has other impacts. A number of rural areas have chosen to tie their economies to prisons, viewing the institutions as recession-proof development engines. Though many local officials cite benefits, broader research suggests that prisons may not generate the nature and scale of benefits municipalities anticipate or may even slow growth in some localities. Record incarceration rates can have longer-term economic impacts by contributing to increased income inequality and more concentrated poverty. The problems are exacerbated by the fact that African Americans and Hispanics are far more likely than whites to be incarcerated. The large prison population also may be affecting distribution of federal dollars. The U.S. Census counts individuals where they reside. Some regions may record a significant population increase due to new prisons, meaning they garner more aid under federal population-based formulas.

The corrections sector is in stress as states seek to reduce prison populations and rein in costs. The efforts have been underway for several years, but have intensified as the recession that began at the end of 2007 has wrought havoc on state budgets. At least 26 states cut corrections spending for FY2010. California Gov. Arnold Schwarzenegger has suggested amending that state's constitution to ensure that spending on prisons cannot exceed spending on higher education. Arizona is preparing to sell prison facilities to private firms. It remains to be seen whether private companies will prosper from state efforts, or incur losses if inmate populations level out or decline. Congress is involved in the debate via federal contracts with private prisons, proposed legislation to create a task force on the prison system, increased funding to reduce recidivism, a proposed bill to allow collective bargaining for public sector correctional workers, proposals to alter rules for the 2010 Census count, and rural development efforts. Legislation introduced in the 111th Congress includes S. 2772, S. 714, S. 1611, H.R. 4080, H.R. 413, and H.R. 2450.

Chapter 2 - At yearend 2008, federal and state correctional authorities had jurisdiction over 1,610,446 prisoners (**figure 1**). *Jurisdiction* refers to the legal authority over a prisoner, regardless of where the prisoner is held.

Chapter 3 - The federal Bureau of Prisons (BOP) is responsible for the custody and care of more than 201,000 federal offenders. To provide housing for the federal prison population, BOP manages the construction and maintenance of its prison facilities and oversees contract facilities. GAO was asked to look into recent increases in estimated costs for Federal Correctional Institution (FCI) construction projects located in Mendota, CA; Berlin, NH; and McDowell, WV, which have led to almost $278 million or 62 percent more being provided in funding than initially estimated. This chapter addresses (1) the reasons for the changes to the estimated costs and (2) the actions BOP has taken—or plans to take—to control future cost increases and delays. GAO reviewed and analyzed BOP's fiscal years 2001 to 2009 budget documents, files for these three projects, and project management guidance. GAO also reviewed government and industry guidance on project management and met with BOP officials.

Chapter 4 - Over the last 10 years, the cost to confine federal Bureau of Prison (BOP) inmates in non-BOP facilities has nearly tripled from about $250 million in fiscal year 1996 to about $700 million in fiscal year 2006. Proponents of using contractors to operate prisons claim it can save money; others question whether contracting is a cost-effective alternative. In response to Conference Report 109-272, accompanying Pub. L. No. 109-108 (2005), this chapter discusses the feasibility and implications of comparing the costs for confining federal inmates in low and minimum security BOP facilities with those managed by private firms for BOP. GAO reviewed available data on a selection of 34 low and minimum security facilities; related laws, regulations, and documents; and interviewed BOP and contract officials.

Chapter 5 - Seven percent of the 1.5 million prisoners in the United States are held in privately operated prisons, according to the most recent survey of prisons published by the

Bureau of Justice Statistics.[1] At midyear 2006, there were 84,867 State inmates and 27,108 Federal inmates in privately operated prisons—a 10-percent increase over the previous year.

The overall percentage of adults in private prisons is relatively small, but the actual impact for some States may be much greater. An article in *The New Mexican,* for example, suggested that New Mexico was overpaying millions of dollars to private providers that were housing more than 40 percent of the State's inmate population.[2]

Thus, it is vital that policymakers have the best possible cost and quality information when they are making decisions regarding privatizing prisons in their jurisdiction. But what criteria should prison administrators and policymakers use when making cost and quality evaluations?

To help answer these questions, the National Institute of Justice (NIJ) assembled researchers, prison officials, private service providers, and proponents and opponents of prison privatization on March 28, 2007, to discuss this complicated and often controversial issue. At the core of the meeting was a rare occurrence: two cost and performance analyses of the same four prisons— one privately operated and three publicly operated—with different findings. The two reports are referred to in this article as the "Taft studies."[3]

One of the Taft studies was conducted by Doug McDonald, Ph.D., principal associate with Abt Associates Inc. (referred to as the "Abt report").[4] The other study, funded by the Bureau of Prisons (BOP), had two components: a performance or quality analysis conducted by Scott Camp, Ph.D., a senior research analyst in BOP's Office of Research and Evaluation,[5] and a cost analysis conducted by Julianne Nelson, Ph.D., an economist with the Center for Naval Analyses (referred to collectively as the "BOP report").[6]

The Taft studies offer the research and public policy communities a rare opportunity to consider the different approaches that were used, why the results were different, and how this can inform not only the prison privatization debate, but in many ways, the government outsourcing, or privatization, issue in general.

In: Prison Growth and Economic Impact
Editor: Lewis C. Sawyer

ISBN: 978-1-61728-864-7
© 2010 Nova Science Publishers, Inc.

Chapter 1

ECONOMIC IMPACTS OF PRISON GROWTH*

Suzanne M. Kirchhoff

SUMMARY

The U.S. corrections system has gone through an unprecedented expansion during the last few decades, with a more than 400% jump in the prison population and a corresponding boom in prison construction. At the end of 2008, 2.3 million adults were in state, local, or federal custody, with another 5.1 million on probation or parole. Of that total, 9% were in federal custody. Globally, the United States has 5% of the world's population but 25% of its prisoners. Prison growth has been fueled by tough drug enforcement, stringent sentencing laws, and high rates of recidivism—the re-arrest, re-conviction, or re-incarceration of an ex-offender.

The historic, sustained rise in incarceration has broad implications, not just for the criminal justice system, but for the larger economy. About 770,000 people worked in the corrections sector in 2008. The U.S. Labor Department expects the number of guards, supervisors, and other staff to grow by 9% between 2008 and 2018, while the number of probation and parole officers is to increase by 16%. In addition to those working directly in institutions, many more jobs are tied to a multi-billion dollar private industry that constructs, finances, equips, and provides health care, education, food, rehabilitation and other services to prisons and jails. By comparison, in 2008 there were 880,000 workers in the entire U.S. auto manufacturing sector. Private prison companies have bounced back from financial troubles in the late 1 990s, buoyed in part by growing federal contracts. Nearly all new U.S. prisons opened from 2000-2005 were private. Private prisons housed 8% of U.S. inmates in 2008, including more than 16% of federal prisoners.

The growth of the corrections sector has other impacts. A number of rural areas have chosen to tie their economies to prisons, viewing the institutions as recession-proof development engines. Though many local officials cite benefits, broader research suggests

---

* This is an edited, reformatted and augmented version of a CRS Report for Congress publication dated April 2010.

that prisons may not generate the nature and scale of benefits municipalities anticipate or may even slow growth in some localities. Record incarceration rates can have longer-term economic impacts by contributing to increased income inequality and more concentrated poverty. The problems are exacerbated by the fact that African Americans and Hispanics are far more likely than whites to be incarcerated. The large prison population also may be affecting distribution of federal dollars. The U.S. Census counts individuals where they reside. Some regions may record a significant population increase due to new prisons, meaning they garner more aid under federal population-based formulas.

The corrections sector is in stress as states seek to reduce prison populations and rein in costs. The efforts have been underway for several years, but have intensified as the recession that began at the end of 2007 has wrought havoc on state budgets. At least 26 states cut corrections spending for FY2010. California Gov. Arnold Schwarzenegger has suggested amending that state's constitution to ensure that spending on prisons cannot exceed spending on higher education. Arizona is preparing to sell prison facilities to private firms. It remains to be seen whether private companies will prosper from state efforts, or incur losses if inmate populations level out or decline. Congress is involved in the debate via federal contracts with private prisons, proposed legislation to create a task force on the prison system, increased funding to reduce recidivism, a proposed bill to allow collective bargaining for public sector correctional workers, proposals to alter rules for the 2010 Census count, and rural development efforts. Legislation introduced in the 111th Congress includes S. 2772, S. 714, S. 1611, H.R. 4080, H.R. 413, and H.R. 2450. This chapter will not be updated.

CORRECTIONS A RISING CONCERN

The U.S. prison system has exploded in size and economic importance during the past three decades, due to a variety of factors including mandatory sentencing laws and tougher drug enforcement efforts. At the end of 2008, more than 2.3 million adults were in local, state, or federal custody, according to the U.S. Department of Justice.[1] More than 5 million more were on probation or parole.[2] Overall, one in every 31 U.S. adults was under the authority of the correctional system in 2007. Globally, the United States has the highest per capita incarceration rate of 218 countries and territories.[3]

The record U.S. prison population is creating pressures on the federal and state governments as spending on corrections claims a larger share of tax dollars, potentially crowding out public investment in other areas. There is growing concern among policymakers across the political spectrum that corrections policy may have reached a point of diminishing returns. Correctional spending has continued rising, even though the crime rate has declined or stabilized since the early 1990s.[4] High rates of recidivism—ex-offenders coming back into the corrections sector for new offenses or violations of probation or parole—indicate that the system may not be effective as desired in deterring or rehabilitating offenders.[5] Responding to these concerns, Congress is considering a variety of actions to alter corrections policy. While state and local governments fund and administer the bulk of corrections-related activity, the federal role is significant. For example, federal contracts are the main source of funding for the private companies. Nearly 17% of federal prisoners are housed in private prisons.[6]

During the 111th Congress, lawmakers have introduced legislation to reduce the size and fiscal impact of the corrections system and to increase scrutiny of prison operators. One measure, S. 2772 (companion bill H.R. 4080), would create a grant program to help states and localities reduce spending on corrections. Another, S. 714, would create a National Criminal Justice Commission to carry out a comprehensive review of the criminal justice system. The FY2010 omnibus spending bill (P.L. 111-117) included $100 million, a $75 million increase from FY2009, for programs authorized by the Second Chance Act that focus on reducing recidivism by supporting a variety of state, local, and tribal offender re-entry programs.

Other congressional initiatives include H.R. 413 and S. 1611 to allow public safety officers to engage in collective bargaining, and H.R. 2450, to make non-federal prisons and private facilities housing federal prisoners comply with the same public disclosure rules as other federal institutions. The Senate Judiciary Committee is reviewing mandatory sentencing laws for some drug-related crimes. Congress is also involved in oversight and funding of the expanding federal prison system.

A number of states are trying to reduce their prison populations.[7] The efforts have been underway for several years, but have accelerated during the recession, which began in 2007 and has reduced tax revenues and forced governors and legislators to cut spending to balance their budgets. States are laying off corrections workers, releasing nonviolent prisoners, closing facilities, changing sentencing laws and considering selling prisons to private firms. More than 26 states reduced their corrections budgets for the 2010 fiscal year; additional cuts are expected for FY2011.[8]

In addition, the Congressional Black Caucus is part of a coalition that has pushed for change in U.S. Census policy. The CBC contends that the practice of counting inmates as residents of the area where they are incarcerated, rather than where they usually reside, drains federal funds that are distributed under population formulas based on Census data from needy urban areas.[9]

This chapter provides an economic overview of the correctional sector as background for the unfolding debate over spending and other policies. It begins with information on the growth in prison populations in public and in private prisons. It also briefly explores the economic impacts of prison location. It is not intended a study of the effectiveness of sentencing and other laws, nor of evolving polices aimed at reducing recidivism and prison populations.[10]

Corrections Sector

The corrections system has expanded during the past three decades into a nationwide network of businesses and workers whose livelihoods are tied to the prison system.[11] The nation spent $68.7 billion on corrections in 2006, a 660% increase from 1982.[12] State governments, on average, spend about 7% of their general fund revenues on incarceration.[13] During the past three decades correctional spending has risen nearly twice as fast as state spending on education, health care, and social service programs.[14] In some states, for example California, the prison system now consumes a larger share of general revenues (10%) than higher education (7%).[15]

About 770,000 people work in U.S. prisons and jails and other institutions, and many additional workers are employed by companies that provide supplies and services to the corrections sector. States have vastly increased their prison capacity in the past 30 years. The South has the highest per-capita imprisonment rate, followed by the West, Midwest, and the

Northeast. States with the largest corrections systems include Texas, Pennsylvania, Florida, California and New York. [16] (**See Figure 1.**)

State and federal correctional functions are often contracted out to a network of private firms that design, build, and manage prisons, arrange financing, and provide health care, transportation, education, and other services. States and the federal officials are becoming more dependent on a small group of companies that build and manage private prisons as they search for potential cost efficiencies. Nationally, more than 8% of all prisoners are now in private institutions. In some states, however, more than 30% of inmates are in for-profit prisons.[17] The federal government has nearly 17% of its inmates and detainees in private facilities. Underscoring the importance of these corporations, nearly all new U.S. prisons opened between 2000 and 2005 were developed by private companies.[18]

Some major investors are anticipating that private industry will assume an even larger role as state and federal officials explore potential cost savings from contracting out more correctional functions.[19] California and Arizona, for example, are debating selling prisons and hiring private firms to provide services, such as inmate health care.[20] But if state legislatures make major changes in drug laws or other policies that reduce the number of individuals going to prison or the length of prison sentences, these private firms could face a potential reduction in profits. The federal government or state officials could experience problems if a private prison company were to face financial distress.

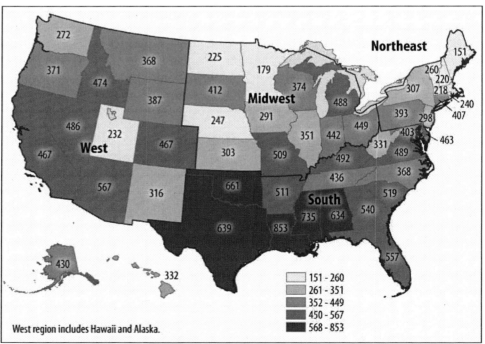

Source: Map prepared by CRS based on DOJ, Bureau of Justice Statistics, *Prisoners in 2008,* Appendix Table 10.

Notes: The imprisonment rate is the number of inmates sentenced to more than one year per 100,000 U.S. residents.

Figure 1. Imprisonment Rates, by State
Prison population per 100,000 residents

Prison populations in a number of states are beginning to stabilize, according to recent data, though the federal system continues to expand. The number of immigrants held by the federal government, for example, rose from 19,515 in 2000 to 34,161 at the end of 2008.[21] President Obama's FY2011 budget calls for a 9% increase from FY2010 in federal funding for detention, predicated on an increased prison population.[22] Federal contracts are now the largest source of revenue for several of the nation's major private prison firms, including the Corrections Corporation of America and the GEO Group.

The prison expansion has other economic impacts. Many rural towns and counties have vied for prisons and the jobs they create, offering financial incentives or even floating bonds to build "speculative" prisons.[23] Recent research questions whether prisons deliver promised economic benefits, and whether some towns have bet their local economies on what may be a corrections bubble that is not sustainable, with failed prison developments ending up as "half-empty white elephants marooned on the American landscape."[24]

While reductions in crime have benefits, academics are questioning whether the system has grown so big, and is imprisoning so many nonviolent offenders, that it has reached a point of diminishing returns.[25] The incarceration rate has continued to increase even though crime rates have leveled off. Research indicates that individuals who serve prison time have lower lifetime earnings and are far less likely to move out of poverty than their peers who do not go to prison.[26] A record 1.7 million children under age 18 now have an imprisoned parent, according to the U.S. Department of Justice. Many incarcerated parents previously were main breadwinners, and the instability and increased poverty resulting from their imprisonment is leading some states to look for ways to cushion the impacts on families.[27]

U.S. CORRECTIONS SYSTEM

The U.S. prison system has gone through a number of changes during its history, as different theories about punishment and rehabilitation moved to the fore or faded. Business interests have played a role in the U.S. justice system since its earliest days, when entrepreneurs arranged to transport convicted felons from Europe to the colonies to work as indentured servants.[28] Initially prison was not the preferred form of punishment in Colonial America. Flogging, public humiliation, and banishment were common penalties, and execution was imposed for a wide range of offenses.[29] After the Revolutionary War, the nation began experimenting with different approaches, and by 1820 most states had limited capital punishment to the most serious offenses. Incarceration became the strategy for rehabilitation and reform, not just retribution. [30]

The first U.S. state prison was established in Philadelphia in 1790. Other prisons followed, with an emphasis on rehabilitation through solitary confinement, daily work and discipline.[31] The nation was considered a world leader in corrections policy, a point underscored by Alexis De Tocqueville's famous 1831 visit to the United States, originally conceived to study the prison system. The idea that enlightened prison management could bring about individual, as well as broader social change, began to break down around the time of the Civil War as institutions became overcrowded, more prisoners were sentenced for violent crimes, and immigrants, a focus of discrimination, became a growing share of the prison population. [32] During Reconstruction, the Convict Lease System was developed.

Inmates were leased to private companies to build railroads and roads, and for mining, logging, and other labor. States were paid a fee by lessees who agreed to feed, clothe, and house the prisoners. Conditions were often brutal, with high mortality rates.[33]

The New York Prison Society in 1867 commissioned what became an influential *Report on the Prisons and Reformatories of the United States and Canada.* The report advocated ending widespread forms of physical punishment and moving away from fixed or mandatory sentences. New York's Elmira Reformatory became a laboratory for such theories, with indeterminate sentencing, parole, and educational programs. The late 1 800s saw the rise of the federal prison system. Construction of the first federal prison, at Leavenworth, KS, began in 1897.[34] After a series of scandals including torture, death and gross mistreatment of predominately African American prisoners, states in the 1920s moved to abolish the convict lease system, which had become particularly entrenched in the South.[35]

In 1965, President Lyndon Johnson, fresh off a presidential campaign in which he was attacked as soft on crime, commissioned a study on the U.S. corrections system. The 1967 report of the President's Commission on Law Enforcement and the Administration of Justice recommended more federal aid to state and local governments.[36] In 1968, Congress passed the Omnibus Crime Control and Safe Streets Act (P.L. 90-351) that included grants to state and local governments for training law enforcement personnel, prison construction, and education. The 1960s saw the rise of the prisoners' rights movement as prisoners won more protections via the courts.

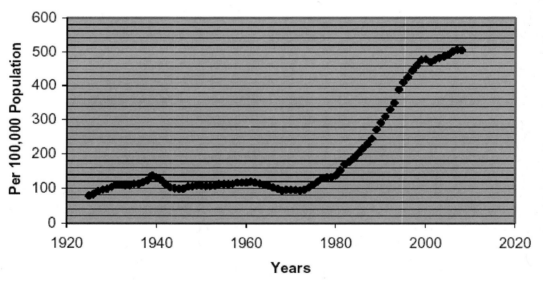

Source: Sabol, William J., Heather C. West, and Matthew Cooper, "Prisoners in 2008," *Bureau of Justice Statistics Bulletin*, December 2009, and Bureau of Justice Statistics, "State and Federal Prisoners 1925-1985," Washington, DC: Bureau of Justice Statistics, 1986.

Notes: Chart details number or prisoners sentenced to state and federal correctional institutions per 1 00,000 of U.S. residents. Data from 1971 onward include adults and youthful offenders serving terms of more than one year.

Figure 2. U.S. Imprisonment Rate, 1925-2008
Number of prisoners per 100,000 residents

PRISONER BOOM

The U.S. prison population remained relatively stable through many of these policy changes. Imprisonment rates even declined in some periods, including during wars when large numbers of men were drafted.[37] (See **Figure 2**.) In 1925, there were fewer than 100,000 inmates in state and federal prisons. By 1975, the figure had grown to about 241,000.[38] Because the nation's population rose during that period, the imprisonment rate—a measure of the number of prisoners relative to the general population—remained stable at about 100 prisoners per 100,000 people.[39]

The prison population began to climb in the late 1970s as states and the federal government cracked down on crime. One turning point was New York State's 1973 imposition of mandatory sentencing laws for drug offenses, under the administration of Gov. Nelson Rockefeller.[40] Other states followed. Initiatives included mandatory sentences for repeat armed career criminals. Congress, in the Sentencing Reform Act of 1984 (18 U.S.C. 3651), repealed federal courts' authority to suspend criminal sentences and made other changes.[41] In 1994, California voters and legislators approved Proposition 184, the so-called Three Strikes Law. Among other things, the law set a minimum sentence of 25 years to life for three-time offenders with prior serious or violent felony convictions.[42]

As this wave of laws took effect, the imprisonment rate—based on the number of adults sentenced to terms of more than one year—jumped from 133 per 100,000 in 1979 to 504 per 100,000 at the end of 2008.[43](See **Figure 2**.) More than 2.3 million people were in the custody of state or federal prisons and local jails at the end of 2008, with another 5 million on probation or parole.[44] The United States, with 5% of the world's population, had about a quarter of all prisoners in 2006.[45]

Taxpayers spent about $68.7 billion in 2008 to feed, clothe, and provide medical care to prisoners in county jails, state and federal prisons and facilities housing legal and illegal aliens facing possible deportation.[46] From 1982 to 2002, state and federal spending on corrections, not adjusted for inflation, rose by 423%, from $40 to $209 per U.S. resident.[47] Corrections spending, as a share of state budgets, rose faster than health care, education, and natural resources spending from 1986 to 2001.[48] The average cost of housing a prisoner for a year was about $24,000 in 2005, though rates vary from state to state.[49]

The increase in the incarceration rate is not due just to the number of arrests, but also because people are staying in prison for longer periods of time under mandatory sentencing laws and are entering prison due to violations in probation or parole.[50] To get a sense of how the length of a sentence affects the prison population, a one-month reduction in the average length of stay of prisoners would reduce the national prison population by about 50,000.[51]

Mandatory sentencing is also contributing to a bulge in the number of older inmates. More than 74,000 people age 55 or older were incarcerated at the end of 2008, with about 16,000 over the age of 65.[52] Research suggests that prisoners develop health problems at an earlier age than the general population and older prisoners are more expensive than younger inmates. In Ohio, for example, the cost for incarcerating older prisoners in 2006 was $81 per day, compared to $69 for the general prison population.[53] Average costs per prisoner were rising at a much faster rate for older inmates. Ohio has a special facility just for older offenders needing acute or long-term care.

Table 1. Prisoners under State and Federal Jurisdiction by Sentence Length, Race, and Gender, 2008

	Total	Male	Female
Prisoners by Sentence Length			
Total under jurisdiction	1,610,446	1,495,594	114,852
Sentenced to over 1 year	1,540,036	1,434,784	105,252
Estimated prisoners by Race			
White	591,900	562,800	29,100
Black	528,200	477,500	50,700
Hispanic	313,100	295,800	17,300

Source: Sabol, William J., Heather C. West, and Matthew Cooper, "Prisoners in 2008," *Bureau of Justice Statistics Bulletin*, December 2009. Table 1.

Note: Race data is based on prisoners sentenced to more than one year. Excludes American Indians, Alaska Natives, Asians, native Hawaiians, other Pacific Islanders and persons identifying two or more races.

Incarceration Trends

There are indications that the state prison population is beginning to stabilize, though wide differences remain from area to area. The federal prison system continues to expand, however.

The U.S. Department of Justice reported a 0.8% annual rise in the prison population in 2008—the smallest in eight years. The average rate of increase from 2000 to 2008 (1.8%) was less than a third of the rate of the previous decade (6.5%).[54] Not only was there a decrease in the number of prison admissions, there was an increase in the number of individuals released, particularly in states that have initiatives to reduce recidivism rates and prison populations.

In 28 states there was a decline in imprisonment rates in 2008, while 20 had increases and two states were flat. The largest decreases were in Massachusetts, Texas, Nevada, Wisconsin and Georgia.[55] Prison populations increased fastest in Pennsylvania, Florida, Alabama, Indiana, Arizona and Tennessee. The South has the highest per-capita imprisonment rate, followed by the West, Midwest and Northeast.

Though state prison populations appear to be leveling, the Federal Bureau of Prisons (BOP) is now operating at well over capacity and estimates that its inmate population will increase during the next several years.[56] The federal prison population, which is 215,000 in FY2010, is forecast to grow by 7,000 by the end of FY2011. President Obama's proposed FY2011 budget includes funds to fill 1,200 prison staffing positions, create additional positions and activate new facilities.[57] Further, the number of individuals held by U.S. Immigration and Customs Enforcement (ICE) increased 12.3% from 2007 to 2008, compared to a 6.6% average growth rate from 2000 to 2007.[58] There were 34,161 immigrants in detention at the end of 2008, compared to 19,515 in 2000. Immigrants are housed in about 250 state, local, and federal prisons and jails and in 41 special ICE facilities.

Kevin Campbell, a senior research analyst for Avondale Partners, LLC, in Nashville, tracks the corrections sector. He notes that the growth of the prison population has slowed significantly. But even a roughly 2% increase in the prison/detention population represents another 40,000 inmates. Campbell estimates that a 1-2% increase in the prison population comes out to another $2.6 billion in spending annually.[59] Campbell also notes the difficulty of achieving deep cuts in prison populations. Early parole policies have backfired in states like Connecticut and Washington after recently released prisoners committed violent crimes when back on the streets.

PRISON EMPLOYMENT

The corrections sector is a large and growing part of the labor force. According to the Census Bureau, more than 770,000 people worked in the U.S. correctional industry in 2008.[60] The U.S. Department of Labor, in its *2010-11 Occupational Outlook Handbook*, estimates there were about 620,000 guards, probation officers, prison supervisors and court bailiffs in 2008.[61]

The Labor Department forecasts a 9% rise in the number of corrections officers and supervisors from 2008 to 2018, compared to an overall 10% rise in the population and workforce.[62] The Labor Department predicts, however, that the number of probation and parole specialists could grow by 19% from 2008 to 2018, faster than the average for all occupations.

> There may be more emphasis in many States on rehabilitation and alternate forms of punishment, such as probation, that will spur demand for probation and parole officers and correctional treatment specialists. Additionally, there will be a need for parole officers to supervise the large number of currently incarcerated people when they are released from prison.[63]

By way of comparison, there were 880,000 workers in the entire U.S. automobile manufacturing industry in 2008.[64]

The median annual salary for U.S. prison guards and jailors was $38,380 in May 2008. Wages are significantly higher for workers in government-run prisons than for those in facilities managed by private prison companies. Federal correctional workers had median wages of $50,830, state workers earned $38,850, local government employees $37,510, and employees at private prison companies $28,900.[65] Staffing costs are the largest share of correctional budgets, accounting for as much as 75-80% of annual costs.[66]

In some states, including those with strong unions or significant overtime hours due to staff shortages, wages can be higher. The California Department of Corrections and Rehabilitation website notes that correctional officers can earn more than $73,000 a year, along with a benefits and retirement package. [67]

Training and educational requirements are generally most stringent in federal correctional facilities. The Federal Bureau of Prisons calls for entry-level correctional officers to have at least a bachelor's degree or three years of full-time experience in a related field. [68] Some state and local entities require at least a high school diploma or equivalent and may specify college credit for some positions. Workers are normally required to undergo additional, specialized training after they are hired.

Table 2. Median Wages and Employment of Correctional Workers, 2008-2018

Category of Correctional Worker	Median Wages	Number of Workers	Projected Employment 2018	2008-2018 Employment Change
Correctional Officers/Jailers	$38,380	454,500	497,500	9%
Supervisors/managers	$57,380	43,500	47,200	9%
Bailiffs	$37,820	20,200	21,900	8%
Probation Officers and Case Workers	$45,910	103,400	123,300	19%

Source: U.S. Department of Labor, Bureau of Labor Statistics, *2010-11 Occupational Outlook Handbook.*

A 2008 study published in *Corrections Today* magazine noted high turnover in the correctional sector and difficulty recruiting qualified personnel.[69] The study, conducted for the American Correctional Association (an industry trade group), predicted that the corrections sector would be second to the health care profession in fields most affected by a shortage of workers in coming years. It also noted that the correctional workforce was predominately white and male, at a time when women and minorities make up a larger share of the overall labor force. About 10% of correctional workers held a bachelor's degree or higher, with slightly more than a third having some college education.

> Study respondents noted that inadequate pay and benefits, burdensome hours and shift work, a shortage of qualified applicants, and undesirable location of correctional facilities are factors that render recruiting difficult.[70]

Unions

Many prison employees have joined unions to negotiate compensation, pension and health care benefits, and other issues. The American Federation of State, County and Municipal Employees (AFSCME) represents about 62,000 corrections officers and 23,000 corrections employees, including those working in minimum and maximum security prisons and county jails.[71] States also have associations. The California Correctional Peace Officers Association (CCPOA), formed in 1957, represents more than 30,000 guards, prison personnel and parole agents.[72] The New York Correctional Officers & Police Benevolent Association represents more than 23,000 workers.[73]

Workers in private prison companies are far less likely to be unionized than their peers in the public sector. According to the 2008 annual report of the Corrections Corporation of America, the nation's largest private prison company, less than 5% of the firm's workers were members of trade organizations.[74] Further, some states prohibit collective bargaining by public employees.[75] AFSCME is among groups that have pushed for federal legislation to allow more public safety workers to engage in collective bargaining.

Unions have taken an active role in the current debate over state and federal correctional policy. CCPOA recently brought a lawsuit against California regarding its plan to require guards to take unpaid furloughs.[76] The New York Correctional Officers & Police Benevolent Association has run advertisements and lobbied against state Gov. David Paterson's proposal to close four minimum security prisons in 2011, warning it will endanger public safety and devastate local communities.[77] AFSCME, in a news release, claimed partial credit for the State of Minnesota's recent decision to close a private prison in Appleton, MN, while expanding operations at a state-owned facility.

Correctional unions have come under criticism for their efforts. For example, CCPOA, which has one of the largest political action committees in California, supported the 1994 "Three Strikes" ballot measure and opposed a 2004 ballot measures to limit the scope of the law.[78] Critics called the moves an effort to maintain high incarceration rates and job security for prison employees.

The unions say their work is a legitimate exercise of political speech, borne from a desire to ensure public safety.

PRISON CONSTRUCTION

The federal government, states, and localities have financed and built hundreds of new prisons during the past three decades in what may be one of the more concerted public works projects in recent history. The number of state and federal adult correction facilities rose from 1,277 in 1990 to 1,821 in 2005, a 43% increase.[79] For a time in the mid-1990s, the peak of the prison construction boom, a new U.S. prison opened every 15 days on average.[80] The pace of construction has begun to slow. According to the DOJ's Bureau of Justice Statistics, the number of state and federal adult correctional facilities increased 9% from mid-2000 to the end of 2005. That compares to a 14% increase from 1995-2000.[81]

In another shift, states and the federal government are relying more on private companies to build and run prisons. Of the 153 prisons and jails that opened between 2000 and 2005, 151 were private institutions. The number of private facilities under contract to states or the federal government rose by 57% during that five-year period.[82] Private facilities accounted for about 23% of adult corrections institutions in 2005, compared to 16% in 2000. Nearly 17% of federal prisoners were in private prisons in 2008, compared to just 3% in 1999.[83]

The South has traditionally had the largest concentration of facilities owned or managed by private corporations. More recently, the West has seen rapid growth in private prison development. In 2008,10 states had more than 20% of state and federal prisoners in their borders housed in private prisons: Alaska, Colorado, Hawaii, Idaho, Mississippi, Montana, New Mexico, Vermont, and Wyoming.[84] Some states have geographically defined clusters of prisons. One such cluster is near Florence, AZ, where there a number of correctional and immigration facilities in a small area. Michigan's Upper Peninsula has a number of institutions, as does northern New York state, for example.

Rural Prisons

Prisons have been sited in both rural and urban counties, though the correctional building surge in the 1980s and 1990s appears to have had an outsized impact in some rural areas.[85] Nearly 60% of new prisons built from 1992 to 1994, in the heat of the prison building boom, were located in rural areas even though such counties accounted for only 20% of the population.[86] From 1980 to 1991, 213 prisons opened in nonmetro counties, housing 53% of all inmates sentenced to new U.S. prisons. By comparison, just 38% of inmates housed in older facilities were located in nonmetro places, and just 23% of the total U.S. population lived in rural areas during that period.

The Pennsylvania Legislature's Center for Rural Pennsylvania found that prisoners were one of the fastest-growing segments of the state's rural population from 1990 to 2000. In a report based on 2000 Census data, the Center estimated that the percentage of people in prisons in rural Pennsylvania rose by 187% from 1990 to 2000, compared to a 46% increase in prisoners in urban areas. In 2000, rural areas had 11 prisoners per 1,000 residents, compared to 5 prisoners per 1,000 for urban areas.[87]

In a separate study, Pennsylvania State University researchers created a special data set to track U.S. prison construction through the end of 1995 and examine institutions by type of facility, location, and other indicators. They found that nearly 40% (576) of the 1,500 prisons in operation at the end of 1995 were located in rural areas. Roughly 210 of those rural prisons, 36%, were built from 1985 to 1995; the height of the prison building boom.[88] (According to Census data, 75% of the population was located in urban areas in 1990, with 25% in rural regions.)[89] Part of the reason that rural counties are home to so many correctional institutions is the fact that many communities actively competed for prisons, as an economic development strategy. (See Economic Impacts below.)

Prison growth is not an exclusively rural issue, but a prison site can have an major impact on a small community. The Urban Institute, in a 2004 study, looked at 10 states with the fastest- growing prison populations during the 1980s and 1990s. The study found that in those states, the majority of institutions were built in metro rather than rural areas. But in an indication of how a prison can alter the demographics of a rural area, 13 counties in the states that were studied— most of non-metro counties—inmates accounted for 20% or more of total population. All the states had at least five counties where 5% or more of the population was incarcerated.[90]

Cost and Overcrowding

As the prison population has grown, states have had a hard time keeping pace. Recent data shows overcrowding is beginning to ease, though it is still a problem in a number of states. The DOJ reported that state prisons were operating at 97% of highest capacity in 2008, down from 114% in 1995.[91] Still, 13 states were operating at more than 100% of highest capacity, while federal institutions were also overcrowded.[92]

California, for example, is grappling with court orders to reduce its prison population.[93] The state is taking steps to deal with its problems, including transferring inmates to other states with excess capacity and building new prisons. In Pennsylvania, which registered a 9% increase in the number of prisoners in state and federal facilities from 2007 to 2008 (the largest of any state), lawmakers recently voted to send 3,000 inmates to institutions in other states until Pennsylvania can open more prisons.[94]

Cornell Companies, one of the nation's largest private prison firms, in releasing its fourth quarter 2009 earnings report on February 24, 2010, noted mounting state budget pressures. But the firm said there was still sufficient state and federal business to support growth.[95] In its 2008 annual report, for example, Cornell said state and federal authorities would need 35,000 to 40,000 beds annually for the next few years, while only about 12,000 to 15,000 a year were in the pipeline. The company also predicted that the weak economy would make it harder for individuals released from prison to find work and avoid situations that could lead them back into confinement:

> At core, demand for beds results from high rates of recidivism among released offenders and an increasing length of sentence for those repeat offenders. Recidivism itself is highly correlated with employment opportunities for offenders; getting a job helps keep an ex-offender straight. Moreover, the probability of employment for an ex-offender increases substantially with in-prison programs for adult basic education, substance abuse treatment and vocational training followed by re-entry via a "halfway house" program. Unfortunately, in this economy, these factors, unemployment and budget cuts to those in-prison treatment, education and vocational programs, lead one to conclude that demand for prison beds will likely remain strong, while the ability of government agencies to build their own beds remains constrained. As an industry, private corrections can provide beds quickly and cost effectively. [96]

Many states are scaling back corrections spending. At least 22 states have shut institutions, reduced the number of beds, halted expansions or delayed opening new facilities, partly in response to state budget problems.[97] New York Gov. Paterson's proposed 2011 budget calls for closing four facilities.[98] Arizona officials in December announced they would transfer some illegal immigrants from state prisons to federal custody for the final months of their sentences; the move is expected to save the state about $6 million a year.[99] Other states are also considering transferring more prisoners who are illegal immigrants to federal custody. California Gov. Schwarzenegger in his State-of-the-State address in January 2010 recommended an amendment to the state constitution to assure that prison spending could not exceed higher education funding, a goal that would be met partially through privatizing some prisons.[100] It is too soon to say whether the budget problems will bring about a fundamental rethinking of the prison system, or less sweeping, temporary changes.

Financing

Though legislators have approved a number of laws instituting tougher, mandatory sentences, they have sometimes been less able to persuade voters to approve financing for the jails and prisons needed to house the rising number of offenders. Further, states may operate under debt caps that limit their ability to issue bonds. In response, state and local governments have developed new methods to finance prisons and other public institutions including courthouses, schools, and equipment. These alternative financing arrangements are generally not subject to voter approval.

A 1999 report prepared for the Association of State Correctional Administrators spelled out some details of the alternative financing arrangements:

> The issuance of general obligation bonds has been the traditional methodology for financing prison facilities, but over time there has been increasing use of revenue bonds and certificates of participation, known as COPs. In the latter two, the debt is not secured by the general obligation of the state or municipality issuing the debt, but by a pledge of the streams of revenues that are generated by use of the facility. In a corrections context the revenue streams are payments made for housing inmates in the facility (per diem or fixed payment amounts), or for the exclusive use of the facility. A revenue bond or COP transaction might be

structured to also include certain tax revenues or user fees as pledged revenues. Revenue Bonds and COPs will generally not be included within the state or local government's overall debt limit.[101]

Voters have challenged alternative financing efforts in court, however. In California, for example, a citizen's group called Taxpayers for Improving Public Safety filed lawsuits challenging the constitutionality of a particular type of bonds for prison finance. The group argued that the bonds would violate California's debt limit because they had not been approved by voters. A California appeals court in March 2009 ruled that the state had the legal power to use the bonds.[102]

State budget documents offer some illustrative examples of prison funding trends. In Oregon, the state's Certificate of Participation (COP) debt rose from $191 million in FY1995 to about $1.1 billion in FY2008. A special state advisory commission reported that the increase was "directly related to the passage of Ballot Measure 11 by Oregon voters in 1994. Measure 11 created mandatory minimum penalties for specified crimes and required that juveniles charged with certain violent crimes be tried and sentenced as adults."[103] Nearly 60% of Oregon COP obligations are related to running the state's prisons, community corrections system, and juvenile justice system.

The State of Colorado had about $130 million of COP debt for prisons outstanding in 2008, out of a total of $383 million in such financing.[104] Colorado in 2006 used COP bonds to fund a new high-security Colorado State Penitentiary. Due to a lawsuit challenging the financing system, in addition to state budget problems, the institution may not open as planned. The state is currently examining financing options to allow it to operate at least part of the prison.[105]

Even though lease revenue and COP bonds are commonly used by states and municipalities, there can be drawbacks. The financing can be more expensive than other conventional bonds because they are viewed by investors as less secure. Even if bonds issued by a municipality are not backed by its taxing authority, a government can suffer via an impaired credit rating if it is unable or unwilling to make scheduled payments.[106] On a related note, the inability or unwillingness of state and local governments to seek voter approval for prison construction has contributed to their increasing reliance on private prison companies, which have their own sources of financing and may not need voter approval to finance new prisons.

PRIVATE SECTOR

As federal, state, and local governments have increased spending on prisons, they have contracted with the private sector for financing, design, construction, management, and staffing of prisons, jails, and other correctional facilities. Private firms also provide services including health care, education, transportation, and counseling. Public-private partnerships are in keeping with a growing trend to contract out government services. They also reflect the long history of private sector involvement in U.S. prisons.

Table 3. Number of State or Federal Prisoners in Private Facilities, 2000-2008

Year	Total	Number of Prisoners		Percent of all Prisoners
		Federal	State	
2000	87,369	15,524	71,845	6.3%
2001	91,828	19,251	72,577	5.8%
2002	93,912	20,274	73,638	6.5%
2003	95,707	21,865	73,842	6.5%
2004	98,628	24,768	73,860	6.6%
2005	107,940	27,046	80,894	7.1%
2006	113,697	27,726	85,971	7.2%
2007	123,942	31,310	92,632	7.8%
2008	128,524	33,162	95,362	8.0%
Average annual change 2000-07	5.1%	10.5%	3.7%	:
Percent change 2007-08	3.7%	5.9%	2.9%	:

Source: Sabol, William J., Heather C. West, and Matthew Cooper, *Prisoners in 2008, Appendix Table 18.*
Note: Figures are as of December 31 for each calendar year.

Advocates of the private correctional industry call it a cost-effective means of providing safe and humane services to inmates. Private prisons, mainly minimum- or medium-security facilities, are newer, less crowded, and more technologically advanced. Critics, including labor unions, religious groups, and prisoners' rights organizations, warn of the rise of a "prison-industrial complex"—a sector dependent on government funds, with a vested interest in the continuation or expansion of the prison system. They call incarceration a core government service and worry that private companies have an incentive to stint on services or staff to increase profits. The debate has been inflamed by high-profile cases at some private prisons, including a 1998 incident when six prisoners escaped from a Corrections Corporation of America prison in Youngstown, OH. A subsequent DOJ investigation showed major problems at the facility.[107] More recently, several deaths and a spate of lawsuits have raised questions about the quality of care provided at facilities holding immigrants pending possible deportation, including at facilities operated by private prison companies.[108]

A debate within the architecture and design community illustrates some of the conflict and crosscurrents regarding corrections privatization. Architecture firms have worked with state and local governments to design jails and prisons that are safer for both guards and prisoners. Innovations include placing housing around a central break room, allowing more movement and natural light, and making the exterior of jail buildings more street friendly, particularly if they are located in urban areas. The American Institute of Architects has an awards competition for justice and correctional projects. But more than 1,000 architects and designers have signed a petition calling for professionals to boycott the design, construction, or renovation of a jail or prison. The petition sponsors say the current incarceration rate is too high and the focus should instead be on finding alternatives to prison.[109]

Further, during the past decade, some college students have urged school administrators to drop food service contracts with firms that also sell services to prisons or to divest from financial funds or products that include private prison company investments.[110]

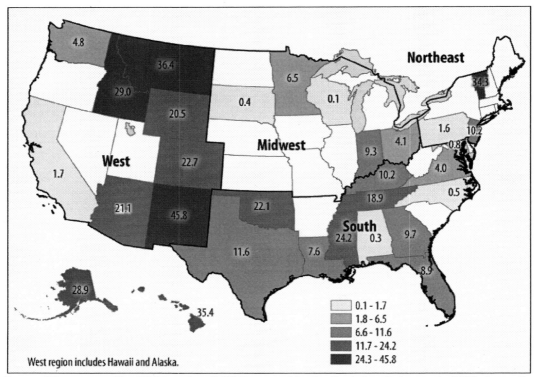

Source: Map prepared by CRS based on DOJ, Bureau of Justice Statistics, *Prisoners in 2008,* Appendix
Table 19.

Notes: Overall, 8% of all U.S. prisoners are in private institutions, including 6.8% of state prisoners and
16.5% of federal inmates.

Figure 3. Percentage of Prisoners in Private Prisons
Percentage of adult incarcerated prisoners in private institutions

Despite the controversy and the possibility of additional reductions in state corrections spending, investors seem to believe private prisons offers growth potential. Private prison companies have reported increased revenues in recent earnings reports.

Private Prison Companies

Private companies that build and manage prisons are probably the most visible part of the private correctional industry. The companies have been experiencing a turnaround since a slump in the late 1990s, when some ran into severe problems due to overbuilding and failed efforts to reorganize as Real Estate Investment Trusts.[111] Private prisons made up 23% of all state and federal institutions in 2005, compared to 16% in 2000.[112] The federal government is the biggest client of the publicly traded prison firms, accounting for about 40% of revenues at the Corrections Corporation of America in recent years and about a third of the business at Cornell Corrections, for example.

Private sector involvement in the prison system, in its most recent incarnation, began in the 1970s when the state and municipal governments began contracting with private companies to house juveniles. It gained momentum during the 1980s as state prisons became overcrowded and the federal government turned to private institutions to house detained immigrants.[113] Even though private sector involvement has grown to the point that private companies oversee 8% of all prisoners, there are conflicting data regarding whether private prisons offer either significant cost savings or increased quality. A 2007 Government Accountability Office (GAO) report said the Federal Bureau of Prisons did not collect enough detailed information to determine whether private prison companies provided long-term cost efficiencies or comparable quality, compared to the expected cost of government management.[114] The Bureau of Prisons responded that it had sufficient data due to its previous work on the issue.

In 1996, lawmakers instructed the Bureau of Prisons to conduct a five-year demonstration project comparing the cost of public prisons versus a private prison in Taft, CA. The Bureau of Prisons did its own follow-up evaluation and also paid for an independent analysis by consulting firm Abt Associates, Inc. The two reports produced findings that were significant enough that DOJ officials in 2008 held a special meeting to discuss approaches in methodology regarding the issue.[115] For example, the Abt report said the private Taft facility was cheaper to run than three comparable public facilities, noting that in 2002 the average cost of the public facilities was 14.8% above that of the private prison. The Bureau of Prisons found, however, that the average cost of the public facilities in 2002 was only 2.2% more than the private prison.[116]

A 2001 report commissioned by the DOJ's Bureau of Justice Assistance concluded that average savings from privatization were about 1%, due mainly to lower labor costs, compared to earlier estimates of as much as 20%. The study found that private companies could build prisons faster and more cheaply, and added that the mere prospect of prison privatization may have made prison administrators more open to certain reforms.[117] A report by Vanderbilt University researchers (partially funded by the prison industry) indicated that private contractors can provide similar outcomes for less money.[118]

The DOJ's Bureau of Justice Assistance study also found three main differences between private and public prisons. Private prisons have lower staff-to-inmate ratios, less sophisticated information management systems, and a higher reported rate of serious incidents involving inmates.[119] Cost savings were not significant in private prisons, according to the study.

Some state data show that private prisons have lower daily per-inmate costs than public institutions. The effectiveness of state oversight is a major factor, however. New Mexico has nearly 46% of its prison population in private facilities, the largest proportion of any state. A 2007 study by the New Mexico legislature found the state was spending more than needed on the facilities. For example, the report found that state spending on private prison contracts had increased 57% since 2001, due to features such as automatic inflation adjustments in contracts, including fixed-price construction contracts.[120]

Kevin Campbell of independent investment firm Avondale Partners says costs and potential cost savings vary widely from state to state. [121] Based on his analysis, some state governments have tight oversight and may post significant savings by contracting out with private firms that pay lower salaries and do not offer pension benefits equivalent to those for public workers. He also says states can realize significant savings by shipping prisoners to existing, private institutions in other states, rather than building new prisons of their own.

The federal government is now the most important single customer for private prison companies. There have been concerns that federal agencies could face problems if private firms were to encounter financial difficulties.[122] There are also concerns in the investment community about potential liability issues as some legislatures tighten oversight of private prisons. A recent report by the Florida legislature noted continuing challenges in setting performance standards for private institutions and ensuring they provided health care and other services comparable to public institutions.[123] Florida in 1993 created a Correctional Privatization Commission to work with private firms to develop private prisons. The Commission was disbanded in 2005 after a series of scandals, including embezzlement and ethics violations. Responsibility for overseeing private prisons was transferred to the State Department of Management Services. States are currently making a new push to contract out prison services, and the federal government is relying more on private prisons, even though there is a lack of consensus in some areas such as how best to compare costs and quality between public and private prisons.

The Private Prison Industry

Three publicly traded private prison companies now dominate the industry and merit special attention.

Corrections Corporation of America

The Corrections Corporation of America (CCA) is the nation's largest private prison firm. The Tennessee-based company controls nearly 87,000 beds (a common capacity measure) at 65 institutions. The company owns 44 facilities and manages the rest. [124] At the end of 2008, CCA had approximately 17,400 employees. The firm reported $1.6 billion in 2008 revenues, nearly double the $887 million in revenues reported for 2001.[125] Federal contracts accounted for about 40% of CCA total revenue in 2008, up from 32% in 2002.[126]

The company has rebounded since the early 2000s, when it took on too much debt,[127] and has increased earnings even during the economic downturn. In the fourth quarter of 2009, the CCA reported a 4% increase in revenues, compared to the same period in 2008. The company had net income of $42.5 million, or 36 cents per share in the fourth quarter of 2009, up from 32 cents per share during the same period in the previous year.[128]

The occupancy rate in CCA-owned or managed facilities, a key gauge, was 91.5% in the fourth quarter of 2009, down from average occupancy of more than 96% from 2006 to 2008. The rise in empty beds was due in part to the opening of new facilities. But the company also noted in its release that it has lost some prison contracts due to tight state budgets. CCA has been building institutions on the premise that a number of state and federal institutions are still so overcrowded that officials will have to turn to the private sector.

In its fourth quarter 2009 earnings report, CCA officials noted that company faced the risk that customers, such as the State of California, might not be able to pay their bills on time, or might ask for concessions. Todd Mullenger, chief financial officer and executive vice president, told financial analysts during a February 2010 conference call: "Debt, along with the risks that other customers delay payments are issues we will monitor ... uncertainty remains related to the general economy and around government budget deficits. This is the primary uncertainty in risk we face in 2010."[129]

New York-based Pershing Square Capital Management, a prominent hedge fund, in December 2009 bought a 9.5% share in CCA. Pershing Square officials in a presentation to investors described CCA as a "high quality real estate business."[130]

In recent weeks, CCA has both profited from, and been buffeted by, state spending decisions. CCA recently secured contracts to house 10,000 California inmates at CCA facilities in Arizona, Mississippi, and Oklahoma.[131] But the company in December 2009 announced it would close an Appleton, MN facility that had been in operation since 1996. Minnesota is consolidating its prison population in existing state facilities. The company in January 2010 announced that the State of Arizona had decided not to renew its contract to house inmates at the CCA 752-bed Huerfano County Correctional Center in Colorado.[132] In early January, the State of Kentucky ordered 400 female inmates removed from the CCA's Otter Creek Correctional Complex to a state-run prison. The state acted in response to allegations of sexual misconduct by CCA guards.[133]

Geo Group

Geo Group, headquartered in Boca Raton, FL, operates prisons and other correctional centers in the United States and overseas.[134] Geo Group owns or manages 61 facilities with 60,000 beds worldwide with more than 13,000 full-time staff. The company also operates a migrant operations center at Guantanamo Bay, Cuba, housing people caught trying to enter the United States illegally. The company provides education and mental health treatment. Revenues were $1.14 billion in 2009, up from $1.04 billion in 2008.[135] The firm expects revenues in the range of $1.11 to $1.13 billion in 2010. The company's average occupancy rate for its corrections operations declined to 93.7% in 2009 from 95.7% in 2008.

According to the company's 2008 *Annual Report*, federal contracts accounted for a third of the company's revenues in 2008, with another 19% from the State of Florida and 12% from overseas operations.[136] The company views provision of mental health services as a key growth area. The firm's GEO Care subsidiary expanded to 1,700 beds and $113.8 million in revenues in 2007 from 325 beds and $31.7 million in revenues in 2004.[137] GEO Group estimates the overall market for state/local mental health services at $6 billion.

The federal government has become an increasingly important customer for the company, including growth in detaining immigrants. In a conference call to discuss fourth quarter 2008 earnings, corporate officials noted that federal contracts account for about half of corporate earnings under some measures, though they make up just 37% of revenues.[138]

Cornell Companies

Cornell Companies runs prisons and juvenile detention centers and provides drug and alcohol counseling, rehabilitation, and education services. The firm has about 70 facilities in 15 states and the District of Columbia, with a total capacity of 21,392 prisoners. The company was running at average occupancy of about 91% during the fourth quarter of 2009, compared to 92% during the same period in the previous year.[139] About 34% of the company's revenues came from contracts with the Federal Bureau of Prisons in 2008. No other customer accounted for more than 10% of company revenues.[140]

Cornell Companies' revenues increased from $277 million in 2004 to $412 million in 2009. Cornell expects the bulk of its future growth to come from institutions housing adult prisoners.[141]

Other Private Firms

Large firms and small businesses across the country provide essential services and products to the corrections sector, from health care to meal trays to surveillance and security equipment. Many companies that contract with prisons and jails are members of the American Correctional Association (ACA), which describes itself as an organization of "professionals representing all levels and facets of corrections and criminal justice, including federal, state and military correctional facilities, county jails and metropolitan detention centers, probation and parole agencies and community corrections/halfway houses." The ACA has 62 chapters and affiliated organizations, with more than 20,000 additional individual members.[142]

The ACA website includes a marketing center with links to hundreds of firms around the country that provide services to the correctional sector. Other correctional business associations include the Detention Equipment Manufacturers Division of the National Association of Architectural Metal Manufacturers and The Association of Correctional Food Service Affiliates.

One of the biggest prison-associated growth areas is the provision of inmate health care. In the case of prisoners, the Supreme Court has held that they are entitled to adequate medical care as a component of protections accorded by the Eighth Amendment to the U.S. Constitution. [143] A 2009 study by Cambridge Health Alliance and Harvard Medical School illustrates the scope of health concerns, and the potential market, in U.S. correctional institutions. The researchers, using 2002 and 2004 DOJ data, found that about 40% of the two million people in U.S. prisons and jails had chronic conditions such as diabetes, asthma or heart problems—a far higher rate than other Americans of a similar age.[144] About a quarter of the inmates had a history of mental illness, including schizophrenia, bipolar disorder or depression, but two-thirds of those in custody were not using prescribed drugs at the time they were incarcerated.

Among private sector firms offering inmate health services is the Tennessee-based America Service Group, which owns Correctional Health Services and Prison Health Services. The company works with federal, state, and local governments, as well as private entities. America Service Group, which announced full year 2009 revenues of $610 million, a 21% increase from the previous year.[145] The company had nearly 4,000 employees at the end of 2008, and estimated that it had about 6.6% of the combined private and non-private market for correctional health care. Other large, private-sector competitors include Correctional Medical Services and Wexford Health Services.[146]

Other notable private-sector firms:

- The New Jersey-based Community Education Centers provides education, counseling, and related services to 30,000 offenders in 19 states. The privately held firm employs more than 4,000 people.[147]
- Aramark, one of the nation's largest food service providers, operates Aramark Correctional Services at more than 600 prisons and jails, preparing more than a million meals a day.[148]
- Tiger Correctional Services of Arkansas, which also provides food services, has doubled in size during the past several years. The company now provides food and commissary services and jail management software to 150 jails in 20 states.[149]

- The Keefe Group, working through affiliates, supplies electronics, clothing and technology to the correctional commissary market. The company has grown to 2,000 employees from two workers in 1975. Among its products is a specialized MP3 player sold to prisons through Access Corrections, a subsidiary. The Access to Entertainment program is one of the top U.S. providers of digital music.
- Cornerstone Detention Products of Alabama builds and renovates correction facilities and sells products, such as furniture, locks, gates, and personal supplies, including toothbrushes and soap. The firm was named one of the nation's fastest growing companies in 2007 by *Inc.* magazine.[150]
- Argyle Security Inc. provides electronic monitoring and construction services to the corrections industry. Argyle, which had about 600 full-time employees in 2008, estimated that the North American electronic security market was $27 billion at the end of 2007, of which 67% was in the commercial-industrial area.[151]

Phone Service

Jails and prisons negotiate exclusive contracts with telephone carriers to serve their institutions. Organizations such as the National Sheriffs Association say such contractual arrangements ensure security and allow them to monitor inmate phone calls. Groups representing prisoners, including the Citizens United for the Rehabilitation of Errants (CURE) and their families, say that telephone providers often pay prison operators a high percentage of the fees they collect for prisoners' collect calls, and then charge inmates well-above general market rates for service. Groups seeking to change the system say commissions on telephone service can be as high as 45- 65% of gross revenues generated by the service.[152] Some states, including New York, have altered their practices in response to complaints. The Federal Communications Commission has been petitioned to set rates for inmate calls. The National Sheriffs Association told Congress in June 2009 that changing the rules could endanger public safety.[153]

ECONOMIC IMPACT

Prisons have been viewed as an economic development tool by a number of small, rural towns. Localities see the facilities as recession-proof tools to stabilize population and employment, while spurring retailing, homebuilding, and associated activities. Rural communities have provided incentives to lure prison development, including infrastructure upgrades and bond financing. Some towns have financed and built their own prisons, counting on forecasts of increasing prison populations to fill the new cells. CCA has been expanding its inventory as well. It has been building prisons based on projections that states and the federal government will not be able to finance and build enough prison beds to alleviate overcrowding, and will have to look to the private sector for a quick solution. CCA officials term their strategy "thoughtful disciplined building of capacity in front of demand." [154] But CCA officials add that given their thousands of empty beds they are pausing on the construction front.

There are relatively sparse data on the long-term economic impact of prison development. Some studies indicate slight economic gains for prison towns, while others suggest that rural areas that have become prison anchors may have grown less rapidly than similar counties without prisons. The idea that prisons are "recession proof" is being tested as states close prisons or release nonviolent offenders to reduce budget gaps caused by a drop in tax revenues. The state efforts have sparked politically charged debates over both public security and the impact on jobs.

The ongoing effort to transfer internees from the U.S. military facility at Guantanamo Bay, Cuba, to a U.S. prison illustrates the issues. Several U.S. rural communities with extra prison space and high unemployment rates expressed interest in taking the detainees to create or preserve jobs.[155] The White House in December 2009 announced the government planned to buy an underused state prison in Thomson, IL, for a joint facility to be run by the military and the Bureau of Prisons. The Illinois facility has been largely empty since it was built at a cost of $120 million in 2001, based on projections for an increasing prison population that did not pan out.[156] In announcing its decision, the White House Council of Economic Advisers released a study of the potential economic impact of the facility on Thomson and surrounding areas.[157] The White House forecast $1.1 billion in additional spending in northern Illinois during the first four years the facility is operational, including construction, pay, operating costs, spending by visitors to the prison, and families transferred to the area. The White House predicted the Thomson project would spur 3,180-3,880 ongoing jobs and 840-910 temporary jobs in its first four years, increasing local earnings by $793 million to $1.02 billion. Local citizens will be candidates for about half the jobs, which could reduce the unemployment rate in Carroll County, IL, where the prison is located, by two percentage points.[158]

The Thomson facility is unique in some respects. For example, the Department of Defense expects its activities to increase employment by 1,960 to 2,660 positions by the fourth year, but expects few direct hires from the local communities. DOD is also expected to spend $40 million on capital improvements to open the facility and a similar amount of capital improvements in subsequent years, a higher dollar amount than is usually spent on correctional facility upkeep and improvements. The Federal Bureau of Prisons anticipates hiring 448 correctional officers and 448 medical personnel, food service workers, and other staff. About half the needed workers are expected to come from local areas.[159] Other studies indicate that many prison jobs are filled from outside the immediate area, particularly the highest-paying, highest skilled positions. The Federal Bureau of Prisons requirements that its correctional officers have some higher education or other outside experience can mean many local residents do not qualify. Further, many prisons centralize their buying from outside sources, rather than local businesses.

Though many local officials credit prisons with stabilizing their economies, some academic studies say prisons have a lesser impact than believed, or even retard economic development by creating a stigma that makes it more difficult to attract other types of investment. A 2007 study by Pennsylvania State University researchers found that prisons have "had no significant economic effect on rural places in general, but ... may have had a positive impact on poverty rates in persistently poor rural counties."[160] Overall, however, the study concluded there was not convincing evidence that the prison development boom resulted in structural economic change in persistently poor rural places. The study examined prison construction in the United States using a special data base tracking prison data through 1995. It also examined changes in poverty populations as well as other indicators of area-wide economic health in localities that had become prison hosts. A 2004 study by researchers at Washington State University also did not find evidence that prison expansion stimulated economic development. [161] Instead, the study suggested that prison construction tamped down growth in rural counties, specifically in counties that were already growing at a slow rate. In higher-growth counties, the impact was not as pronounced. The study looked at 3,100 counties in 48 states, assessing the impact of prison development on growth in earnings, per capita income, and employment.

A 2004 study by Iowa State University researchers examined prisons opened in rural towns between 1990 and 2000. [162] The study looked at 274 new state prisons in 248 small towns, defined as incorporated places with fewer than 10,000 residents. It compared them to nearly 20,000 similar towns that did not have prisons. The researchers found that small towns that acquired a state prison during the1990s had higher poverty levels, higher unemployment, lower household wages and lower housing values than similar towns without a prison.

Prisons as Drivers of Economic Development

Although there is a significant debate about the costs and benefits of prisons to local economies, the examples of two small towns, Shelby and Hardin, in Montana illustrate the possibilities and perils of prisons as an economic development tool.

Shelby, MT
Shelby, located in Toole County (population 3,541), Montana, in the northern part of the state, is host to a 660-bed maximum security prison, the Crossroads Correctional Center, which was financed, built, and operated by CCA.

Every five years, Shelby city officials publish a review of the economic impacts of the institution. [163] According to the most recent review, covering a period through 2008, the prison employs 181 people from Shelby and the surrounding area. It generates $100,000 to $150,000 in annual billings for the local medical center, which serves the prison population and people who moved to the area to work at the prison. The prison buys only 5% of its supplies from local Toole County, though it contracts for another 75% from Montana-based businesses. Property values in the county have increased, in contrast to other rural Montana communities which have shown significant declines. It is not possible to say whether the improvement is due to the prison or other factors, such as energy-related development in the area.

The prison has created some strains, including an increase in the number of cases heard at the courthouse. The local police force has had to devote about 1,320 hours from 2005 through 2008 on prison-related work, such as investigating in-prison assaults and serving warrants or civil court summons. There have been fights and gang activity at the prison and, in 2008, CCA had a national security company bring employees in from out of state to fill jobs at the prison. [164] But officials say the costs are more than balanced by the nearly $500,000 in annual property taxes paid by the prison, and Shelby Mayor Larry Bonderud said the town continues to attract business and has experienced no stigma from the maximum-security facility. Mayor Bonderud said he preferred the higher security institution, in part because it requires higher staffing levels and therefore more local jobs. [165]

Hardin, MT

The story is much different in Hardin (pop 3,600) in the southeastern part of the state. The Hardin facility, a speculative prison, has stood vacant since it was completed in 2007, forcing a technical default on $27.4 million in revenue bonds.[166]

According to an audit prepared for the Montana Legislature, the Two Rivers Regional Authority (a port authority created by Hardin for economic development) in 2006 entered into a deal with the Municipal Capital Markets Group, Herbert J. Sims & Co., a construction firm, and other businesses to use the proceeds from $27 million in bonds to build the prison (which cost about $19 million), create a debt reserve, and pay other expenses. Fees for housing prisoners were to be used to pay off facility and operating costs. (The price tag included a $1.6 million fee for arranging the financing). The memorandum noted that a feasibility study prepared by an outside group for the project contained assumptions "that appear to be unfounded." The audit further noted that the companies that worked with Hardin officials had proposed and built other facilities in other states that had run into financial problems.[167]

Rather than spurring development in the small town, the empty prison is impeding efforts by Two Rivers officials to attract new business to the area. The economic development entity's ability to raise money is clouded by the outstanding bonds. Negative press about the prison has created a sense of notoriety about Hardin.[168]

CHALLENGES FOR POLICYMAKERS

There is growing unease among public officials that the U.S. correctional system is too expensive, too punitive, and too large. U.S. Supreme Court Justice Anthony Kennedy, in a speech in California, criticized the state's three strikes laws, noting that U.S. sentences were much longer than in other countries. [169] Missouri Chief Justice William Ray Price, in an address to that state's legislature in February 2010, said Missouri could not afford to continue incarcerating so many nonviolent offenders.

> We are following a broken strategy of cramming inmates into prisons and not providing the type of drug treatment and job training that is necessary to break their cycle of crime. Any normal business would have abandoned this failed practice years ago, and it is costing us our shirts.[170]

In Congress, the growth of the prison system and more recent tension about costs and effectiveness, have given rise to a number of initiatives. The Congressional efforts range from broad efforts to examine the correctional system, to more targeted bills aimed a specific issues such as the cost of inmate telephone service, as well as efforts to monitor inmate communications.

In Congress, the Senate Judiciary Committee favorably ordered to be reported with an amendment in the nature of a substitute the National Criminal Justice Commission Act of 2009 (S. 714), which would establish a commission to (1) review all areas of federal and state criminal justice costs, practices, and policies; (2) make specified findings relating to incarceration, prison administration, the impact of gang activity, drug policy, mental illness among prisoners and the role of the military in crime prevention; (3) make recommendations for changes in policies and laws to address findings; (4) consult with government and nongovernmental leaders, including state and local law enforcement officials; and (5) submit a final report to Congress and the President and make such report public.

In the House, the Family Telephone Connection Protection Act of 2009 (H.R. 1133) was introduced on February 23, 2010, and referred to the Committee on Energy and Commerce. The bill, if enacted into law, would amend the Communications Act of 1934 to direct the Federal Communications Commission (FCC) to consider the following types of regulation of inmate telephone service: (1) prescribing a maximum uniform per-minute rate (paid to telephone service providers); (2) prescribing a maximum uniform service connection or other per-call rate; (3) prescribing variable maximum rates depending on factors such as carrier costs or the size of the correctional facility; (4) requiring providers of inmate telephone service to offer both collect calling and debit account services; (5) prohibiting the payment of commissions by such providers to administrators of correctional facilities; and (6) requiring such administrators to allow more than one service provider at a facility so that prisoners have a choice. As of April 2, 2010, the bill had not been reported out of committee, although a hearing has been held at subcommittee level.

Another bill, the Safe Prisons Communications Act of 2009 (H.R. 560), was introduced on January 15, 2009. The bill, which was referred to the House Energy and Commerce Committee and the House Judiciary Committee, would amend the Communications Act of 1934 to authorize the director of the Federal Bureau of Prisons or the chief executive officer of a state to petition the Federal Communications Commission (FCC) to permit the installation of devices to prevent, jam, or interfere with wireless communications within the geographic boundaries of a specific prison, penitentiary, or correctional facility under his or her jurisdiction.

The Criminal Justice Reinvestment Act of 2009 (H.R. 4080/S. 2772) would authorize the Attorney General to make grants to states, local governments, territories, or Indian tribes to: (1) analyze and improve the cost-effectiveness of state and local spending on prisons, jails, and community corrections; and (2) assist in managing the growth in spending on corrections and increase public safety. Both bills were introduced on November 16, 2009. S. 2772 was referred to the Judiciary Committee. On March 11, 2010, the bill was ordered to be reported favorably with an amendment in the nature of a substitute. On March 22, 2010, the bill was so reported as the Criminal Justice Reinvestment Act of 2010 and placed on the Senate Legislative Calendar. The House has not taken action on the bill.

State legislatures, during their 2010 sessions, are poised to debate proposals to reduce the size and cost of the corrections system, responding in large part to major budget shortfalls. In addition to spending cuts and layoffs approved in 2009, 13 states commissioned task forces or studies related to sentencing and supervision and legislatures this year could act on their recommendations.[171] New York has rolled back its three strikes law. Congress as part of the FY20 10 appropriations instructed a federal panel that advises the judiciary to review mandatory sentencing policies.[172]

As states expanding their use of strategies such as early release for nonviolent offenders and greater use of probation and parole, several have been able to realize large reductions in their prison populations. Still, the prison population remains historically high and it is not clear how far-reaching any changes will be. The Vera Institute on Justice points out that budget pressures have also forced reductions in some state programs to reduce recidivism.[173] The Oregon House recently voted to suspend an early release program for inmates until mid-2011, after complaints that some prisoners incarcerated for violent crimes had been released. [174] In Michigan, Gov. Jennifer Granholm also faces a fight over her plan to further reduce the size of the state prison population.

The federal prison system is still expanding. Private prison companies are anticipating that key states and the federal government will continue to need more prison beds than they can build— and will rely on private firms that have available space and can secure their own financing, thus avoiding thorny financing debates. CCA President and CEO Damon Hininger, in a February conference call, noted that states had "done a little tinkering around the edges" of the prison system.[175]

> Wholesale changes in policy, we haven't seen a lot of activity," Hininger said, adding that while California was talking about new initiatives regarding probation and parole, so far there was not much real activity. "But that ...potentially would be a risk and something we'll monitor in the short-term, Hininger said.

Though states initially took the lead in efforts to reduce prison spending and incarceration rates, Congress appears poised to assume a larger role. U.S. lawmakers have provided funding for state efforts to reduce recidivism and experiment with alternatives to incarceration. Some members of Congress are scrutinizing federal prison financing and sentencing laws. The scope of further changes will depend on several factors, including the effectiveness of emerging state policies and the health of the economy, which has a direct bearing on federal and state budgets. State and federal decisions, in turn, will likely have wide repercussions, including potential financial impacts on the large and growing number of private companies that serve the prison sector.

End Notes

[1] Sabol, William J., Heather C. West, and Matthew Cooper, "Prisoners in 2008," *Bureau of Justice Statistics Bulletin*, Washington, DC: U.S. Department of Justice (DOJ), Office of Justice Programs (OJP), Bureau of Justice Statistics (BJS), December 2009, p. 8. http://bjs.ojp.usdoj.gov/content/pub/pdf/p08.pdf (viewed on April 2, 2010).

[2] Glaze, Lauren E. and Thomas P. Bonzcar, "Probation and Parole in the United States, 2006," *Bureau of Justice Statistics Bulletin*, Washington, DC: DOJ/OJP/BJS, Revised July 2008. http://bjs.ojp.usdoj.gov/ content/ pub/pdf/ ppus08.pdf (viewed on April 2, 2010).

[3] Walmsey, Roy, *World Prison Population List*, 8th ed., King's College London, International Centre for Prison Studies, 2008. http://www.kcl.ac.uk/depsta/law/research/icps/downloads/wppl-8th_41.pdf (Viewed on April 2, 2010).

[4] Austin, James and Tony Fabelo, *The Diminishing Returns of Increased Incarceration: A Blueprint to Improve Public Safety and Reduce Costs,* The JFA Institute, Washington, DC, July 2004, p. 2. http://www.jfa-associates.com/publications/srs/BlueprintFinal.pdf (viewed on April 2, 2010).

[5] CRS Report RL34287, *Offender Reentry: Correctional Statistics, Reintegration into the Community, and Recidivism,* by Nathan James.

[6] Sabol, William J., Heather C. West, and Matthew Cooper, "Prisoners in 2008," *Bureau of Justice Statistics Bulletin*, Washington, DC: Department of Justice, Office of Justice Programs, December 2009, p. 8. http://bjs.ojp.usdoj.gov/ content/pub/pdf/p08.pdf (Viewed on April 2, 2010).

[7] Lawrence, Alison, *Cutting Corrections Costs: Earned Time for State Prisoners*, Denver, CO: National Conference of State Legislatures, July 2009, p. 1. http://www.ncsl.org/documents/cj/Earned_time_report.pdf (Viewed on April 2, 2010).

[8] Scott-Hayward, Christine, *The Fiscal Crisis in Correction: Rethinking Policies and Practices*, Washington, DC: Vera Institute of Justice, July 2009, p. 2. http://www.vera.org/files/The-fiscal-crisis-in-corrections_July-2009.pdf (Viewed on April 2, 2010).

[9] National Urban League, "The Fight for a Fair Count in the 2010 Census," Press Release, December 18, 2009. http://www.nul.org/content/fight-fair-count-2010-census (Viewed on April 2, 2010).

[10] For background on those issues refer to CRS Report RL32766, *Federal Sentencing Guidelines: Background, Legal Analysis, and Policy Options*, by Lisa M. Seghetti and Alison M. Smith, and CRS Report RL34287, *Offender Reentry: Correctional Statistics, Reintegration into the Community, and Recidivism*, by Nathan James. Another, related issue beyond the scope of this chapter is the expansion of prison-based industries. For more information on that topic, refer to CRS Report RL32380, *Federal Prison Industries*, by Nathan James.

[11] U.S. Census Bureau, *Government Employment & Payroll, 2008*. http://www.census.gov/govs/apes/ (Viewed on April 2, 2010). The data are derived from an annual survey of state, local and federal government entities.

[12] DOJ/OJP, Bureau of Justice Statistics, *Justice Expenditure and Employment Extracts, 2006*, December 1, 2008. http://bjs.ojp.usdoj.gov/content/glance/exptyp.cfm (Viewed on April 2, 2010). The DOJ report is based on data from the Census Bureau's *Annual Government Finance Survey and Annual Survey of Public Employment*. The corrections population includes people in prisons, jails, and other facilities. The term prison usually refers to facilities for inmates serving terms longer than a year, while jails house prisoners serving shorter sentences. State prisons are for violations of state laws, while federal prisons are for violations of federal statues. Immigration review is a growing area of confinement. U.S. Immigration and Customs Enforcement (ICE) operates more than 350 U.S. prison or detention facilities either on its own or through lease arrangements.

[13] National Governors Association/National Association of State Budget Officers, *The Fiscal Survey of the States*, December 2009. http://www.nasbo.org/Publications/FiscalSurvey/tabid/65/Default.aspx

[14] Hughes, Kristen A., "Justice Expenditure and Employment in the United States, 2003," *Bureau of Justice Statistics Bulletin*, Washington, DC: DOJ/OJP,BJS, April 2006, p. 4. http://bjs.ojp.usdoj.gov/ content/pub/pdf/jeeus03.pdf (These numbers are not adjusted for inflation). (Viewed on April 8, 2010).

[15] State of California, Office of the Governor, "Fact Sheet: State of the State 2010—Reshaping our Priorities to Shift Funding From Prisons to Universities," January 6, 2010. http://gov.ca.gov/index.php?/fact-sheet/14126/ (Viewed on April 2, 2010).

[16] Stephan, James J., *Census of State and Federal Correctional Facilities, 2005*, Washington, DC: DOJ/OJP,BJS, October 2008, Appendix Table 1. http://bjs.ojp.usdoj.gov/content/pub/pdf/csfcf05.pdf Texas, with 132 prisons, topped the list in terms of prison facilities in 2005. Texas has been working to reduce recidivism and overhaul corrections policy. (Viewed on April 2, 2010).

[17] Sabol, William J., Heather C. West, and Matthew Cooper, "Prisoners in 2008," *Bureau of Justice Statistics Bulletin*, Washington, DC: DOJ/OJP/BJS, December 2009, p. 10. http://bjs.ojp.usdoj.gov/content/ pub/pdf/p08.pdf (Viewed on April 2, 2010).

[18] Stephan, James J., *Census of State and Federal Correctional Facilities, 2005*, Washington, DC: DOJ/OJP/BJS, October 2008, p. 1. www. bjs.ojp.usdoj.gov/content/pub/pdf/csfcf05.pdf (Viewed on April 2, 2010).

[19] Pershing Square Capital Management, L.P., *Prisons Dilemma*, October 20, 2009, http://www.scribd.com/doc/21624762/Bill-Ackman-s-Presentation-on-Corrections-Corp-of-America-CXW-the-ValueInvesting-Congress+ http://vjsm.com/investor resources/vjsm/ackman/21624762-Bill-Ackman-s-Presentation-on-Corrections-Corp-ofAmerica-CXW-the-Value-Investing-Congress.pdf (Viewed on April 7, 2010).

[20] Goldmacher, Shane and Larry Gordon, "Governor's Call for Giving Colleges Priority over Prisons Faces Hard Political Tests," *Los Angeles Times*, January 7, 2010. http://articles.latimes.com/2010/jan/07/local/la-me-educationprison7-20 10jan07 (Viewed on April 8, 2010).

[21] Sabol, William J., Heather C. West, and Matthew Cooper, "Prisoners in 2008," *Bureau of Justice Statistics Bulletin*, Washington, DC: DOJ/OJP/BJS, December 2009, p. 10. http://bjs.ojp.usdoj.gov/content/pub/pdf/p08.pdf (viewed on April 2, 2010). For further information, see CRS Report RL32369, *Immigration-Related Detention: Current Legislative Issues*, by Chad C. Haddal and Alison Siskin.

[22] DOJ, "2011 Budget Summary," *2011 Budget and Performance Summary*. http://www.justice 2011summary/pdf/doj-budget-summary.pdf (Viewed on April 2, 2010).

[23] Speculative prisons are prisons that are built by private companies in anticipation of housing state and federal prisoners in the future. Some private prison companies are currently increasing their supply of beds, with the idea that the need by states and the federal government for more prison space will exceed the governmental entities' ability to finance and build it.

[24] Clement, Douglas "Big House on the Prairie," *FedGazette*, Federal Reserve Bank of Minneapolis, January 2002. http://www.minneapolisfed.org/publications_papers/pub_display.cfm?id=2048 (Viewed on April 2, 2010).

[25] Austin, James and Tony Fabelo, *The Diminishing Returns of Increased Incarceration: A Blueprint to Improve Public Safety and Reduce Costs*, The JFA Institute, July 2004, p. 2. http://www.jfa-associates.com/publications/srs/ BlueprintFinal.pdf (Viewed on April 2, 2010).

[26] Western, Bruce and Becky Pettit, *Incarceration and Social Inequality*, Workshop in Race and Inequality, December 8, 2009. http://www.econ.brown.edu/econ/events/daedalus01.pdf (Viewed on April 2, 2010).

[27] Christian, Steve, *Children of Incarcerated Parents*, National Conference of State Legislatures, March 2009. http://www.ncsl.org/documents/cyf/childrenofincarceratedparents.pdf (Viewed on April 2, 2010).

[28] Austin, James and Garry Coventry, *Emerging Issues on Privatized Prisons*, Bureau of Justice Assistance, Washington, DC: DOJ/OJP, February 2001, p. 9. http://www.ncjrs.gov/pdffiles1/bja/181249.pdf (Viewed on April 2, 2010).

[29] Morris, Norval and David J. Rothman, eds., *The Oxford History of the Prison: The Practice of Punishment in Western Society*, Oxford: Oxford University Press, 1995, p. 112.

[30] Pillsbury, Samuel, H., "Understanding Penal Reform: The Dynamic of Change," *The Journal of Criminal Law and Criminology*, vol. 80, No. 3, Autumn 1989, P. 730.

[31] Morris, Norval and David J. Rothman, eds., *The Oxford History of the Prison: The Practice of Punishment in Western Society*, Oxford University Press, 1995, p.1 17.

[32] Ibid, p. 127; Pillsbury, Samuel, H., "Understanding Penal Reform: The Dynamic of Change," *The Journal of Criminal Law and Criminology*, vol. 80, No. 3, Autumn 1989, P. 730.

[33] Morris, Norval and David J. Rothman, eds., *The Oxford History of the Prison: The Practice of Punishment in Western Society*, Oxford: Oxford University Press, 1995, p. 176.

[34] Ibid, p. 87.

[35] Florida Department of Corrections, *Florida Corrections: Centuries of Progress, Timeline 1821-2003*, http://www.dc.state.fl.us/oth/timeline/1921.html (viewed on April 2, 2010). Bureau of Justice Statistics, *Prisoners 1925-1985*. Washington, DC: Bureau of Justice Statistics, 1986; Curtin, Mary Ellen, "Convict-Lease System," *Encyclopedia of Alabama*, Auburn University and Alabama Humanities Foundation, January 22, 2010. http://www.encyclopediaofalabama.org/face/Article.jsp?id=h-1346 (viewed on April 2, 2010).

[36] Feucht, Thomas E. and Edwin Zedlewski, "The 40th Anniversary of the Crime Report," *NIJ Journal*, DOJ/OJP, National Institutes of Justice, No. 257, June 2007. http://www.ojp.usdoj.gov/nij/journals/257/40th-crime-report.html#commission (viewed on April 2, 2010).

[37] Austin, James, *Reducing America's Correctional Populations: a Strategic Plan*, National Institute of Corrections, 2009, p. 2. http://www.nicic.gov/PopulationReduction (viewed on April 2, 2010); Bureau of Justice Statistics, "State and Federal Prisoners 1925-1985," *Bureau of Justice Statistics Bulletin*, October 1986. Note: The DOJ Bureau of Justice Statistics prior to 2006 used the term incarceration rate to refer to the total number of inmates in custody in state or federal prison or local jails per 100,000 population as well as the number of sentenced prisoners per 100,000 population, where sentenced prisoners was defined as those sentenced to a term of a year or more. The BJS recently altered its terminology. Incarceration rate now refers to the total number of inmates, while the imprisonment rate refers to inmates sentenced to a year or more.

[38] DOJ/OJP, Bureau of Justice Statistics, "State and Federal Prisoners, 1925-1985," *Bureau of Justice Statistics Bulletin*, October 1986.

[39] Blumstein, Alfred and Allen J. Beck, "Population Growth in U.S. Prisons, 1980-1996," *Crime and Justice*, vol. 26, 1999, p. 19. http://www.jstor.org/stable/1147683 ; Michael J. Brown, Kentucky Justice & Public Safety Cabinet Secretary, "Population Trends and Cost Drivers," Presentation to National Governors' Association. http://www.nga.org/Files/pdf/0805SENTENCEPRES4.PDF (Viewed on April 7, 2010).

[40] Tinto, Eda Katharine, "The Role of Gender and Relationship in Reforming the Rockefeller Drug Laws," *New York University Law Review*, 76 NYUL, 2001, p. 911. http://heinonline.org/HOL/Page?handle=hein.journals/nylr76&div= 3 1&g_sent=1&collection=journals#93 1 (Viewed on April 2, 2010).

[41] CRS Report RL32040, *Federal Mandatory Minimum Sentencing Statutes*, by Charles Doyle, December 27, 2007.

[42] Brown, Brian and Greg Jolivette, *A Primer: Three Strikes, The Impact After More Than a Decade*, California Legislative Analyst's Office, October 2005, http://www.lao.ca.gov/2005/3_strikes/3_strikes_102005.htm# (Viewed on April 2, 2010).

[43] Western, Bruce, *From Prison to Work*, Presentation at Brookings Institution Symposium, December 2008. http://www.brookings.edu/~/media (viewed on April 2, 2010); Sabol, William J., Heather C. West, and Matthew Cooper, "Prisoners in 2008," *Bureau of Justice Statistics Bulletin*, Washington, DC: DOJ/OJP/BJS, December 2009, p. 16. Under another measure, which includes people in jails, as well as those in state or federal prisons, the 2008 incarceration rate was 754 per 100,000. This measure is sometimes used in studies showing the United States with the world's highest incarceration rate. Many other countries include their jail populations in their incarceration rate.

[44] Sabol, William J., Heather C. West, and Matthew Cooper, "Prisoners in 2008," *Bureau of Justice Statistics Bulletin*, December 2009, p. 8. The figure includes about 1.6 million people in state and federal prisons and 785,558 in jails. The total incarcerated population is 2.42 million counting those held U.S. Immigration and Customs Enforcement (ICE) facilities, juvenile facilities, and jails in Indian country.

[45] Holmes, Nigel, "Lock Up, U.S.A.," *American History*, October 2009, p. 44; Walmsey, Roy, *World Prison Population List*, 8th ed., International Centre for Prison Studies, King's College London, 2008. http://www.kcl.ac.uk/ depsta/law/research/icps/downloads/wppl-8th_41 .pdf (Viewed on April 2, 2010).

[46] Bureau of Justice Statistics, *Justice Expenditure and Employment Extracts, 2006*. http://bjs.ojp.usdoj.gov/index.cfm? ty=pbdetail&iid=1022 (Viewed on April 2, 2010).

[47] Bureau of Justice Statistics, "Justice Expenditure and Employment in the United States, 2003," *Bureau of Justice Statistics Bulletin*, April 2006, p. 2. http://bjs.ojp.usdoj.gov/index.cfm?ty=pbdetail&iid=1017 (Viewed on April 2, 2010).

[48] Stephan, James J., "State Prison Expenditures, 2001," *Bureau of Justice Statistics Special Report*, Washington, DC: DOJ/OJP, June 2004, p. 2. http://www.ojp.usdoj.gov/bjs/pub/pdf/spe01.pdf (Viewed on April 2, 2010).

[49] The Pew Center on the States, *One in 100: Behind Bars in America in 2008*, February 2008, p. 11. http://www.pewcenteronthestates.org/uploadedFiles/One%20in%20100.pdf (Viewed on April 2, 2010).

[50] Austin, James, *Reducing America's Correctional Populations, a Strategic Plan 2009*, National Institute of Corrections, 2009. http://community. (Viewed on April 2, 2010).

[51] Austin, James and Tony Fabelo, *The Diminishing Returns of Increased Incarceration: A Blueprint to Improve Public Safety and Reduce Costs*, The JFA Institute, July 2004, p. 12. http://www.jfa-associates.com/BlueprintFinal.pdf (Viewed on April 2, 2010).

[52] Sabol, William J., Heather C. West, and Matthew Cooper, "Prisoners in 2008," *Bureau of Justice Statistics Bulletin*, December 2009, Appendix Table 13.

[53] Sterns, Anthony A., Greta Lax, Chad Sed, Patrick Keohane and Ronni S. Sterns, "The Growing Wave of Older Prisoners: A National Survey of Older Prisoner Health, Mental Health and Programming," *Corrections Today*, Vol. 70, no. 4 (August 2008), pp. 70-76. http://www.aca.org/fileupload/177/ahaidar/Stern_Keohame.pdf (Viewed on April 2, 2010).

[54] Sabol, William J., Heather C. West, and Matthew Cooper, "Prisoners in 2008," *Bureau of Justice Statistics Bulletin*, December 2009, p. 1; National Institute of Corrections, *Reducing America's Correctional Populations, a Strategic Plan*, 2009, p. 2. http://community. (Viewed on April 2, 2010).http://www.nicic.gov/PopulationReduction

[55] U.S. Congress, House, Committee on Appropriations, Subcommittee on Commerce, Justice, Science, and Related Agencies, *Justice Reinvestment*, Statement by Secretary Roger Werholtz, Kansas Department of Corrections, Hearing, April 1, 2009. http://appropriations.house.gov/Witness_testimony/CJS/Roger_Werholtz_04_01_09.pdf (Viewed on April 2, 2010).

[56] U.S. Congress, House, Committee on Appropriations, Subcommittee on Commerce, Justice, Science, and Related Agencies. *Major Challenges Facing Federal Prisons, Part I*, Statement by Harley G. Lappin, Director, Federal Bureau of Prisons, Hearing, March 10, 2009. http://appropriations.house.gov/Witness_testimony/CJS/harley_lappin_03_10_09.pdf (Viewed on April 2, 2010).

[57] DOJ, "Maintain Prisons, Detention, Parole and Judicial and Courthouse Security," *FY 2011 Budget Request*, Factsheet. http://www.justice (Viewed on April 2, 2010).

[58] Sabol, William J., Heather C. West, and Matthew Cooper, "Prisoners in 2008," *Bureau of Justice Statistics Bulletin*, December 2009, p. 10.

[59] Interview with Kevin Campbell, Avondale Partners, February 19, 2010.

[60] U.S. Census Bureau, *Government Employment & Payroll, 2008*, http://www.census.gov/govs/apes/ (viewed on April 2, 2010). The data are derived from an annual survey of state, local and federal government entities. Of that total, there are 36,770 federal correction workers, 475,587 state workers and 258,317 state employees.

[61] U.S. Department of Labor (DOL), Bureau of Labor Statistics (BLS), *Occupational Outlook Handbook, 2010-1 1 Edition: Correctional Officers*, December 2009. http://www.bls.gov/oco/ocos156.htm (Viewed on April 2, 2010). The Labor Department occupational survey provides employment statistics by industry. The survey covers wage and salary workers in approximately 725,000 nonfarm establishments in 400 detailed industries.

[62] Ibid.

[63] DOL, BLS, *Occupational Outlook Handbook, 2010-11 Edition: Probation Officers and Correctional Treatment Specialists*, December 2009, http://www.bls.gov/oco/ocos265.htm (Viewed on April 2, 2010).

[64] CRS Report RL34297, *Motor Vehicle Manufacturing Employment: National and State Trends and Issues*, by Michaela D. Platzer.

[65] DOL, BLS, *Occupational Outlook Handbook, 2010-11 Edition: Correctional Officers*, December 2009. http://www.bls.gov/oco/ocos156.htm (Viewed on April 2, 2010).

[66] Scott-Hayward, Christine, *The Fiscal Crisis in Correction: Rethinking Policies and Practices*, Vera Institute of Justice, July 2009, p. 2. http://www.vera.org/files/The-fiscal-crisis-in-corrections_July-2009.pdf (Viewed on April 2, 2010).

[67] California Department of Corrections and Rehabilitation, *Peace Officer Careers*. http://www.cdcr.ca.gov/Career_Opportunities/POR/COIndex.html (Viewed on April 2, 2010).

[68] DOJ, Federal Bureau of Prisons, BOP Career Opportunities: Correctional Officers. http://www.bop.gov/jobs job_descriptions/correctional_officer.jsp (Viewed on April 2, 2010).

[69] Sumter, Melvina "The Correctional Work Force Faces Challenges in the 21st Century," *Corrections Today*, August 2008. http://www.aca.org/research/pdf/ResearchNotes_Aug08.pdf (Viewed on April 2, 2010).

[70] Ibid.

[71] AFSCME website, *Jobs We Do, Corrections*. http://www.afscme.org/workers (Viewed on April 2, 2010).

[72] California Correctional Peace Officers Association, Resources: Furlough. http://www.ccpoa.org/members/resources category/furlough/ (Viewed on April 2, 2010).

[73] New York State Correctional Officers & Police Benevolent Association (NYSCOPBA). NYSCOPBA Fighting Staffing Cuts and Facility Closures. http://www.nyscopba.org/fightingclosures (Viewed on April 2, 2010).

[74] Corrections Corporation of America, *2008 Annual Report*, p. 20. http://phx.corporate-ir.net/External.File?item= UGFyZW50SUQ9MTg3MDJ8Q2hpbGRJRD0tMXxUeXBlPTM=&t=1 (Viewed on April 2, 2010).

[75] CRS Report R40738, *The Public Safety Employer-Employee Cooperation Act*, by Jon O. Shimabukuro and Gerald Mayer.

[76] California Correctional Peace Officers Association, Resources: Furlough. http://ccpoa.org/news/tags/tag/furloughs (Viewed on April 2, 2010).

[77] Beam, Andrew, "Corrections officers use radio, TV to fight prison closings," *LegislativeGazette.com*, February 16, 2010. http://www.legislativegazette.com/Articles-c-2010-02-16-65492.113 122_Corrections_officers_use_radio_TV_to_fight_prison_closings.html (Viewed on April 2, 2010); Office of New York Gov. David Paterson, "Governor Paterson Announces Agency Cuts, Facility Closures And Other Measures to Streamline Government, Save Taxpayer Dollars," Press Release, January 19, 2010. http://www.state.ny.us/ governor/press/press_01 191005.html (Viewed on April 2, 2010).

[78] University of California at Berkeley, Institute of Government Studies, *California Correctional Peace Officers Association*, January 31, 2008. http://igs.berkeley.edu/library/htCaliforniaPrisonUnion.htm#Topic2 (Viewed on April 2, 2010).

[79] DOJ, "Prison Construction Keeping Pace with Population Growth," Press Release, August 7, 1997. http://bjs.ojp.usdoj.gov/content/pub/press/CSFCF95.PR(viewed on April 2, 2010); Stephan, James J., *Census of State and Federal Correctional Facilities, 2005*, Washington, DC: Bureau of Justice Statistics, p. 1. http://bjs.ojp.usdoj.gov/ content/pub/pdf/csfcf05.pdf (Viewed on April 2, 2010).; Unseem, Bert and Anne Morrison Piehl, *Prison State: The Challenge of Mass Incarceration*, Cambridge Studies in Criminology, Cambridge: Cambridge University Press, 2008. The 2005 DOJ figures include facilities that house primarily state or federal prisoners including prisons, prison farms, prison hospitals, boot camps, community correctional centers, centers for alcohol and drug treatment, centers for parole violators and other prisoners returned to custody, institutions for juveniles and geriatric inmates. The study did not include city, county, and regional jails; private facilities that did not house primarily state or federal inmates; military or immigration facilities, institutions operated by the Bureau of Indian Affairs, U.S. Marshals Service; or hospital wards not operated by correctional authorities.

[80] Beale, Calvin L., "Rural Prisons: An Update", *Rural Development Perspectives*, vol. 11, no. 2, March 2001, p. 25. http://www.ers.usda.gov/publications/RDP (Viewed on April 2, 2010).

[81] Stephan, James J. and Jennifer C. Karberg, , *Census of State and Federal Correctional Facilities, 2000*, Bureau of Justice Statistics, August 2003, p. 2. http://bjs.ojp.usdoj.gov/content/pub/pdf/csfcf00.pdf (viewed on April 2, 2010). Most prisons are medium- or minimum-security facilities. Maximum-security prisons make up about a fifth of the total. Most prisons have fewer than 500 inmates, though there has been a increase in the number of institutions housing 2,500 inmates or more.

[82] Ibid, p. 1. Private firms built 154 institutions between 1995 to 2000, out of the 204 adult correctional facilities built during that period.

[83] Sabol, William J., Heather C. West, and Matthew Cooper, "Prisoners in 2008," *Bureau of Justice Statistics Bulletin*, December 2009, p. 39.

[84] Ibid.

[85] Beale, Calvin, L. "Rural Prisons: An Update", *Rural Development Perspectives*, vol. 11, no. 2, March 2001, Washington, DC: Department of Agriculture, Economic Research Service. p. 25. http://www.ers.usda.gov/publications/ RDP/RDP296/rdp296d.pdf (Viewed on April 2, 2010)..

[86] Ibid. The findings follow earlier research by Beale who found that from 1980 to 1991, 213 prisons opened in nonmetro counties. The rural prisons held 53% of all prisoners sentenced to new prisons around the country. By comparison, only 38% of inmates in older facilities were located in nonmetro places, and 23% of the total U.S. population lived in nonmetro counties

[87] The Center for Rural Pennsylvania, *Newsletter*, November/December 2001. http://www.rural.palegislature.us/ news1 101.html. The report found that from 1990 to 2000, Pennsylvania's rural county population grew by 5.4%. If prisoners were not included in the rural population count, the growth rate would have been 4.7% in rural areas—a 0.7 percentage point difference. By comparison, factoring out the prison population would have reduced the growth rate in urban counties by less than 0.2 percentage points. (Viewed on April 2, 2010).

[88] Glasmeier, Amy K. and Tracey Farrigan, "The Economic Impacts of the Prison Development Boom on Persistently Poor Rural Places," *International Regional Science Review*, Vol. 30, No. 3 (2007), p. 4. A version of this paper is available at http://www.povertyinamerica.psu.edu/products/publications/prison_development/prison_development.pdf (Viewed on April 2, 2010).

[89] U.S. Census Bureau, *1990 Census of Population and Housing,* "Population: 1790 to 1990," http://www.census.gov/ population/www/censusdata/files/table-4.pdf (Viewed on April 2, 2010).

[90] Lawrence, Sarah and Jeremy Travis, *The New Landscape of Imprisonment: Mapping America's Prison Expansion*, Urban Institute Justice Policy Center, April 2004, p. 1. http://www.urban.org/UploadedPDF/ 410994_mapping_prisons.pdf (Viewed on April 2, 2010).

[91] Sabol, William J., Heather C. West, and Matthew Cooper, "Prisoners in 2008," *Bureau of Justice Statistics Bulletin*, December 2009. p. 9. http://bjs.ojp.usdoj.gov/content/pub/pdf/p08.pdf According to the Bureau of Justice Statistics, "Highest capacity is the sum of the maximum number of beds and inmates reported by the

states and the federal system across the three capacity measures." The three measures are: *rated capacity*, *operational capacity*, and *design capacity*.

[92] Ibid.

[93] *Coleman v. Schwarzenegger*, No. CIV S-90-0520 LKK JFM P, Three-Judge Court and *Plata v. Schwarzenegger*, No. C01-1351 TEH, Three-Judge Court, United States District Court for the Eastern District of California, August 4, 2009. See also: *Plata v. Schwarzenegger*, 560 F.3d 976 (9th Cir. Cal., 2009). The Order of the Three Judge Court is at http://www.ca9.uscourts.gov/datastore/general/2009/08/04/Opinion%20&%20Order%20FINAL.pdf (viewed on April 2, 2010). Moore, Solomon, "Court Orders California to Cut Prison Population," *New York Times*, February 9, 2009. http://www.nytimes.com/2009/02/10/us/10prison.html (Viewed on April 2, 2010).

[94] Sabol, William J., Heather C. West, and Matthew Cooper, "Prisoners in 2008," *Bureau of Justice Statistics Bulletin*, December 2009, p. 17; Jackson, Peter, "Pa. plans to send inmates away," *Associated Press*, November 23, 2009. http://www.philly.com/inquirer/local/pa/20091123_Pa_plans_to_send_inmates_away.html (Viewed on April 2, 2010).

[95] Cornell Companies, "Cornell Companies Reports Fourth-Quarter Earnings Above Guidance," Press Release, February 24, 2010. http://phx.corporate-ir.net/phoenix.zhtml?c=94469&p=irol-newsArticle&ID=1395235&highlight= (Viewed on April 2, 2010).

[96] Cornell Companies, *2008 Annual Report*, Introduction, p. 2. http://phx.corporate-ir.net/External.File?item=UGFyZW50SUQ9MzM3NDI3fENoaWxkSUQ9MzIyMDEwfFR5cGU9MQ==&t=1 (Viewed on April 2, 2010).

[97] Scott-Hayward, Christine, *The Fiscal Crisis in Correction: Rethinking Policies and Practices*, Vera Institute of Justice, July 2009, p. 6. http://www.vera.org/files/The-fiscal-crisis-in-corrections_July-2009.pdf (Viewed on April 2, 2010). Not all states are in a position to close facilities. States that have taken action to reduce their prison populations have been able to carry out such moves.

[98] Office of New York Gov. David Paterson, "Governor Paterson Announces Agency Cuts, Facility Closures And Other Measures to Streamline Government, Save Taxpayer Dollars," Press Release, January 19, 2010. http://www.state.ny.us/governor/press/press_01191005.html (Viewed on April 2, 2010).

[99] Steinhauer, Jennifer, "Arizona Prisons Plan to Transfer Illegal Immigrants to Federal Authority," *New York Times*, December 21, 2009. http://www.nytimes.com/2009/12/22/us/22arizona.html (Viewed on April 2, 2010).

[100] California, Office of the Governor, "Fact Sheet: State of the State 2010 Reshaping our Priorities to Shift Funding From Prisons to Universities," January 6, 2010. http://gov.ca.gov/index.php?/fact-sheet/14126/ (Viewed on April 2, 2010).

[101] Gold, Martin E., *Alternatives for Financing Prison Facilities*, Report for the Association of State Correctional Administrators by Brown & Wood LLP, 1999, p. iii. http://www.asca.net/documents/alt_main_000.pdf (Viewed on April 2, 2010).

[102] Saskal, Rich, "California Appeals Court Upholds Lease Revenue Bond Holding, *Bond Buyer*, March 31, 2009.

[103] Oregon State Debt Policy Advisory Commission, *2009 Legislative Update*, January 9, 2009, p. 17. http://www.ost.state.or.us/divisions/DMD/SDPAC/SDPAC.Report.2009.pdf (Viewed on April 2, 2010).

[104] Colorado, Department of the Treasury, *Public Finance and Debt Issuance*. http://www.colorado.gov/cs/Satellite/Treasury/TR/1 190709088150 (Viewed on April 2, 2010).

[105] Alexander, Rachel, "CSP II Will Open This Year," *Canon City Daily Record*, February 19, 2010. http://www.canoncitydailyrecord.com/Top-Story.asp?ID=12998 (Viewed on April 2, 2010).

[106] Provus, Stan, *CDFA Spotlight: Lease/Appropriation-Backed Bonds*, Council of Development Finance Agencies. http://www.cdfa.net/cdfa/cdfaweb.nsf/pages/tlcjan2006.html (Viewed on April 2, 2010).

[107] Clark, John L., *Report to the Attorney General: Independent Review of the Management and Operations of the Northeast Ohio Correctional Center (NEOCC) in Youngstown, Ohio, Owned and Operated by the Corrections Corporation of America (CCA)*. Washington, DC: Office of the Corrections Trustee for the District of Columbia, November 25, 1998. Available at http://www.justice (viewed on April 2, 2010). General Accounting Office (GAO), *District of Columbia: Issues Related to the Youngstown Prison Report and Lorton Closure Process*, GAO/GCD-0086. Available at http://www.gao.gov/archive/2000/gg00086.pdf (Viewed on April 2, 2010).

[108] Priest, Dana and Amy Goldstein, "System of Neglect," *Washington Post*, May 11, 2008. http://www.washingtonpost.com/wp-srv/nation

[109] Dickinson, Elizabeth, "The Future of Incarceration," *Architect*, June 2008. http://www.architectmagazine.com/Design/the-future-of-incarceration.aspx?page=1 (Viewed on April 2, 2010).

[110] Cray, Charlie, "Behind the Lines: No to Prison Food," *Multinational Monitor*, Vol. 22, No. 6, June 2001. http://www.multinationalmonitor.org/mm2001/062001/lines.html (Viewed on April 2, 2010).

[111] Berestein, Leslie, "A once ailing private-prison sector is now a revenue maker," *Copley News Service*, May 2008, http://www.hermes-press.com/prison0.htm (Viewed on April 2, 2010).

[112] Stephan, James J., *Census of State and Federal Correctional Facilities, 2005*, Washington, DC: Bureau of Justice Statistics, p. 1. http://bjs.ojp.usdoj.gov/content/pub/pdf/csfcf05.pdf (Viewed on April 2, 2010).

[113] Austin, James and Garry Coventry, *Emerging Issues on Privatized Prisons*, Washington, DC: Department of Justice, Bureau of Justice Assistance, February 2001, p. 12. Available at http://www.ncjrs.gov/pdffiles1/bja/181249.pdf (Viewed on April 2, 2010).

[114] U. S. Government Accountability Office, *Cost of Prisons: Bureau of Prisons Needs Better Data to Assess Alternatives for Acquiring Low and Minimum Security Facilities Cost*, Report GAO-08-6, October 2007, p. 4. http://www.gao.gov/new.items/d086.pdf (Viewed on April 2, 2010).

[115] Gaes, Gerry, "Cost, Performance Studies Look at Prison Privatization," *NIJ Journal*, No. 259, Washington, DC: Department of Justice, National Institute of Justice, March 18, 2008. http://www.ncjrs.gov/pdffiles1/nij/221507.pdf (Viewed on April 2, 2010).

[116] Ibid.

[117] Austin, James and Garry Coventry, *Emerging Issues on Privatized Prisons*, Washington, DC: Department of Justice, Bureau of Justice Assistance, February 2001, available at http://www.ncjrs.gov/pdffiles1/bja/181249.pdf (Viewed on April 2, 2010).

[118] Blumstein, James, Mark A. Cohen and Susan Seth, "Do Government Agencies Respond to Market Pressure? Evidence from Private Prisons," *Virginia Journal of Social Policy and the Law*, Vol. 15(3), p. 446 - 477, Spring 2008. Initial work on the study was funded in part by the Corrections Corporation of America and the Association for Private Correctional and Treatment Organizations. Later research was funded by the Owen Graduate School of Management and Vanderbilt Law School. This article is available at http://www.correctionscorp.com/static/assets Blumstein_Cohen_Study.pdf (Viewed on April 2, 2010).

[119] Austin, James and Garry Coventry, *Emerging Issues on Privatized Prisons*, Washington, DC: Department of Justice, Bureau of Justice Assistance, February 2001, p, 52, available at http://www.ncjrs.gov/pdffiles1/bja/181249.pdf (Viewed on April 2, 2010).

[120] New Mexico, Legislative Finance Committee, *Corrections Department: Review of Facility Planning Efforts and Oversight of Private Prisons and Health Programs*, Report #07-04, May 23, 2007. http://www.nmlegis.gov/lcs/lfc/ lfcdocs/perfaudit/CorrectionsFacilities0507.pdf (Viewed on April 2, 2010).

[121] Interview with Kevin Campbell, February Feb 19, 2010.

[122] DOJ, Office of the Inspector General, *The Department of Justice's Reliance on Private Contractors for Prison Services*, Report No. 01-16, July 31, 2001, http://www.justice (Viewed on April 2, 2010). The 2001 audit by the DOJ Office of Inspector General noted that federal entities were becoming more dependent on private prisons and stressed the need for contingency plans in the event private firms ran into financial difficulties that could make it hard for them to fulfill contracts.

[123] Florida, Legislature, Office of Program Policy Analysis & Government Accountability, *While DMS Has Improved Monitoring, It Needs to Strengthen Private Prison Oversight and Contracts*, December 2008, available at http://www.oppaga.state.fl.us/reports/pdf/0871rpt.pdf (Viewed April 2, 2010).

[124] Corrections Corporation of America, http://www.correctionscorp.com/ (Viewed on April 2, 2010).

[125] Corrections Corporation of America, *2008 Annual Report*, p. 29 and *2005 Annual Report*, p. 11, http://ir.correctionscorp.com/phoenix.zhtml?c=117983&p=irol-reportsannual (Viewed on April 2, 2010).

[126] Corrections Corporation of America, *2008 Annual Report*, p. 11, http://ir.correctionscorp.com/phoenix.zhtml?c= 1 17983 &p=irol-reportsannual.

[127] Pershing Square Capital Management, L.P., *Prisons' Dilemma*, October 20, 2009. PowerPoint presentation at http://www.scribd.com/doc/21624762/Bill-Ackman-s-Presentation-on-Corrections-Corp-of-America-CXW-the-ValueInvesting-Congress (Viewed on April 2, 2010).

[128] Corrections Corporation of America, "CCA Announces Fourth Quarter and Full Year 2009 Financial Results," Press Release, February 9, 2010 http://ir.correctionscorp.com/phoenix.zhtml?c=117983&p=irol-newsArticle&ID=1385706& highlight= (Viewed on April 2, 2010).

[129] *Seeking Alpha*, "Corrections Corporation of America Q4 2009 Earnings Call Transcript," February 10, 2010, http://seekingalpha.com/article/187861-corrections-corporation-of-america-q4-2009-earnings (Viewed on April 2, 2010).

[130] Barr, Alistair, "Ackman Highlights Corrections as top real estate play," *Marketwatch*, Oct 20, 2009, http://www.marketwatch.com/story/fund-manager-ackman-highlights-corrections-corp-2009-10-20 (Viewed on April 2, 2010).

[131] Morain, Dan, "Private prisons? A sweet deal for some," *Sacramento Bee*, January 7, 2010, http://www.sacbee.com/ 1 190/story/2443722.html (Viewed on April 2, 2010).

[132] Correction Corporation of America, News Releases, http://ir.correctionscorp.com/phoenix.zhtml?c=117983&p=irolnews&nyo=0 (viewed April 2, 2010).

[133] Gee, Brandon, "Sexual misconduct allegations threaten CCA contract," *Nashville Business Journal*, March 1, 2010, http://www.bizjournals.com/nashville/stories/2010/03/01/daily6.html (Viewed on April 2, 2010).

[134] GEO Group, "Who We Are," http://www.thegeogroupinc.com/about.asp (Viewed on April 2, 2010).

[135] GEO Group, "The GEO Group Reports Fourth Quarter 2009 Results and Announces $80.0 Million Stock Repurchase Program," Press Release, February 22, 2010, http://phx.corporate-ir.net/phoenix.zhtml?c=9 133 1&p=irolnewsArticlejrint&ID=1393451&highlight= (Viewed on April 2, 2010).

[136] GEO Group, *2008 Annual Report*, p. 1, http://phx.corporate-ir.net/phoenix.zhtml?c=9 133 1&p=irol-reportsAnnual (Viewed on April 2, 2010).

[137] GEO Group, *2007 Annual Report*, p. 5, http://phx.corporate-ir.net/phoenix.zhtml?c=9 133 1&p=irol-reportsAnnual (Viewed on April 2, 2010).

[138] *Seeking Alpha*, "The GEO Group Inc. Q4 2008 Earnings Call Transcript, February 12, 2009," http://seekingalpha.com/article/120353-the-geo-group-inc-q4-2008-earnings (Viewed on April 2, 2010).

[139] Cornell Companies, "Cornell Companies Reports Fourth Quarter Earnings Above Guidance," Press Release, February 24, 2010 http://phx.corporate-ir.net/phoenix.zhtml?c=94469&p=irol-newsArticlejrint&ID=1395235& highlight= (Viewed on April 2, 2010).

[140] Cornell Companies, *2008 Annual Report*, p. 55, http://phx.corporate-ir.net/External.File?item= UGFyZW50SUQ9MzM3NDI3fENoaWxkSUQ9MzIyMDEwfFR5cGU9MQ==&t=1 (Viewed on April 2, 2010).

[141] Ibid.

[142] American Correctional Association, http://www.aca.org/advertise/audience.asp (Viewed on April 2, 2010).

[143] CRS Report R40846, *Health Care: Constitutional Rights and Legislative Powers*, by Kathleen S. Swendiman, p. 5.

[144] Wilper, Andrew P., Steffie Woolhandler, J. Wesley Boyd, Karen E. Lasser, Danny McCormick, David H. Bor, and David U. Himmelstein, "The Health and Health Care of U.S. Prisoners: A Nationwide Survey," *American Journal of Public Health*, Vol. 99, No. 4, 2009, pp. 666-672.

[145] America Service Group, "America Service Group Announces Fourth Quarter and Year End Results," Press Release, March 2, 2010, at http://investor.asgr.com/phoenix.zhtml?c=117621&p=irol-newsArticle&ID=1397878&highlight= (Viewed on April 2, 2010).

[146] America Service Group, *2008 Annual Report*, p. 8, at http://www.asgr.com/ (Viewed on April 2, 2010).

[147] Community Education Centers, http://www.cecintl.com/About/Message.htm (Viewed on April 2, 2010).

[148] Aramark Correctional Services, http://www.aramarkcorrections.com/ (Viewed on April 2, 2010).

[149] Tiger Correctional Services, http://www.tigercommissary.com/about-tiger-commissary.html (Viewed on April 2, 2010).

[150] Cornerstone Detention Products. http://www.cornerstonedetention.com/ (Viewed onApril 2, 2010).

[151] Argyle Security Inc., *2008 Annual Report*, p. 11. http://phx.corporate-ir.net/External.File?item= UGFyZW50SUQ9Mzk4OHxDaGlsZElEPS0xfFR5cGU9Mw==&t=1 (viewed April 2, 2010).

[152] U.S. Congress, House, Committee on Energy and Commerce, Subcommittee on Communications, Technology and the Internet, *Legislative Hearing on H.R. 1147, the Local Community Radio Act of 2009, H.R. 1133, the Family Telephone Connection Protection Act of 2009, and H.R. 1084, the Commercial Advertisement Loudness Mitigation Act (CALM Act)*: Testimony of Frank Krogh, Representing the Washington Lawyers' Committee for Civil Rights and Urban Affairs, June 11, 2009. http://energycommerce.house.gov/Press_111/20090611/testimony_krogh.pdf (viewed April 2, 2010).

[153] U.S. Congress, House, Committee on Energy and Commerce, Subcommittee on Communications, Technology and the Internet, *Legislative Hearing on H.R. 1147, the Local Community Radio Act of 2009, H.R. 1133, the Family Telephone Connection Protection Act of 2009, and H.R. 1084, the Commercial Advertisement Loudness Mitigation Act (CALM Act)*, Testimony of Sheriff David Goad, president National Sheriffs' Association, June 11, 2009. http://www.sheriffs.org/userfiles/File/Congressional%20Testimony/Microsoft _NSA_Sheriff_Goad_Testimony_on_H_R__1 133.pdf (Viewed on April 2, 2010).

[154] *Seeking Alpha*, "Corrections Corporation of America Fourth Quarter 2009 Earnings Call Transcript." http://seekingalpha.com/article/187861-corrections-corporation-of-america-q4-2009-earnings

[155] *National Public Radio*, "Michigan Town Weighs Moving Guantanamo Detainees Next Door," September 1, 2009. http://www.pbs.org/newshour/bb/terrorism (viewed April 2, 2010).

[156] Carton, Tony, "Sparse Attendance at COGFA Marathon Hearing for Thomson Prison Closing," *Prairie Advocate News*, December 30, 2009. http://www.prairie-advocate-news.com/12-30-09/thomsonprison12_30_09.html (viewed April 2, 2010).

[157] Executive Office of the President, Council of Economic Advisers, *Technical Memorandum*. November 21, 2009, see http://www.illinois.gov/publicincludes/statehome/gov/documents/White%20House% 20Thomson% 20economic%20analysis.pdf (viewed on April 2, 2010); *Chicago Sun-Times*, "Illinois, Guantanamo north? White House releases economic impact study," November 21, 2009.

[158] Carton, Tony, "Sparse Attendance at COGFA Marathon Hearing for Thomson Prison Closing," *Prairie Advocate News*, December 30, 2009. http://www.prairie-advocate-news.com/12-30-09/thomsonprison12_30_09.html (Viewed on April 2, 2010).

[159]   Council of Economic Advisers, *Technical Memorandum.* November 21, 2009, http://www.illinois.gov/publicincludes/statehome/gov/documents/White%20House%20Thomson%20economic%20analysis.pdf.

[160]   Glasmeier, Amy K. and Tracey Farrigan, "The Economic Impacts of the Prison Development Boom on Persistently Poor Rural Places," *International Regional Science Review*, Vol. 30, No. 3 (2007), p. 1. A version of this paper is available at http://www.povertyinamerica.psu.edu/products/publications/prison_development/prison_development.pdf (Viewed on April 2, 2010).

[161]   Hooks, Gregory, Clayton Mosher, Thomas Totolo and Linda Lobao, "The Prison Industry: Carceral Expansion and Employment in U.S. Counties, 1969-1994," *Social Science Quarterly*, Vol. 85, No. 1, 2004. pp. 37-57.

[162]   Besser, Terry L. and Margaret M. Hanson. "Development of Last Resort: The Impact of New State Prisons on Small Town Economies in the United States," *Community Development*, vol. 35, Issue 2, (2004). pp. 1-16.

[163]   City of Shelby, Montana, *Corrections at the Crossroads, 5-Year Analysis, 10-Year Analysis, Crossroads Correctional Center*, at http://www.shelbymt.com/Brownsfield/CCC%20Analysis.pdf (Viewed on April 2, 2010).

[164]   Johnson, Peter, "Supporters want Shelby prison in running for expansion," *Great Falls Tribune*, September 14, 2009.

[165]   Telephone interview with Larry Bonderud, Mayor, Shelby, MT, February 1, 2010.

[166]   Telephone interview with Jeffrey S. McDowell, Executive Director, Hardin Two Rivers Port Authority, January 27, 2010.

[167]   Montana, Legislative Audit Division, *Two Rivers Regional Detention Center in Hardin, Montana*, Memorandum, November 27, 2007. http://www.cor.mt.gov/content/Resources/CorAdvCouncil/Archive/February2008/ AuditorReport.pdf (Viewed on April 2, 2010).

[168]   Telephone interview with Jeffrey S. McDowell, Executive Director, Hardin Two Rivers Port Authority, January 27, 2010.

[169]   Williams, Carol J., "Justice Kennedy laments the state of prisons in California, U.S.," *Los Angeles Times*, February 4, 2010, see http://articles.latimes.com/2010/feb/04/local/la-me-kennedy4-2010feb04 (Viewed on April 2, 2010).

[170]   *Kansas City Star*, "Judge Price Delivers State of the Judiciary Address." http://primebuzz.kcstar.com/?q=node/21240 (viewed on April 2, 2010).

[171]   National Conference of State Legislatures, Significant State Sentencing and Corrections Legislation in 2009, January 19, 2010. http://www.ncsl.org/?TabId=19122 (Viewed on April 2, 2010).

[172]   Fields, Gary, "U.S. Commission to Assess Mandatory Sentences," Wall Street Journal, November 12, 2009. http://online.wsj.com/article/SB125798793160144461.html (Viewed on April 2, 2010).

[173]   Scott-Hayward, Christine, *The Fiscal Crisis in Corrections, Rethinking Policies and Practices*, Vera Institute of Justice, July 2009, p. 2 http://www.vera.org/files/The-fiscal-crisis-in-corrections_July-2009.pdf.

[174]   Gustafson, Alan, "House Votes to Suspend Early Release, *Salem Statesman Journal*, February 17, 2010, http://www.statesmanjournal.com/article/20100217/LEGISLATURE/2170439/1042.

[175]   *Seeking Alpha*, "Corrections Corporation of America Q4 2009 Earnings Call Transcript, February 10, 2010, http://seekingalpha.com/article/187861-corrections-corporation-of-america-q4-2009-earnings (Viewed on April 2, 2010).

PRISONERS IN 2008: BUREAU OF JUSTICE STATISTICS*

United States Department of Justice

At yearend 2008, federal and state correctional authorities had jurisdiction over 1,610,446 prisoners (**figure 1**). *Jurisdiction* refers to the legal authority over a prisoner, regardless of where the prisoner is held.

The prison population increased by 12,201 prisoners from 2007 to 2008, the smallest annual increase since 2000. The 0.8% growth during 2008 was the second year of decline in the rate of growth and the slowest growth in eight years. From 2000 to 2008 the growth of the prison population (1.8% per year on average) was less than a third of the rate observed during the 1990s (6.5% per year on average) (not shown in figure).

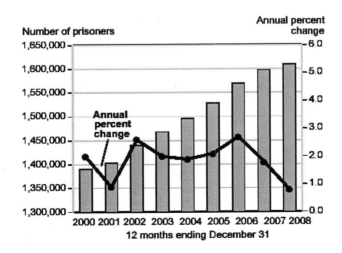

Figure 1. Prisoners under state or federal jurisdiction at yearend, 2000-2008

---

* This is an edited, reformatted and augmented version of a U. S. Department of Justice publication dated April 2010.

State correctional authorities had jurisdiction over 1,409,166 prisoners at yearend 2008, an increase of 10,539 state prisoners during the year. Federal correctional authorities (or the federal prison system) had jurisdiction over 201,280 prisoners, up 1,662 federal prisoners from the previous year. While the numbers of state and federal prisoners reached all-time yearend highs in 2008, the respective growth rates for each slowed to 0.8% (**figure 2**). This was the second smallest annual rate of growth in the state prison population (0.1% growth occurred in 2001) and the lowest rate for the federal prison population since 2000.

HIGHLIGHTS

- The U.S. prison population grew at the slowest rate (0.8%) since 2000, reaching 1,610,446 prisoners at yearend 2008.
- Growth of the prison population since 2000 (1.8% per year on average) was less than a third of the average annual rate during the 1990s (6.5% per year on average).
- Slower growth in the state prison population was associated with fewer new court commitments during 2007 and 2008, reversing the trend of steady growth of state prison admissions witnessed from 2000 to 2006.
- An increase in the number of prison releases was led by offenders released to the community without supervision.
- Between 2000 and 2008 the number of blacks in prison declined by 18,400, lowering the imprisonment rate to 3,161 men and 149 women per 100,000 persons in the U.S. resident black population.
- The U.S. imprisonment rate declined for the second time since yearend 2000; about 1 in every 198 persons in the U.S. resident population was incarcerated in state or federal prison at yearend 2008.

Twenty states reported a decline in the number of prisoners under their jurisdiction in 2008 for a total decrease of 9,719 prisoners (appendix table 2). New York (down 2,273 prisoners), Georgia (down 1,537), and Michigan (down 1,495) reported the largest reductions, accounting for more than half (54.6%) of the decline in the total number of prisoners. New York (down 3.6%) recorded the largest rate of decrease in its prison population during 2008, followed by Kentucky (down 3.3%), and New Jersey (down 3.3%).

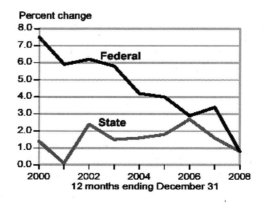

Figure 2. Percent change in number of prisoners under state or federal jurisdiction, 2000-2008

Twenty-nine states and the federal prison system reported a combined increase of 21,920 prisoners at yearend. Pennsylvania (up 4,178 prisoners) and Florida (up 4,169) had the largest increases, followed by Arizona (1,843), the federal prison system (1,662), and North Carolina (1,512). Combined, these five jurisdictions accounted for 61% of the growth among jurisdictions holding more prisoners at yearend. Pennsylvania also reported the fastest rate of growth (up 9.1%) for 2008.

SLOWER GROWTH IN THE STATE PRISON POPULATION ASSOCIATED WITH FEWER NEW COURT COMMITMENTS

Several factors contributed to slowing the growth of the state and federal prison populations from 2006 to 2008, including a decrease in the number of prison admissions, a decline in the number of new court commitments to state prison, and an increase in the number released from both state and federal prison. Prison admissions have declined for the past two years as the number of admissions dropped by about 6,923 sentenced offenders during 2007 and by 3,743 prisoners during 2008 (**table 3**).

The number of offenders released from state and federal prisons rose by 2.0% to reach 735,454 prisoners while the number of admissions declined by 0.5% (down 3,743).

Among the states, admissions and releases of sentenced prisoners have converged since 2006 as admissions declined and releases of state prisoners increased (**figure 3**). In 2008, 30 states reported a decrease in prisons admissions, totaling 19,019 prisoners. The remaining 20 states reported an increase in prison admissions, totalling 15,783 prisoners. Four states accounted for 40.7% of the total decrease in prison admissions from 2007 to 2008 (**appendix table 11**). Georgia (down 2,509) reported the largest absolute decrease, followed by Mississippi (down 1,841), Kansas (down 1,408), and Washington (down 1,229).

Fewer new court commitments to state prison accounted for the declining number of state prison admissions in 2007 and 2008, reversing the trend in the increasing number of state prison admissions observed from 2000 to 2006 (**figure 4**).[1] The number of new court commitments to state prison dropped by 10,587 in 2007 and 2,189 in 2008 as the total number of state prison admissions declined by 3,046 and 3,787, respectively. The number of parole violators admitted to state prison increased during 2008 at a slower rate than during the previous two years, offsetting some of the effect of the decline in new court commitments on the total number of state prison admissions.

SELECTED CHARACTERISTICS OF THE PRISON POPULATION UNDER STATE AND FEDERAL JURISDICTION

- Men were 93% of prisoners under state or federal jurisdiction, and women were 7% (**table 1**).
- About 34% of all sentenced prisoners were white, 38% were black, and 20% were Hispanic.
- Males were imprisoned at a rate about 15 times higher than females (**table 2**).
- Black males were imprisoned at a rate six and half times higher than white males.

Table 1. Number of Prisoners Under State and Federal Jurisdiction, by Sentence Length, Race, Hispanic Origin, and Gender, 2008

	Total	Male	Female
Prisoners by sentence length			
Total under jurisdiction	1,610,446	1,495,594	114,852
Sentenced to more than 1 year	1,540,036	1,434,784	105,252
Estimated prisoners by race[a]			
White[b]	591,900	562,800	50,700
Black[b]	528,200	477,500	29,100
Hispanic	313,100	295,800	17,300

[a]Based on prisoners sentenced to more than 1 year. Excludes American Indians, Alaska Natives, Asians, Native Hawaiians, other Pacific Islanders, and persons identifying two or more races.
[b]Excludes persons of Hispanic or Latino origin.

Table 2. Imprisonment Rate Per 100,000 Person in the U.S. Resident Population, by Race, Hispanic Origin, and Gender, 2008

	Male	Female
Total[a]	952	68
White[b]	487	50
Black[b]	3,161	149
Hispanic	1,200	75

Note: Imprisonment rates are the number of prisoners under state or federal jurisdiction sentenced to more than 1 year per 100,000 persons in the U.S. resident population in the referenced population group. See *Methodology* for estimation method.
[a]Total includes American Indians, Alaska Natives, Asians, Native Hawaiians, other Pacific Islanders, and persons identifying two or more races.
[b]Excludes persons of Hispanic or Latino origin.

NUMBER AND RATE OF PRISON RELEASES INCREASED IN 2008

The number of offenders released from state and federal prisons increased by 2% (or 14,293 releases) during 2008 to reach 735,454. In total, 29 states and the federal system reported increases in the number of prison releases totaling 23,524 offenders. This increase was offset by a total decrease of 9,034 releases in the remaining 21 states (**appendix table 11**). The increase in the number of prison releases was led by an 8% (or 16,883 releases) increase in the number of prisoners released unconditionally during 2008.[2]

Table 3. Number of Sentenced Prisoners Admitted to and Released from State and Federal Jurisdiction, 2000-2008

Year	Admissions			Releases		
	Total	Federal	State	Total	Federal	State
2000	625,219	43,732	581,487	604,858	35,259	569,599
2001	638,978	45,140	593,838	628,626	38,370	590,256
2002	661,712	48,144	613,568	630,176	42,339	587,837
2003	686,437	52,288	634,149	656,384	44,199	612,185
2004	699,812	52,982	646,830	672,202	46,624	625,578
2005	733,009	56,057	676,952	701,632	48,323	653,309
2006	749,798	57,495	692,303	713,473	47,920	665,553
2007	742,875	53,618	689,257	721,161	48,764	672,397
2008	739,132	53,662	685,470	735,454	52,348	683,106
Average annual change, 2000-2007	2.5%	3.0%	2.5%	2.5%	4.7%	2.4%
Percent change, 2007-2008	-0.5	0.1	-0.5	2.0	7.3	1.6

Note: Totals based on prisoners with a sentence of more than 1 year. Totals exclude transfers, escapes, and AWOLS.

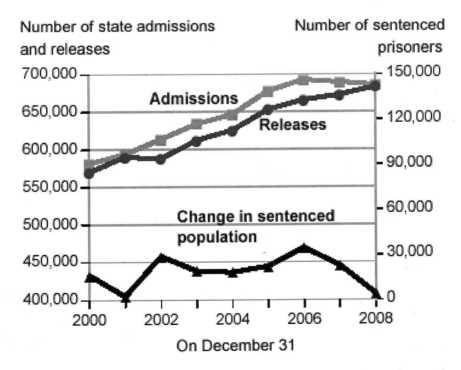

Figure 3. Number of state admissions and releases and change in number of sentenced state prisoners, December 2000-2008

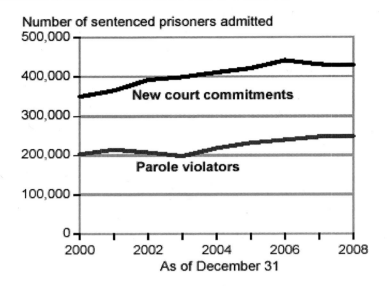

Figure 4. Sentenced admissions into state prisons, by type of admission, 2000-2008

Table 4. Number of Sentenced Prisoners Released from State Prisons, by Type of release, 2000-2008

Year	Releases		
	Total[a]	Conditional[b]	Unconditional[c]
2000	569,599	425,887	118,886
2001	590,256	437,251	130,823
2002	587,837	440,842	127,389
2003	612,185	442,168	127,386
2004	625,578	480,727	123,147
2005	653,309	495,370	133,943
2006	665,553	497,801	148,114
2007	672,397	504,181	152,589
2008	683,106	505,168	165,568

[a]Totals based on prisoners with a sentence of more than 1 year. Totals exclude transfers, escapes, and AWOLS.

[b]Total conditional releases include releases to probation, parole, supervised mandatory releases, and other unspecified conditional releases.

[c]Total unconditional releases include expirations of sentence, commutations, and other unconditional releases.

Unconditional releases from state prisons accounted for 91% of the increase in the total number of prisoners released unconditionally (not shown in a table). During 2008 the number released unconditionally from state prisons increased by about 13,000 (or 8.5%), while conditional releases from state prisons increased by fewer than 1,000 (or about 0.2%) (**table 4**).[3] As a result of the increase in unconditional releases from state prisons, the share of all state prison admissions accounted for by unconditional releases reached 24% in 2008, a higher share than any year since 2000.

SLOWER GROWTH IN THE PRISON POPULATION SINCE 2000 WAS ASSOCIATED WITH A DECLINE IN THE NUMBER OF SENTENCED BLACK PRISONERS

A decrease in the number of sentenced black offenders has been associated with slower growth in the size of the state and federal prison populations. The number of imprisoned blacks has declined by about 18,400 since yearend 2000, reducing the total number of blacks in prison to about 591,900 at yearend 2008 (**table 5**). Conversely, the numbers of sentenced white and Hispanic offenders have increased since 2000. the number of imprisoned whites has risen by 57,200 since 2000 to reach 528,200 at yearend 2008. The total number of imprisoned Hispanics rose by 96,200 to reach 313,100 during this period.

A decrease in the black imprisonment rates accompanied the decline in the number of imprisoned black offenders (**table 6**). Between 2000 and 2008 the imprisonment rate for black men decreased from 3,457 per 100,000 in the U.S. resident population to 3,161, and the imprisonment rate for black women declined from 205 per 100,000 in the U.S. resident population to 149. For Hispanic men the imprisonment rate remained relatively steady at about 1,200 per 100,000 in the U.S. resident population during this period. For white men the imprisonment rate increased from 449 per 100,000 in the U.S. resident population in 2000 to 487 per 100,000 in 2008.

The decline in the black imprisonment rate since 2000 means that an estimated 61,000 fewer blacks were in state or federal prisons than expected at yearend 2008 if the imprisonment rate for blacks had remained at its 2000 level (not shown in table). In contrast, the increase in the imprisonment rate for whites resulted in about 54,000 more sentenced white prisoners at yearend 2008 than expected if their rate of imprisonment had remained unchanged since 2000. The number of imprisoned Hispanics and the Hispanic U.S. resident population experienced about the same rates of growth from 2000 to 2008. Consequently, there was relatively little difference (3,600) between the number of sentenced Hispanics who would have been in prison in 2008 if the Hispanic imprisonment rate had remained at its 2000 level.

FEWER BLACKS IMPRISONED FOR DRUG OFFENSES ACCOUNTED FOR MOST OF THE DECLINE IN THE NUMBER OF SENTENCED BLACKS IN STATE PRISON

From 2000 to 2006 (the most recent offense data available), the total number of sentenced offenders in state prisons increased by 124,700 to reach 1,331,100 state prisoners. Offenders convicted of a violent offense accounted for 63% of the growth in the state prison population; offenders convicted of a drug offense accounted for about 12% (**table 7**). The number of sentenced blacks in state prisons fell to 508,700 in 2006, declining by 53,300 prisoners since 2000. More than half of this decline (56%) was made up of 29,600 fewer blacks imprisoned for drug offenses.

Table 5. Estimated Number of Sentenced Prisoners under State or Federal Jurisdiction, by Race and Hispanic Origin, December 31, 2000-2008

Year	Total number of prisoners			
	Total[a]	White[b]	Black[b]	Hispanic
2000	1,321,200	471,000	610,300	216,900
2001	1,344,500	485,400	622,200	209,900
2002	1,380,300	472,200	622,700	250,000
2003	1,409,300	493,400	621,300	268,100
2004	1,433,800	491,800	583,400	275,600
2005	1,461,100	505,500	577,100	294,900
2006	1,502,200	527,100	562,800	308,000
2007	1,532,800	521,900	586,200	318,800
2008	1,540,100	528,200	591,900	313,100

Note: Totals based on prisoners with a sentence of more than 1 year. See *Methodology* for estimation method.
[a]Includes American Indians, Alaska Natives, Asians, Native Hawaiians, other Pacific Islanders, and persons identifying two or more races.
[b]Excludes persons of Hispanic or Latino origin.

Table 6. Estimated Rate of Sentenced Prisoners under State or Federal Jurisdiction, Per 100,000 U.S. Residents, by Gender, Race, and Hispanic Origin, December 31, 2000-2008

Year	Males				Females			
	Total[a]	White[b]	Black[b]	Hispanic	Total[a]	White[b]	Black[b]	Hispanic
2000	904	449	3,457	1,220	59	34	205	60
2001	896	462	3,535	1,177	58	36	199	61
2002	912	450	3,437	1,176	61	35	191	80
2003	915	465	3,405	1,231	62	38	185	84
2004	926	463	3,218	1,220	64	42	170	75
2005	929	471	3,145	1,244	65	45	156	76
2006	943	487	3,042	1,261	68	48	148	81
2007	955	481	3,138	1,259	69	50	150	79
2008	952	487	3,161	1,200	68	50	149	75

Note: Totals based on prisoners sentenced to more than 1 year. Imprisonment rates are per 100,000 U.S. residents in each reference population group. See *Methodology* for estimation method.
[a]Includes American Indians, Alaska Natives, Asians, Native Hawaiians, other Pacific Islanders, and persons identifying two or more races.
[b]Excludes persons of Hispanic or Latino origin.

The number of sentenced white and Hispanic prisoners convicted of a drug offense increased from 2000 to 2006, offsetting the decline in the number of imprisoned black drug offenders. Imprisoned white drug offenders increased by 13,800 prisoners during this period; the number of Hispanic drug offenders increased by 10,800. Consequently, the overall number of sentenced drug offenders in state prison increased by 14,700 prisoners.

Table 7. Change in Number of Sentenced Prisoners in State Prisons, 2000 to 2006, by Race and Hispanic Origin and Offense

Race and Hispanic origin	Number of prisoners in 2006	Change since 2000	Percent of total change
Total offenses	1,331,100	124,700	100.0 %
Violent	667,900	78,800	63.2
Property	277,900	39,400	31.6
Drugs	265,800	14,700	11.8
Other[b]	119,500	-8,200	-6.6
White[a]	474,200	37,500	100%
Violent	227,500	15,100	40.3
Property	126,200	17,600	46.9
Drugs	72,000	13,800	36.8
Other[b]	48,500	-9,000	-24.0
Black[a]	508,700	-53,300	100%
Violent	267,900	-5,500	10.3
Property	89,700	-7,100	13.3
Drugs	115,700	-29,600	55.5
Other[b]	35,400	-11,100	20.8
Hispanic or Latino	248,900	70,400	100%
Violent	141,600	54,500	77.4
Property	32,800	4,400	6.3
Drugs	54,100	10,800	15.3
Other[b]	20,400	700	1.0

Note: Data are for inmates sentenced to more than 1 year under the jurisdiction of state correctional authorities. The estimates for gender were based on jurisdiction counts at yearend (NPS 1B). The estimates by race and Hispanic origin were based on data from the 2004 Survey of Inmates in State Correctional Facilities and updated by yearend jurisdiction counts; estimates within offense categories were based on offense distributions from the National Corrections Reporting Program, 2006, updated by yearend jurisdiction counts. All estimates were rounded to the nearest 100. Detail may not add to total due to rounding.

[a]Excludes persons of Hispanic or Latino origin.
[b]Includes public order and other unspecified offenses.

Changes in the types of drugs involved in drug offenses could not be identified in the available data. BJS's most recent survey focusing on the types of drugs involved in drug offenses was conducted in 2004. The data collected through inmate interviews revealed an increase in the percentage of state prisoners serving time for drug law violations involving stimulants, such as methamphetamines. About 10% of the drug offenders in state prison in 2004 were convicted of a drug offense involving stimulants, up from 10% in 1997. Additionally, the percentage of state prisoners convicted of a cocaine-related drug offense declined from 72% in 1997 to 62% in 2004.[4]

THE U.S. IMPRISONMENT RATE DECREASED FOR THE SECOND TIME SINCE YEAREND 2000

The imprisonment rate at yearend 2008 was 504 per 100,000 U.S. residents, a decrease from 506 per 100,000 at yearend 2007 (**appendix table 10**). About 1 in every 198 persons in the U.S. resident population was incarcerated in state or federal prison at yearend 2008. *Imprisonment rate* refers to the number of prisoners sentenced to more than 1 year per 100,000 U.S. residents.

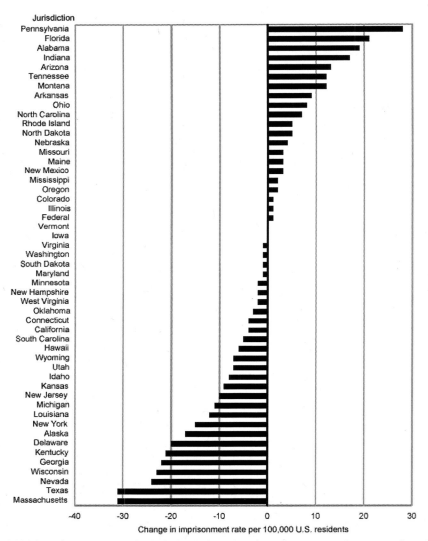

Note: The 2008 imprisonment rate included 4,012 male prisoners sentenced to more than 1 year but held in local jails or houses of corrections in the Commonwealth of Massachusetts; the 2007 imprisonment rate included 6,200 sentenced males held in local jails or houses of corrections. *See Methodology.*

Figure 5. Change in imprisonment rate, 2007-2008

SELECTED CHARACTERISTICS OF THE CUSTODY POPULATION AT YEAREND 2008

On December 31, 2008—

- State and federal prisons and local jails had custody or physical guardianship over 2,304,115 inmates, an increase of 0.3% from yearend 2007 (**table 8**).
- About 1 in every 133 U.S. residents was in custody of state or federal prisons or local jails.
- The incarceration rate—the number of inmates held in custody of state or federal prisons or in local jails per 100,000 U.S. residents—decreased to 754 inmates at yearend 2008, down from 756 inmates at yearend 2007.
- The total incarcerated population reached 2,424,279 inmates—up 0.2% or 5,038 inmates from yearend 2007 (**table 9**).
- Populations held in ICE facilities (up 2.4%) and in local jails (up 0.7%) increased during 2008. The largest absolute increase of inmates occurred in local jails (5,382), followed by state and federal prisons (692).
- Populations held in military facilities (down 8.0%), prisons in U.S. territories (down 7.5%), and jails in Indian country (down 1.3%) decreased. The largest absolute decrease of 1,102 inmates occurred in the U.S. territories during 2008.

Table 8. Inmates Held in Custody in State or Federal Prisons or in Local Jails, December 31, 2000, 2007, and 2008

Inmates in custody	Number of inmates			Percent of inmates	
	12/31/2000	12/31/2007	12/31/2008	Average annual change, 2000-2007	Percent change, 2007-2008
Total[a]	1,937,482	2,298,041	2,304,115	2.5 %	0.3 %
Federal prisoners[b]					
Total	140,064	197,285	198,414	5.0 %	0.6 %
Prisons	133,921	189,154	189,770	5.1	0.3
Federal facilities	124,540	165,975	165,252	4.2	-0.4
Privately operated facilities	9,381	23,179	24,518	13.8	5.8
Community Corrections Centers[c]	6,143	8,131	8,644	4.1	6.3
State prisoners[a]	1,176,269	1,320,582	1,320,145	1.7 %	0.0 %
Local jails[d]	621,149	780,174	785,556	3.3 %	0.7 %
Incarceration rate[a,e]	684	756	754	1.4 %	-0.3 %

[a]Total includes all inmates held in state or federal prison facilities or in local jails. It does not include inmates held in U.S. territories, military facilities, U.S. Immigration and Customs Enforcement (ICE) facilities, jails in Indian country, and juvenile facilities.

[b]After 2001 the responsibility for sentenced felons from the District of Columbia was transferred to the Federal Bureau of Prisons.
[c]Non-secure, privately operated community corrections centers.
[d]Counts for inmates held in local jails are for the last weekday of June in each year. Counts were estimated from the Annual Survey of Jails. See *Methodology*.
[e]The total number in custody of state or federal prison facilities or local jails per 100,000 U.S. residents. Resident population estimates were as of January 1 of the following year for December 31 estimates.

Table 9. Total Incarcerated Population, December 31, 2007 and 2008

Incarcerated population	Number of inmates		Percent change, 2007-2008
	2007	2008	
Total[a]	2,419,241	2,424,279	0.2%
Federal and state prisons	1,517,867	1,518,559	0.0
Territorial prisons	14,678	13,576	-7.5
Local jails[b]	780,174	785,556	0.7
ICE facilities	9,720	9,957	2.4
Military facilities	1,794	1,651	-8.0
Jails in Indian country	2,163	2,135	-1.3
Juvenile facilities[c]	92,845	92,845	:

:Not calculated.
[a]Total includes all inmates held in state or federal public prison facilities, local jails, U.S. territories, military facilities, U.S. Immigration and Customs Enforcement (ICE) owned and contracted facilities, jails in Indian country, and juvenile facilities.
[b]Counts for inmates held in local jails are for the last weekday of June in each year.
[c]Data are from the 2006 Census of Juveniles in Residential Placement (CJRP), conducted by the Office of Juvenile Justice Delinquency Prevention, Office of Justice Programs, U.S. Department of Justice.

A decrease in the imprisonment rate resulted from a lower rate of growth in the sentenced prison population (0.5% increase) than in the U.S. resident population (0.8% increase). This was the second decline in the U.S. imprisonment rate since 2000.

Twenty-eight states reported a decrease in their imprisonment rates, 20 states reported an increase, and two states reported no change to their imprisonment rates at yearend 2008 (**figure 5**). Massachusetts and Texas (both down 31 prisoners per 100,000 U.S. residents) reported the largest declines in their imprisonment rates.

Pennsylvania (up 28 prisoners per 100,000), Florida (up 21 prisoners per 100,000), and Alabama (up 19 prisoners per 100,000) reported the largest increases in their imprisonment rates at yearend.

MEN AGES 30 TO 34 AND WOMEN AGES 35 TO 39 HAD THE HIGHEST IMPRISONMENT RATES

At yearend 2008, 1,434,800 men and 105,300 women were serving prison sentences of more than one year (**appendix table 13**). Men ages 25 to 29 represented the largest share (17.2%) of sentenced male prisoners in state or federal prison. The imprisonment rate for men was highest for those ages 30 to 34 (2,366 per 100,000 men in the U.S. resident population), followed by men ages 25 to 29 (2,238 per 100,000) (**appendix table 14**).

Women ages 35 to 39 made up the largest percentage (19.8%) of sentenced female prisoners under state or federal jurisdiction. The imprisonment rate for women was also highest for those ages 35 to 39 (201 per 100,000 women in the U.S. resident population), followed by women ages 30 to 34 (190 per 100,000) (**appendix table 14**).

STATE PRISON CAPACITIES WERE HIGHER IN 2008 THAN IN 2000; PERCENT OF CAPACITY OCCUPIED DECREASED IN 2008

State and federal correctional authorities provide three measures of their facilities' capacity.

Rated capacity is the number of beds or inmates assigned by a rating official to institutions within the jurisdiction.

Operational capacity is the number of inmates that can be accommodated based on a facility's staff, existing programs, and services.

Design capacity is the number of inmates that planners or architects intended for the facility.

Highest capacity is the sum of the maximum number of beds and inmates reported by the states and the federal system across the three capacity measures. Lowest capacity is the minimum of these three capacity measures reported by the states and the federal system. Estimates of prison populations as a percentage of capacity are based on the jurisdiction's custody population. In general a jurisdiction's capacity and custody counts exclude inmates held in private facilities. Some states include prisoners held in private facilities as part of the capacity of their prison systems. Where this occurs, prison population as a percent of capacity includes private prisoners.

The federal system reported a rated capacity of 122,479 beds at yearend 2008 (appendix table 24). The highest capacity reported by the states was 1,272,345, and the lowest capacity reported was 1,139,927 (**table 10**). These capacities are between 10% and 14% higher than the capacities reported by the states in 2000.

In 2008 the percent of capacity occupied in state prisons decreased. States were operating at 97% of their highest capacity and over 8% of their lowest capacity at yearend. Eighteen states were operating at more than 100% of highest capacity by yearend 2008, and 24 were operating at more than 100% of lowest capacity.

Table 10. Number of Inmates Held in Custody of State Prisons, as a Percent of Capacity, 1995 and 2000-2008

Year	Highest capacity	Lowest capacity
1995	114%	125%
2000	100	115
2001	101	116
2002	101	117
2003	100	116
2004	99	115
2005	99	114
2006	98	114
2007	96	113
2008	97	109
State capacity, 2008	1,272,345	1,139,927

Note: Capacity excludes prisoners held in local jails and in privately operated facilities, with exceptions. See NPS jurisdiction notes.

TRENDS IN THE ICE POPULATION

At yearend 2008, U.S. Immigration and Customs Enforcement (ICE) had custody over 34,161 detainees, up 14,646 detainees from yearend 2000 and up 3,730 detainees from yearend 2007 (**table 11**). The 12.3% growth in the number of detainees in custody of ICE during 2008 was greater than the average annual growth rate (6.6%) of the number of detainees held from 2000 to 2007.

More than half (57.5%) of all detainees were held in facilities in Texas (8,695), California (3,694), Arizona (2,975), Florida (2,195), and Georgia (2,075). The number of detainees held in Texas has increased by 5,080 since 2000, representing 34.7% of the growth in the number of detainees held nationwide (14,646 detainees) during this period.

Nationwide, the overall number of ICE detainees held per facility (state, federal, local, or ICE) has doubled since 2000 (not shown in table). Approximately 53 detainees were held per facility in 2000, compared to about 115 in 2008. The number of state, federal, and local jails responsible for holding this growing population declined from 347 to 256 during this period, and the average number of detainees held per facility increased from approximately 37 to 95. ICE increased its number of facilities from 24 in 2000 to 41 in 2008, while its average number of detainees held per facility fell from about 276 to 243. Texas has independently added a net of three ICE/INS-owned or -contracted facilities since 2000, and increased the number of detainees held in the average Texas facility from approximately 79 in 2000 to 248 in 2008.

Mexican citizens represented over a third (36.2% or 12,360 detainees) of the detainee population in 2008, followed by El Salvadorans (10.3% or 3,521 detainees), Guatemalans (9.4% or 3,227 detainees), and Hondurans (8.1% or 2,780) (**figure 6**). Among these groups the fastest growth occurred in the Mexican detainee population, increasing from 4,267 ICE detainees in 2000 to 4,623 in 2005. From 2005 to 2007 the Mexican detainee population more than doubled from 4,623 to 10,358 ICE detainees. The number of Mexican detainees increased at a slower pace in 2008, reaching 12,360 at yearend.

Table 11. Selected characteristics of ICE detainees and facilities, 2000, 2007, and 2008

Characteristics	Number of detainees			Average annual change, 2000-2007	Percent change, 2007-2008
	2000	2007	2008		
Total	19,515	30,431	34,161	6.6 %	12.3 %
States holding the largest number of detainees					
Texas	3,615	7,842	8,695	11.7 %	10.9 %
California	3,210	3,702	3,694	2.1	-0.2
Arizona	1,685	2,943	2,975	8.3	1.1
Florida	1,491	1,861	2,195	3.2	17.9
Georgia	596	1,452	2,075	13.6	42.9
Facility type					
Intergovernmental service agreement and Bureau of Prisons	12,904	20,711	24,204	7.0 %	16.9 %
ICE owned and contracted	6,611	9,720	9,957	5.7	2.4
Number of facilities	371	326	297		
Intergovernmental service agreement and Bureau of Prisons	347	292	256		
ICE owned and contracted	24	34	41		

Note: Only select characteristics are detailed; categories may not add to totals.

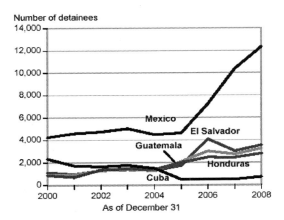

Figure 6. ICE detainees held, by country of origin, 2000-2008

While the El Salvadoran detainee population experienced a similar pattern of growth, the population increased at a slower pace during these same periods. The El Salvadoran detainee population rose from 1,125 in 2000 to 1,727 in 2005. From 2005 to 2007 this detainee population increased from 1,727 to 3,005 ICE detainees. During 2008 the El Salvadoran detainee population increased at a slower pace, reaching 3,521 at yearend.

METHODOLOGY

National Prisoner Statistics

Begun in 1926 under a mandate from Congress, the National Prisoner Statistics (NPS) program collects statistics on prisoners at midyear and yearend. The Census Bureau serves as the data collection agent for the Bureau of Justice Statistics (BJS). BJS depends entirely upon the voluntary participation by state departments of corrections and the Federal Bureau of Prisons for NPS data.

The NPS distinguishes between prisoners in custody and prisoners under jurisdiction. To have custody of a prisoner, a state or federal prison must hold that prisoner in one of its facilities. To have jurisdiction over a prisoner, a state or federal prison must have legal authority over the prisoner. Some states are unable to provide prisoner counts that distinguish between custody and jurisdiction.

The NPS jurisdiction counts include prisoners serving a sentence within a jurisdiction's facilities. These facilities include prisons, penitentiaries, correctional facilities, halfway houses, boot camps, farms, training/treatment centers, and hospitals. Jurisdiction counts include inmates who are—

- temporarily absent (less than 30 days), out to court, or on work release
- housed in privately-operated facilities, local jails, other state or federal facilities
- serving concurrent sentences for more than one correctional authority.

The NPS custody counts include all inmates held within a respondent's facilities, including inmates housed for other correctional facilities. The custody counts exclude inmates held in local jails and in other jurisdictions. With a few exceptions for several respondents, the NPS custody counts exclude inmates held in privately-operated facilities.

Additionally, NPS data include counts of inmates in combined jail-prison systems in Alaska, Connecticut, Delaware, Hawaii, Rhode Island, and Vermont. The District of Columbia has operated only a jail system since yearend 2001. Prisoners sentenced under the District of Columbia criminal code are housed in federal facilities. Selected previously published prisoner counts and percent population change statistics include DC jail inmates for 2001, the last year of collection. Additional information is provided in notes to the tables, where applicable.

Nevada was not able to provide 2007 data. Estimates were calculated using ratio estimates. All numbers were reviewed and approved by individuals at the Nevada Department of Corrections.

Additional information about the data collection instruments instruments is available online at <http://bjs.ojp.usdoj.gov>.

Military Corrections Statistics

BJS obtains yearend counts of prisoners in the custody of U.S. military authorities from the Department of Defense Corrections Council. The council, composed of representatives from each branch of the military services, adopted a standardized report (DD Form 2720) with a common set of items and definitions in 1994. This chapter obtains data on persons held in U.S. military confinement facilities inside and outside of the continental United States, by branch of service, gender, race, Hispanic origin, conviction status, sentence length, and offense. It also provides data on the number of facilities and their design and rated capacities.

Other Inmate Counts

In 1995 BJS began collecting yearend counts of prisoners from the department of corrections in the U.S. Territories (American Samoa, Guam, and the U.S. Virgin Islands) and U.S. Commonwealths (Northern Mariana Islands and Puerto Rico). These counts include all inmates for whom the territory or Commonwealth had legal authority or jurisdiction and all inmates in physical custody (held in prison or local jail facilities). The counts are collected by gender, race, Hispanic origin, and sentence length. Additionally, BJS obtains reports on the design and rated and operational capacities of these correctional facilities.

BJS obtains yearend counts of persons detained by U.S. Immigration and Customs Enforcement (ICE), formerly the U.S. Immigration and Naturalization Service. Located within the Department of Homeland Security, ICE is responsible for holding persons for immigration violations. ICE holds persons in federal, state, and locally operated prisons and jails, as well as privately operated facilities under exclusive contract and ICE-operated facilities.

Data on the number of inmates held in the custody of local jails are from the BJS Annual Survey of Jails (ASJ). The ASJ provides data on inmates in custody at midyear. For more information about the ASJ. (See *Methodology* in *Jail Inmates at Midyear 2008 – Statistical Tables,* BJS Web. 9 Mar. 2009.)

Federal prisoner data used to calculate race and offense distributions are obtained from BJS' Federal Justice Statistics Program (FJSP). The FJSP obtains its data from the Federal Bureau of Prisons. These data include individual-level records of prisoners in federal facilities as of September 30. Specifically, the FJSP provides counts of sentenced federal inmates by gender, race, Hispanic origin, and offense.

Guam did not submit data for 2008. Data for 2008 are estimates based on the percent change from 2006 to 2007 as reported by Guam's Department of Corrections.

Estimates of juvenile inmates for 2007 and 2008 are based on data from 2006 as reported by the Office of Juvenile Justice and Delinquency Prevention (OJJDP), Office of Justice Programs, U.S. Department of Justice.

Estimating Changes in Admissions and Releases

Technically, the change in the prison population from the beginning of the year to the end of the year should equal the difference between the number of admissions and releases during the year. The formula used to calculate this change is $P(t) - P(t-1) = A(t) - R(t)$. Within this formula, t equals the year referenced, $P(t-1)$ equals the start of the year population, $P(t)$ equals the end of the year population, $A(t)$ equals admissions during the year, and $R(t)$ equals releases during the year. However, throughout this chapter, the references to differences in prison populations refer to the differences between two yearend differences, such as the difference between December 31, 2007, and December 31, 2008. Hence, comparisons of admissions and releases during the year with two yearend population counts may be equal, as there may be changes in the prisoner counts between the last count of the year (December 31) and the first count of the following year (January 1). Also, due to information- system processing issues within states, the two sets of differences do not always equal the difference between the number of admissions and releases for various reasons, such as the final data on admissions and releases may be logged into systems after the surveys have been submitted to BJS. During the 2008 collections, all but three states submitted data in which the differences between the start of year and yearend populations equaled the difference between admissions and releases.

Estimating Age-Specific Incarceration Rates

Estimates are provided for the number of sentenced prisoners under state or federal jurisdiction by gender. Further, prisoners are characterized within genders by age group, race (non- Hispanic white and non-Hispanic black), and Hispanic origin. The detailed race and Hispanic origin categories exclude estimates of persons identifying two or more races.

Estimates were produced separately for prisoners under state or federal jurisdiction and then combined to obtain a total estimated population for 2000 and 2007. State estimates were prepared by combining information about the gender of prisoners from the NPS with information reported during inmate interviews on race and Hispanic origin in the 2004 Survey of Inmates of State Correctional Facilities.

For the estimates of federal prisoners, the distributions of FJSP counts of sentenced federal prisoners by gender, age, race, and Hispanic origin on September 30, 2008, were applied to the NPS counts of sentenced federal prisoners by gender at yearend 2008.

Estimates of the U.S. resident population for January 1, 2009, by age, gender, race, and Hispanic origin, were generated by applying the December 31, 2008, age distributions within gender, race, and Hispanic origin groups to the January 1, 2009, population estimates by gender. The population estimates were provided by the U.S. Census Bureau.

Age-specific rates of imprisonment for each demographic group were calculated by dividing the estimated number of sentenced prisoners within each age group by the estimated number of U.S. residents in each age group. That number was multiplied by 100,000, and then rounded to the nearest whole number. Totals by gender include all prisoners and U.S. residents regardless of racial or Hispanic origin. Detailed race and Hispanic origin imprisonment rates exclude persons identifying two or more races.

DEFINITIONS

Average annual change—arithmetic average (mean) annual change across a specific time period.

Custody—physical location in which an inmate is held regardless of which entity has legal authority over an inmates. For example, a local jail may hold, or have custody over, a state-sentenced prisoner who may be held there because of overcrowding. The custody population refers to the number of inmates held in state or federal public prisons or local jails, regardless of sentence length or the state having jurisdiction

Design capacity— the number of inmates that planners or architects intended for a facility.

Highest capacity—the sum of the maximum number of beds reported across three capacity measures: design capacity, operational capacity, and rated capacity.

Imprisonment rate—the number of prisoners under state or federal jurisdiction sentenced to more than 1 year, per 100,000 U.S. resident population.

Incarceration rate—see total incarceration rate.

Inmates—individuals held in the custody of state or federal prisons or in local jails.

Jail—confinement facilities usually administered by a local law enforcement agency, intended for adults but sometimes holding juveniles, before or after adjudication. Facilities include jails and city/county correctional centers, special jail facilities such as medical treatment or release centers, halfway houses, work farms, and temporary holding or lockup facilities that are part of the jail's combined function. Inmates sentenced to jail facilities usually have a sentence of 1 year or less.

Jails in Indian country—jails, confinement facilities, detention centers, and other facilities operated by tribal authorities or the Bureau of Indian Affairs.

Jurisdiction—the entity having legal authority over a prisoner, regardless of where that prisoner is held. The prison population under jurisdiction refers to the number of prisoners under state or federal correctional authority regardless of the facility in which a prisoner is held. For example, state-sentenced prisoners held in local jails are under the jurisdiction of state correctional authorities.

Lowest capacity—the sum of the minimum number of beds across three capacity measures: design capacity, operational capacity, and rated capacity.

Operational capacity—the number of inmates that can be accommodated based on a facility's staff, existing programs, and services.

Prisons—compared to jail facilities, prisons are longer-term facilities run by a state or the federal government typically holding felons and prisoner with sentences of more than 1 year. However, sentence length may vary by state. Connecticut, Rhode Island, Vermont, Delaware, Alaska, and Hawaii operate integrated systems that combine prisons and jails.

Prisoners—individuals confined in correctional facilities under the legal authority (jurisdiction) of state and federal correctional officials.

Rated capacity—the number of beds or inmates assigned by a rating official to institutions within the jurisdiction.

Sentenced prisoner—a prisoner sentenced to more than 1 year.

Total incarceration rate—the number of inmates held in the custody of state or federal prisons or in local jails, per 100,000 U.S. residents.

Total inmates in custody—includes inmates held in any public facility run by a state or the Federal Bureau of Prisons, including halfway houses, camps, farms, training/treatment centers, and hospitals. This number also includes the number of inmates held in local jails as reported by correctional authorities in the Annual Survey of Jails. Data for jails are as of the last weekday of June.

NPS JURISDICTION NOTES

Alaska—Prisons and jails form one integrated system. All NPS data include jail and prison populations housed in state and out of state. Jurisdictional counts exclude inmates held in local jails that are operated by communities.

Arizona—Population counts are based on custody data and inmates in contracted beds.

California—Jurisdiction counts include felons and unsentenced inmates who are temporarily absent, i.e. housed in local jails, hospitals, etc. This definition is comparable to the 1998 NPS 1b definition.
Discrepancies between admissions and releases and within-year change in the prison population are due to incomplete data about inmate movements, such as inmates out to court or readmitted on violations.

Colorado—Counts include 222 inmates in the Youthful Offender System, which was established primarily for violent juvenile offenders. Capacity figures exclude seven privately run facilities under contract with the Department of Corrections.

Delaware—Prisons and jails form one integrated system. All NPS data include jail and prison populations.

Federal—Custody counts include inmates housed in secure facilities where the BOP had a direct contract with a private operator or a sub-contract with a private provider at a local government facility. Custody includes inmates held in non-secure privately operated community corrections centers or Halfway Houses and inmates held on home confinement

Florida—Counts are not comparable to 2006 counts due to new methods of data collection beginning in 2007.
Georgia—Counts are based on custody data.

Hawaii—Prisons and jails form one integrated systems. All NPS data include jail and prison populations

Iowa—Population counts are based on custody data. Population counts for Inmates with a sentence of more than 1 year include an undetermined number of inmates with a sentence of less than 1 year and unsentenced inmates. Iowa does not differentiate between these groups in its data system. Due to a change in reporting in 2006, out of state inmates have been included in jurisdiction counts. Discrepancies between admissions and releases and within-year change in the prison population are due to data entry corrections made throughout the year.

Kansas—Admission and release data are based on the custody population. Due to a new, computerized reporting system, 2007 admission and release data is not comparable to previous years' counts.

Louisiana—Counts for 2007 are as of December 27, 2007. Custody and jurisdiction counts include evacuees from Hurricane Katrina and other pre-trial offenders from Orleans and Jefferson parish jails.

Maryland—The number of prisoners identifying their race as unknown has increased due to changes in the information system.

Massachusetts—By law, offenders may be sentenced to terms of up to 2.5 years in locally-operated jails and correctional institutions. Such populations are included in counts and rates for local jails and correctional institutions. Counts exclude 4,012 inmates with sentences of more than 1 year held in local jails in 2008 and 6,200 inmates in 2007. Jurisdiction and custody counts include an undetermined number of inmates who were remanded to court, transferred to the custody of another state, federal, or locally-operated system, and subsequently released.

Minnesota—Counts include inmates temporarily housed in local jails or private contract facilities, or on work release and community work crew programs.

Mississippi—Operational and design capacities include private prison capacities.

Missouri—Design capacities are not available for older prisons. Operational capacity is defined as the number of available beds include those temporarily offline. Missouri Department of Corrections does not have updated design capacity for prison extension or improvements.

Montana—Population counts include a small number of inmates with unknown sentence lengths.

Capacity figures include two county operated regional prisons (an estimated 300 beds), one private prison (500 beds), and a state operated boot camp (60 beds). In 2006, the Department of Corrections changed its method of accounting for community corrections offenders placed in residential treatment programs. To track growth patterns, a new standard process was applied to historic populations, resulting in some changes to previous years' counts.

Nevada—Due to an information system conversion that occurred during 2007, Nevada officials were unable to report data for 2007. All 2007 data were estimated from 2006 reported data. All estimates were reviewed by individuals at the Nevada Department of Corrections.

New Hampshire—Due to a system conversion, detailed information on prisoners sentenced to 1 year or less, unsentenced males, and specific types of admission and releases cannot be captured.

New Jersey—Counts of inmates with a sentence of more than 1 year include an undetermined number of inmates with sentences of 1 year. The Department of Corrections has no jurisdiction over inmates with sentences of less than 1 year or over unsentenced inmates. Rated capacity figures are not maintained.

North Carolina—Capacity figures refer to standard operating capacity, based on single occupancy per cell and 50 square feet per inmate in multiple occupancy units.

Ohio—Counts of inmates with a sentence of more than 1 year include an undetermined number of inmates with sentences of 1 year or less. Due to a system conversion, admission and release data may vary from past years. Returns and conditional releases involving Transitional Control inmates are reported only after movement from confinement to actual release status occurs.

Oklahoma—Population counts for inmates with sentences of less than 1 year consist mainly of offenders ordered by the court to the Delayed Sentencing Program for Young Adults pursuant to 22 O.S. 996 through 996.3. As of November 4, 1998, Oklahoma has one type of capacity, which includes state prisons, private prisons, and contract jails.

Oregon—Counts include an undetermined number of inmates with sentences of 1 year or less. County authorities retain jurisdiction over the majority of these types of inmates.

Pennsylvania—As of May 31, 2004, the Department began using a new capacity reporting system based on design as well as other crucial factors such as facility infrastructure, support services, and programming.

Rhode Island—Prisons and jails form one integrated system. Data reported include jail and prison populations. Improved methods were used to measure admissions and releases during 2007. Admission and release data for 2000 and 2007 are not comparable.

South Carolina—Population counts include 36 inmate who were unsentenced, under safekeeping, or ICC status. As of July 1, 2003, South Carolina Department of Corrections (SCDC) began releasing inmates due for release and housed in SCDC institutions on the 1st day of each month. Since January 1, 2008 was a holiday, inmates eligible for release on January 1 were released on December 31, 2007. Therefore, the inmate count was at its lowest point for the month on December 31, 2007.

South Dakota—Discrepancies between admissions and releases and within-year change in the prison population result because admission and release data is gathered in a separate database than the jurisdiction population data.

Texas—Jurisdiction counts include inmates serving time in a pre-parole transfer (PPT) or intermediary sanctions facility (ISF), substance abuse felony punishment facility (SAFPF), private facilities, halfway houses, temporary releases to counties, and paper- ready inmates in local jails.

Vermont—Prisons and jails form one integrated system. Data reported include jail and prison populations. Improved methods were used to measure admissions and releases during 2007. Admission and release data for 2000 and 2007 are not comparable.

Virginia—Jurisdiction counts are as of December 28, 2007. Rated capacity is the Department of Corrections' count of beds, which takes into account the number of inmates that can be accommodated based on staff, programs, services and design.

Washington—A recently revised law allows increasing numbers of certain inmates with sentences of less than 1 year to be housed in prison.

Wisconsin—Operational capacity excludes contracted local jails, federal and other state and private facilities.

Appendix Table 1. Prisoners under the Jurisdiction of State or Federal Prisons or in the Custody of State or Federal Prisons or Local Jails, December 31, 2000-2008

Year	Prisoners under jurisdiction							Incarceration rate[c]
	Total	Federal	State	Male	Female	Sentenced to more than 1 year[a]	Imprisonment rate[b]	
2000	1,391,261	145,416	1,245,845	1,298,027	93,234	1,331,278	478	684
2001	1,404,032	156,993	1,247,039	1,311,053	92,979	1,345,217	470	685
2002	1,440,144	163,528	1,276,616	1,342,513	97,631	1,380,516	476	701
2003	1,468,601	173,059	1,295,542	1,367,755	100,846	1,408,361	482	712
2004	1,497,100	180,328	1,316,772	1,392,278	104,822	1,433,728	486	723
2005	1,527,929	187,618	1,340,311	1,420,303	107,626	1,462,866	491	737
2006	1,569,945	193,046	1,376,899	1,457,486	112,459	1,504,660	501	751
2007	1,598,245	199,618	1,398,627	1,483,740	114,505	1,532,850	506	756
2008	1,610,446	201,280	1,409,166	1,495,594	114,852	1,540,036	504	754
Average annual change, 2000-2007	2.0%	4.6%	1.7%	1.9%	3.0%	2.0%	0.8%	1.4
Percent change, 2007-2008	0.8	0.8	0.8	0.8	0.3	0.5	-0.3	-0.2

Note: Jurisdiction refers to the legal authority over a prisoner, regardless of where the prisoner is held. Custody refers to where an inmate is held, regardless of which entity has jurisdiction over the inmate.

[a] Includes prisoners under the legal authority of state or federal correctional officials with sentences of more than 1 year, regardless of where they are held.

[b] Imprisonment rate is the number of prisoners sentenced to more than 1 year under state or federal jurisdiction per 100,000 U.S. residents. Resident population estimates are from the U.S. Census Bureau for January 1 of the following year for the yearend rates.

[c] Incarceration rate is the total number of inmates held in custody of state or federal prisons or local jails per 100,000 U.S. residents.

Appendix Table 2. Prisoners under the Jurisdiction of State or Federal Correctional Authorities, by Jurisdiction, December 31, 2000, 2007 and 2008

Region and jurisdiction	Number of prisoners			Average annual change, 2000-2007	Percent change, 2007-2008
	12/31/2000	12/31/2007	12/31/2008		
U.S. total	1,391,261	1,598,245	1,610,446	2.0%	0.8%
Federal	145,416	199,618	201,280	4.6	0.8
State	1,245,845	1,398,627	1,409,166	1.7	0.8
Northeast	174,826	179,030	179,776	0.3%	0.4%
Connecticut[a]	18,355	20,924	20,661	1.9	-1.3
Maine	1,679	2,148	2,195	3.6	2.2
Massachusetts	10,722	11,436	11,408	0.9	-0.2
New Hampshire	2,257	2,943	2,904	3.9	-1.3
New Jersey	29,784	26,827	25,953	-1.5	-3.3
New York	70,199	62,620	60,347	-1.6	-3.6
Pennsylvania	36,847	45,969	50,147	3.2	9.1
Rhode Island[a]	3,286	4,018	4,045	2.9	0.7
Vermont[a]	1,697	2,145	2,116	3.4	-1.4
Midwest	237,378	263,039	263,811	1.5%	0.3%
Illinois	45,281	45,215	45,474	0.0	0.6
Indiana	20,125	27,132	28,322	4.4	4.4
Iowa[b]	7,955	8,732	8,766	1.3	0.4
Kansas	8,344	8,696	8,539	0.6	-1.8
Michigan	47,718	50,233	48,738	0.7	-3.0
Minnesota	6,238	9,468	9,406	6.1	-0.7
Missouri	27,543	29,857	30,186	1.2	1.1
Nebraska	3,895	4,505	4,520	2.1	0.3
North Dakota	1,076	1,416	1,452	4.0	2.5
Ohio	45,833	50,731	51,686	1.5	1.9
South Dakota	2,616	3,311	3,342	3.4	0.9
Wisconsin	20,754	23,743	23,380	1.9	-1.5
South	561,214	639,578	647,312	1.9%	1.2%
Alabama	26,332	29,412	30,508	1.6	3.7
Arkansas	11,915	14,314	14,716	2.7	2.8
Delaware[a]	6,921	7,276	7,075	0.7	-2.8
District of Columbia	7,456	~	~	:	:
Florida	71,319	98,219	102,388	4.7	4.2
Georgia[b]	44,232	54,256	52,719	3.0	-2.8
Kentucky	14,919	22,457	21,706	6.0	-3.3
Louisiana	35,207	37,540	38,381	0.9	2.2
Maryland	23,538	23,433	23,324	-0.1	-0.5
Mississippi	20,241	22,431	22,754	1.5	1.4
North Carolina	31,266	37,970	39,482	2.8	4.0
Oklahoma	23,181	25,849	25,864	1.6	0.1
South Carolina	21,778	24,239	24,326	1.5	0.4
Tennessee	22,166	26,267	27,228	2.5	3.7
Texas	166,719	171,790	172,506	0.4	0.4
Virginia	30,168	38,069	38,276	3.4	0.5

Appendix Table 2. (Continued)

Region and jurisdiction	12/31/2000	12/31/2007	12/31/2008	Average annual change, 2000-2007	Percent change, 2007-2008
West Virginia	3,856	6,056	6,059	6.7	0.0
West	272,427	316,980	318,267	2.2%	0.4%
Alaska[a]	4,173	5,167	5,014	3.1	-3.0
Arizona[b]	26,510	37,746	39,589	5.2	4.9
California	163,001	174,282	173,670	1.0	-0.4
Colorado	16,833	22,841	23,274	4.5	1.9
Hawaii[a]	5,053	5,978	5,955	2.4	-0.4
Idaho	5,535	7,319	7,290	4.1	-0.4
Montana	3,105	3,462	3,607	1.6	4.2
Nevada[c]	10,063	13,400	12,743	:	:
New Mexico	5,342	6,466	6,402	2.8	-1.0
Oregon	10,580	13,948	14,167	4.0	1.6
Utah	5,637	6,515	6,546	2.1	0.5
Washington	14,915	17,772	17,926	2.5	0.9
Wyoming	1,680	2,084	2,084	3.1	0.0

~ Not applicable. After 2001, responsibility for sentenced felons from the District of Columbia was transferred to the Federal Bureau of Prisons.

: Not calculated.

[a] Prisons and jails form one integrated system. Data include total jail and prison populations.

[b] Prison population based on custody counts.

[c] Includes estimates for Nevada for December 31, 2007. *See Methodology.*

Appendix Table 3. Male Prisoners under the Jurisdiction of State or Federal Correctional Authorities, by Jurisdiction, December 31, 2000, 2007 and 2008

Region and jurisdiction	Number of male prisoners			Average annual change, 2000-2007	Percent change, 2007-2008
	12/31/2000	12/31/2007	12/31/2008		
U.S. total	1,298,027	1,483,740	1,495,594	1.9%	0.8%
Federal	135,171	186,280	188,007	4.7	0.9
State	1,162,856	1,297,460	1,307,587	1.6	0.8
Northeast	165,744	169,336	169,932	0.3%	0.4%
Connecticut[a]	16,949	19,428	19,159	2.0	-1.4
Maine	1,613	2,009	2,039	3.2	1.5
Massachusetts	10,059	10,646	10,657	0.8	0.1
New Hampshire	2,137	2,741	2,670	3.6	-2.6
New Jersey	28,134	25,417	24,654	-1.4	-3.0
New York	66,919	59,866	57,760	-1.6	-3.5
Pennsylvania	35,268	43,506	47,193	3.0	8.5
Rhode Island[a]	3,048	3,736	3,802	3.0	1.8
Vermont[a]	1,617	1,987	1,998	3.0	0.6
Midwest	222,780	245,110	246,070	1.4%	0.4%
Illinois	42,432	42,391	42,753	0.0	0.9
Indiana	18,673	24,837	25,829	4.2	4.0
Iowa[b]	7,363	8,015	8,017	1.2	0.0
Kansas	7,840	8,071	7,970	0.4	-1.3
Michigan	45,587	48,153	46,781	0.8	-2.8

Appendix Table 3. (Continued)

Region and jurisdiction	Number of male prisoners			Average annual change, 2000-2007	Percent change, 2007-2008
	12/31/2000	12/31/2007	12/31/2008		
Minnesota	5,870	8,866	8,778	6.1	-1.0
Missouri	25,550	27,335	27,737	1.0	1.5
Nebraska	3,629	4,106	4,130	1.8	0.6
North Dakota	1,008	1,269	1,292	3.3	1.8
Ohio	43,025	46,909	47,773	1.2	1.8
South Dakota	2,416	2,942	2,987	2.9	1.5
Wisconsin	19,387	22,216	22,023	2.0	-0.9
South	521,562	591,075	598,262	1.8%	1.2%
Alabama	24,506	27,254	28,277	1.5	3.8
Arkansas	11,143	13,248	13,656	2.5	3.1
Delaware[a]	6,324	6,699	6,518	0.8	-2.7
District of Columbia	7,100	~	~	:	:
Florida	67,214	91,365	95,237	4.5	4.2
Georgia[b]	41,474	50,711	49,027	2.9	-3.3
Kentucky	13,858	20,016	19,436	5.4	-2.9
Louisiana	32,988	35,082	35,865	0.9	2.2
Maryland	22,319	22,249	22,264	0.0	0.1
Mississippi	18,572	20,469	20,773	1.4	1.5
North Carolina	29,363	35,344	36,704	2.7	3.8
Oklahoma	20,787	23,242	23,340	1.6	0.4
South Carolina	20,358	22,635	22,693	1.5	0.3
Tennessee	20,797	24,344	25,099	2.3	3.1
Texas	153,097	157,859	158,653	0.4	0.5
Virginia	28,109	35,136	35,309	3.2	0.5
West Virginia	3,553	5,422	5,411	6.2	-0.2
West	252,770	291,939	293,323	2.1 %	0.5 %
Alaska[a]	3,889	4,603	4,511	2.4	-2.0
Arizona[b]	24,546	34,286	35,823	4.9	4.5
California	151,840	162,654	162,050	1.0	-0.4
Colorado	15,500	20,506	20,980	4.1	2.3
Hawaii[a]	4,492	5,232	5,227	2.2	-0.1
Idaho	5,042	6,519	6,532	3.7	0.2
Montana	2,799	3,161	3,244	1.8	2.6
Nevada[c]	9,217	12,221	11,761	:	:
New Mexico	4,831	5,890	5,833	2.9	-1.0
Oregon	9,984	12,888	13,058	3.7	1.3
Utah	5,256	5,883	5,906	1.6	0.4
Washington	13,850	16,258	16,522	2.3	1.6
Wyoming	1,524	1,838	1,876	2.7	2.1

~ Not applicable. After 2001, responsibility for sentenced felons from the District of Columbia was transferred to the Federal Bureau of Prisons.

[a] Prisons and jails form one integrated system. Data include total jail and prison populations.

[b] Prison population based on custody counts.

[c] Includes estimates for Nevada for December 31, 2007. See *Methodology*.

Appendix Table 4. Females Prisoners under the Jurisdiction of State or Federal Correctional Authorities, by Jurisdiction, December 31, 2000, 2007 and 2008

Region and jurisdiction	Number of female prisoners			Average annual change, 2000-2007	Percent change, 2007-2008
	12/31/2000	12/31/2007	12/31/2008		
U.S. total	93,234	114,505	114,852	3.0 %	0.3 %
Federal	10,245	13,338	13,273	3.8	-0.5
State	82,989	101,167	101,579	2.9	0.4
Northeast	9,082	9,694	9,844	0.9 %	1.5 %
Connecticut[a]	1,406	1,496	1,502	0.9	0.4
Maine	66	139	156	11.2	12.2
Massachusetts	663	790	751	2.5	-4.9
New Hampshire	120	202	234	7.7	15.8
New Jersey	1,650	1,410	1,299	-2.2	-7.9
New York	3,280	2,754	2,587	-2.5	-6.1
Pennsylvania	1,579	2,463	2,954	6.6	19.9
Rhode Island[a]	238	282	243	2.5	-13.8
Vermont[a]	80	158	118	10.2	-25.3
Midwest	14,598	17,929	17,741	3.0 %	-1.0 %
Illinois	2,849	2,824	2,721	-0.1	-3.6
Indiana	1,452	2,295	2,493	6.8	8.6
Iowa[b]	592	717	749	2.8	4.5
Kansas	504	625	569	3.1	-9.0
Michigan	2,131	2,080	1,957	-0.3	-5.9
Minnesota	368	602	628	7.3	4.3
Missouri	1,993	2,522	2,449	3.4	-2.9
Nebraska	266	399	390	6.0	-2.3
North Dakota	68	147	160	11.6	8.8
Ohio	2,808	3,822	3,913	4.5	2.4
South Dakota	200	369	355	9.1	-3.8
Wisconsin	1,367	1,527	1,357	1.6	-11.1
South	39,652	48,503	49,050	2.9 %	1.1 %
Alabama	1,826	2,158	2,231	2.4	3.4
Arkansas	772	1,066	1,060	4.7	-0.6
Delaware[a]	597	577	557	-0.5	-3.5
District of Columbia	356	~	~	:	:
Florida	4,105	6,854	7,151	7.6	4.3
Georgia[b]	2,758	3,545	3,692	3.7	4.1
Kentucky	1,061	2,441	2,270	12.6	-7.0
Louisiana	2,219	2,458	2,516	1.5	2.4
Maryland	1,219	1,184	1,060	-0.4	-10.5
Mississippi	1,669	1,962	1,981	2.3	1.0
North Carolina	1,903	2,626	2,778	4.7	5.8
Oklahoma	2,394	2,607	2,524	1.2	-3.2
South Carolina	1,420	1,604	1,633	1.8	1.8

Appendix Table 4. (Continued)

Region and jurisdiction	Number of female prisoners			Average annual change, 2000-2007	Percent change, 2007-2008
	12/31/2000	12/31/2007	12/31/2008		
Tennessee	1,369	1,923	2,129	5.0	10.7
Texas	13,622	13,931	13,853	0.3	-0.6
Virginia	2,059	2,933	2,967	5.2	1.2
West Virginia	303	634	648	11.1	2.2
West	19,657	25,041	24,944	3.5%	-0.4%
Alaska[a]	284	564	503	10.3	-10.8
Arizona[b]	1,964	3,460	3,766	8.4	8.8
California	11,161	11,628	11,620	0.6	-0.1
Colorado	1,333	2,335	2,294	8.3	-1.8
Hawaii[a]	561	746	728	4.2	-2.4
Idaho	493	800	758	7.2	-5.3
Montana	306	301	363	-0.2	20.6
Nevada[c]	846	1,179	982	:	:
New Mexico	511	576	569	1.7	-1.2
Oregon	596	1,060	1,109	8.6	4.6
Utah	381	632	640	7.5	1.3
Washington	1,065	1,514	1,404	5.2	-7.3
Wyoming	156	246	208	6.7	-15.4

~ Not applicable.After 2001, responsibility for sentenced felons from the District of Columbia was transferred to the Federal Bureau of Prisons.

: Not calculated.

[a] Prisons and jails form one integrated system. Data include total jail and prison populations.

[b] Prison population based on custody counts.

[c] Includes estimates for Nevada for December 31, 2007. See *Methodology*.

Appendix Table 5. Sentenced Prisoners under the Jurisdiction of State or Federal Correctional Authorities, by Jurisdiction, December 31, 2000, 2007 and 2008

Region and jurisdiction	Number of sentenced prisoners			Average annual change, 2000-2007	Percent change, 2007-2008
	12/31/2000	12/31/2007	12/31/2008		
U.S. total	1,331,278	1,532,850	1,540,036	2.0 %	0.5%
Federal	125,044	179,204	182,333	5.3	1.7
State	1,206,234	1,353,646	1,357,703	1.7	0.3
Northeast	166,632	167,694	168,340	0.1 %	0.4%
Connecticut[a]	13,155	14,397	14,271	1.3	-0.9
Maine	1,635	1,950	1,985	2.5	1.8
Massachusetts	9,479	9,872	10,166	0.6	3.0
New Hampshire	2,257	2,930	2,904	3.8	-0.9
New Jersey[b]	29,784	26,827	25,953	-1.5	-3.3
New York	70,199	62,174	59,959	-1.7	-3.6

Appendix Table 5. (Continued)

Region and jurisdiction	Number of sentenced prisoners			Average annual change, 2000-2007	Percent change, 2007-2008
	12/31/2000	12/31/2007	12/31/2008		
Pennsylvania	36,844	45,446	48,962	3.0	7.7
Rhode Island[a]	1,966	2,481	2,522	3.4	1.7
Vermont[a]	1,313	1,617	1,618	3.0	0.1
Midwest	236,458	261,391	261,397	1.4 %	0.0%
Illinois[b]	45,281	45,215	45,474	0.0	0.6
Indiana	19,811	27,114	28,301	4.6	4.4
Iowa[b,c]	7,955	8,732	8,766	1.3	0.4
Kansas[b]	8,344	8,696	8,539	0.6	-1.8
Michigan	47,718	50,233	48,738	0.7	-3.0
Minnesota	6,238	9,468	9,406	6.1	-0.7
Missouri	27,519	29,844	30,175	1.2	1.1
Nebraska	3,816	4,329	4,424	1.8	2.2
North Dakota	994	1,416	1,452	5.2	2.5
Ohio[b]	45,833	50,731	51,686	1.5	1.9
South Dakota	2,613	3,306	3,333	3.4	0.8
Wisconsin	20,336	22,307	21,103	1.3	-5.4
South	538,997	615,535	617,161	1.9 %	0.3%
Alabama	26,034	28,605	29,694	1.4	3.8
Arkansas	11,851	14,310	14,660	2.7	2.4
Delaware[a]	3,937	4,201	4,067	0.9	-3.2
District of Columbia	5,008	~	~	:	:
Florida	71,318	98,219	102,388	4.7	4.2
Georgia[c]	44,141	54,232	52,705	3.0	-2.8
Kentucky	14,919	21,823	21,059	5.6	-3.5
Louisiana	35,207	37,341	37,804	0.8	1.2
Maryland	22,490	22,780	22,749	0.2	-0.1
Mississippi	19,239	21,502	21,698	1.6	0.9
North Carolina	27,043	33,016	34,229	2.9	3.7
Oklahoma	23,181	24,197	24,210	0.6	0.1
South Carolina	21,017	23,314	23,456	1.5	0.6
Tennessee	22,166	26,267	27,228	2.5	3.7
Texas	158,008	161,695	156,979	0.3	-2.9
Virginia	29,643	37,984	38,216	3.6	0.6
West Virginia	3,795	6,049	6,019	6.9	-0.5
West	264,147	309,026	310,805	2.3 %	0.6%
Alaska[a]	2,128	3,072	2,966	5.4	-3.5
Arizona[c]	25,412	35,490	37,188	4.9	4.8
California	160,412	172,856	172,583	1.1	-0.2
Colorado[b]	16,833	22,841	23,274	4.5	1.9

Appendix Table 5. (Continued)

Region and jurisdiction	12/31/2000	12/31/2007	12/31/2008	Average annual change, 2000-2007	Percent change, 2007-2008
Hawaii[a]	3,553	4,367	4,304	3.0	-1.4
Idaho	5,535	7,319	7,290	4.1	-0.4
Montana	3,105	3,431	3,579	1.4	4.3
Nevada[d]	10,063	13,245	12,743	:	:
New Mexico	4,666	6,225	6,315	4.2	1.4
Oregon[b]	10,553	13,918	14,131	4.0	1.5
Utah	5,541	6,421	6,422	2.1	0.0
Washington	14,666	17,757	17,926	2.8	1.0
Wyoming	1,680	2,084	2,084	3.1	0.0

Note: Totals based on prisoners with a sentence of more than 1 year.

~ Not applicable. After 2001, responsibility for sentenced felons from the District of Columbia was transferred to the Federal Bureau of Prisons.

: Not calculated

[a] Prisons and jails form one integrated system. Data include total jail and prison populations.

[b] Includes some prisoners sentenced to 1 year or less.

[c] Prison population based on custody counts.

[d] Includes estimates for Nevada for December 31, 2007. See *Methodology*.

Appendix Table 6. Number of Sentenced Male Prisoners under the Jurisdiction of State and Federal Correctional Authorities, December 31, 2000-2008

Year	Number of sentenced male prisoners			Percent of all sentenced prisoners
	Total	Federal	State	
2000	1,246,234	116,647	1,129,587	93.6%
2001	1,260,033	127,519	1,132,514	93.7
2002	1,291,450	133,732	1,157,718	93.5
2003	1,315,790	142,149	1,173,641	93.4
2004	1,337,730	148,930	1,188,800	93.3
2005	1,364,178	155,678	1,208,500	93.3
2006	1,401,317	162,417	1,238,900	93.1
2007	1,427,064	167,676	1,259,388	93.1
2008	1,434,784	170,755	1,264,029	93.2
Average annual change, 2000-2007	2.0%	5.3%	1.6%	:
Percent change, 2007-2008	0.5	1.8	0.4	:

Note: Totals based on prisoners with a sentence of more than 1 year.
: Not calculated.

Appendix Table 7. Sentenced Male Prisoners under the Jurisdiction of State or Federal Correctional Authorities, by Jurisdiction, December 31, 2000, 2007 and 2008

Region and jurisdiction	Number of sentenced male prisoners			Average annual change, 2000-2007	Percent change, 2007-2008
	12/31/2000	12/31/2007	12/31/2008		
U.S. total	1,246,234	1,427,064	1,434,784	2.0%	0.5%
Federal	116,647	167,676	170,755	5.3	1.8
State	1,129,587	1,259,388	1,264,029	1.6	0.4
Northeast	158,815	159,390	160,004	0.1%	0.4%
Connecticut[a]	12,365	13,581	13,468	1.3	-0.8
Maine	1,573	1,831	1,856	2.2	1.4
Massachusetts	9,250	9,438	9,724	0.3	3.0
New Hampshire	2,137	2,733	2,670	3.6	-2.3
New Jersey[b]	28,134	25,417	24,654	-1.4	-3.0
New York	66,919	59,482	57,412	-1.7	-3.5
Pennsylvania	35,266	43,024	46,261	2.9	7.5
Rhode Island[a]	1,902	2,367	2,418	3.2	2.2
Vermont[a]	1,269	1,517	1,541	2.6	1.6
Midwest	221,902	243,615	243,822	1.3%	0.1%
Illinois[b]	42,432	42,391	42,753	0.0	0.9
Indiana	18,364	24,819	25,808	4.4	4.0
Iowa[b,c]	7,363	8,015	8,017	1.2	0.0
Kansas[b]	7,840	8,071	7,970	0.4	-1.3
Michigan	45,587	48,153	46,781	0.8	-2.8
Minnesota	5,870	8,866	8,778	6.1	-1.0
Missouri	25,531	27,326	27,729	1.0	1.5
Nebraska	3,560	3,963	4,048	1.5	2.1
North Dakota	940	1,269	1,292	4.4	1.8
Ohio[b]	43,025	46,909	47,773	1.2	1.8
South Dakota	2,413	2,937	2,979	2.8	1.4
Wisconsin	18,977	20,896	19,894	1.4	-4.8
South	503,025	571,128	573,111	1.8%	0.3%
Alabama	24,244	26,575	27,567	1.3	3.7
Arkansas	11,084	13,244	13,606	2.6	2.7
Delaware[a]	3,692	3,989	3,862	1.1	-3.2
District of Columbia	4,924	~	~	:	:
Florida	67,213	91,365	95,237	4.5	4.2
Georgia[c]	41,390	50,687	49,014	2.9	-3.3
Kentucky	13,858	19,500	18,906	5.0	-3.0
Louisiana	32,988	34,890	35,324	0.8	1.2
Maryland	21,429	21,640	21,777	0.1	0.6
Mississippi	17,709	19,667	19,855	1.5	1.0
North Carolina	25,654	31,115	32,218	2.8	3.5

Appendix Table 7. (Continued)

Region and jurisdiction	Number of sentenced male prisoners			Average annual change, 2000-2007	Percent change, 2007-2008
	12/31/2000	12/31/2007	12/31/2008		
Oklahoma	20,787	21,786	21,761	0.7	-0.1
South Carolina	19,716	21,858	21,995	1.5	0.6
Tennessee	20,797	24,344	25,099	2.3	3.1
Texas	146,374	149,995	146,262	0.3	-2.5
Virginia	27,658	35,055	35,249	3.4	0.6
West Virginia	3,508	5,418	5,379	6.4	-0.7
West	245,845	285,255	287,092	2.1 %	0.6%
Alaska[a]	2,031	2,800	2,704	4.7	-3.4
Arizona[c]	23,623	32,377	33,874	4.6	4.6
California	149,815	161,551	161,220	1.1	-0.2
Colorado[b]	15,500	20,506	20,980	4.1	2.3
Hawaii[a]	3,175	3,863	3,829	2.8	-0.9
Idaho	5,042	6,519	6,532	3.7	0.2
Montana	2,799	3,133	3,218	1.6	2.7
Nevada[d]	9,217	12,068	11,761	:	:
New Mexico	4,322	5,686	5,747	4.0	1.1
Oregon[b]	9,959	12,860	13,026	3.7	1.3
Utah	5,180	5,805	5,803	1.6	0.0
Washington	13,658	16,249	16,522	2.5	1.7
Wyoming	1,524	1,838	1,876	2.7	2.1

Note: Totals based on prisoners with a sentence of more than 1 year.

~ Not applicable. After 2001, responsibility for sentenced felons from the District of Columbia was transferred to the Federal Bureau of Prisons.

: Not calculated

[a] Prisons and jails form one integrated system. Data include total jail and prison populations.

[b] Includes some prisoners sentenced to 1 year or less.

[c] Prison population based on custody counts.

[d] Includes estimates for Nevada for December 31, 2007. See *Methodology.*

Appendix Table 8. Number of Sentenced Female Prisoners under the Jurisdiction of State or Federal Correctional Authorities, December 31, 2000-2008

Year	Number of sentenced female prisoners			Percent of all sentenced prisoners
	Total	Federal	State	
2000	85,044	8,397	76,647	6.4%
2001	85,184	8,990	76,194	6.3
2002	89,066	9,308	79,758	6.5
2003	92,571	9,770	82,801	6.6
2004	95,998	10,207	85,791	6.7
2005	98,688	10,495	88,193	6.7
2006	103,343	11,116	92,227	6.9

Appendix Table 8. (Continued)

Year	Number of sentenced female prisoners			Percent of all sentenced prisoners
	Total	Federal	State	
2007	105,786	11,528	94,258	6.9
2008	105,252	11,578	93,674	6.8
Average annual change, 2000-2007	3.2%	4.6%	3.0%	:
Percent change, 2007-2008	-0.5	0.4	-0.6	:

Note: Totals based on prisoners with a sentence of more than 1 year.
: Not calculated.

Appendix Table 9. Sentenced Female Prisoners under the Jurisdiction of State or Federal Correctional Authorities, by Jurisdiction, December 31, 2000, 2007 and 2008

Region and jurisdiction	Number of sentenced female prisoners			Average annual change 2000-2007	Percent change, 2007-2008
	12/31/2000	12/31/2007	12/31/2008		
U.S. total	85,044	105,786	105,252	3.2%	-0.5%
Federal	8,397	11,528	11,578	4.6	0.4
State	76,647	94,258	93,674	3.0	-0.6
Northeast	7,817	8,304	8,336	0.9%	0.4 %
Connecticut[a]	790	816	803	0.5	-1.6
Maine	62	119	129	9.8	8.4
Massachusetts	229	434	442	9.6	1.8
New Hampshire	120	197	234	7.3	18.8
New Jersey[b]	1,650	1,410	1,299	-2.2	-7.9
New York	3,280	2,692	2,547	-2.8	-5.4
Pennsylvania	1,578	2,422	2,701	6.3	11.5
Rhode Island[a]	64	114	104	8.6	-8.8
Vermont[a]	44	100	77	12.4	-23.0
Midwest	14,556	17,776	17,575	2.9%	-1.1%
Illinois[b]	2,849	2,824	2,721	-0.1	-3.6
Indiana	1,447	2,295	2,493	6.8	8.6
Iowa[b,c]	592	717	749	2.8	4.5
Kansas[b]	504	625	569	3.1	-9.0
Michigan	2,131	2,080	1,957	-0.3	-5.9
Minnesota	368	602	628	7.3	4.3
Missouri	1,988	2,518	2,446	3.4	-2.9
Nebraska	256	366	376	5.2	2.7
North Dakota	54	147	160	15.4	8.8
Ohio[b]	2,808	3,822	3,913	4.5	2.4
South Dakota	200	369	354	9.1	-4.1
Wisconsin	1,359	1,411	1,209	0.5	-14.3

Appendix Table 9. (Continued)

Region and jurisdiction	Number of sentenced female prisoners			Average annual change 2000-2007	Percent change, 2007-2008
	12/31/2000	12/31/2007	12/31/2008		
South	35,972	44,407	44,050	3.1%	-0.8%
Alabama	1,790	2,030	2,127	1.8	4.8
Arkansas	767	1,066	1,054	4.8	-1.1
Delaware[a]	245	212	205	-2.0	-3.3
District of Columbia	84	~	~	:	:
Florida	4,105	6,854	7,151	7.6	4.3
Georgia[c]	2,751	3,545	3,691	3.7	4.1
Kentucky	1,061	2,323	2,153	11.8	-7.3
Louisiana	2,219	2,451	2,480	1.4	1.2
Maryland	1,061	1,140	972	1.0	-14.7
Mississippi	1,530	1,835	1,843	2.6	0.4
North Carolina	1,389	1,901	2,011	4.6	5.8
Oklahoma	2,394	2,411	2,449	0.1	1.6
South Carolina	1,301	1,456	1,461	1.6	0.3
Tennessee	1,369	1,923	2,129	5.0	10.7
Texas	11,634	11,700	10,717	0.1	-8.4
Virginia	1,985	2,929	2,967	5.7	1.3
West Virginia	287	631	640	11.9	1.4
West	18,302	23,771	23,713	3.8 %	-0.2 %
Alaska[a]	97	272	262	15.9	-3.7
Arizona[c]	1,789	3,113	3,314	8.2	6.5
California	10,597	11,305	11,363	0.9	0.5
Colorado[b]	1,333	2,335	2,294	8.3	-1.8
Hawaii[a]	378	504	475	4.2	-5.8
Idaho	493	800	758	7.2	-5.3
Montana	306	298	361	-0.4	21.1
Nevada[d]	846	1,177	982	:	:
New Mexico	344	539	568	6.6	5.4
Oregon[b]	594	1,058	1,105	8.6	4.4
Utah	361	616	619	7.9	0.5
Washington	1,008	1,508	1,404	5.9	-6.9
Wyoming	156	246	208	6.7	-15.4

Note: Totals based on prisoners with a sentence of more than 1 year.

~ Not applicable. After 2001 the responsibility for sentenced felons from the District of Columbia was transferred to the Federal Bureau of Prisons.

: Not calculated

[a] Prisons and jails form one integrated system. Data include total jail and prison populations.

[b] Includes some prisoners sentenced to 1 year or less.

[c] Priso n population based on custody counts.

[d] Includes estimates for Nevada for December 31, 2007. See *Methodology*.

Appendix Table 10. Imprisonment Rates of Sentenced Prisoners under Jurisdiction of State and Federal Correctional Authorities, by Gender and Jurisdiction, December 31, 2007 and 2008

Region and jurisdiction	Imprisonment rate					
	2007			2008		
	Total	Male	Female	Total	Male	Female
U.S. total[a]	506	955	69	504	952	68
Federal	59	112	8	60	113	7
State[a]	447	844	61	445	840	61
Northeast[b]	306	598	30	306	597	30
Connecticut[c]	410	794	45	407	787	45
Maine	148	284	18	151	289	19
Massachusetts[b]	249	499	13	218	434	13
New Hampshire	222	420	29	220	410	35
New Jersey[d]	308	597	32	298	578	29
New York	322	635	27	307	605	25
Pennsylvania	365	710	38	393	762	42
Rhode Island[c]	235	463	21	240	475	19
Vermont[c]	260	495	32	260	504	24
Midwest	393	743	52	392	741	52
Illinois	350	668	42	351	669	41
Indiana	426	791	71	442	818	77
Iowa[e,d]	291	542	47	291	538	49
Kansas[d]	312	584	44	303	570	40
Michigan	499	971	41	488	951	39
Minnesota	181	341	23	179	336	24
Missouri	506	948	83	509	957	81
Nebraska	243	449	41	247	455	42
North Dakota	221	394	46	225	400	50
Ohio[d]	442	838	65	449	851	66
South Dakota	413	736	92	412	738	87
Wisconsin	397	748	50	374	709	43
South	556	1,050	79	552	1,043	77
Alabama	615	1,180	85	634	1,215	88
Arkansas	502	949	73	511	969	72
Delaware[c]	482	945	47	463	906	45
Florida	535	1,013	73	557	1,054	76
Georgia[e]	563	1,069	72	540	1,021	74
Kentucky	512	934	107	492	902	98
Louisiana	865	1,664	111	853	1,642	109
Maryland	404	793	39	403	796	33
Mississippi	734	1,385	121	735	1,389	121
North Carolina	361	696	41	368	707	42

Appendix Table 10. (Continued)

Region and jurisdiction	Imprisonment rate					
	Total			Male		
	Total	Male	Female	Total	Male	Female
Oklahoma	665	1,211	131	661	1,203	132
South Carolina	524	1,009	64	519	1,000	63
Tennessee	424	804	61	436	824	66
Texas	669	1,244	97	639	1,191	87
Virginia	490	921	74	489	918	75
West Virginia	333	610	68	331	604	69
West[f]	438	807	67	436	803	67
Alaska[c]	447	785	82	430	752	79
Arizona[e]	554	1,009	97	567	1,031	101
California	471	880	62	467	872	62
Colorado[d]	465	829	96	467	834	93
Hawaii[c]	338	594	79	332	585	74
Idaho	483	854	106	474	844	99
Montana	356	649	62	368	660	74
Nevada[f]	:	:	:	486	880	76
New Mexico	313	580	54	316	583	56
Oregon[d]	369	686	56	371	688	58
Utah	239	428	46	232	415	45
Washington	273	500	46	272	501	43
Wyoming	394	686	95	387	687	79

Note: Imprisonment rate is the number of prisoners sentenced to more than 1 year per 100,000 U.S. residents.

[a] The 2008 imprisonment rate includes 4,012 male prisoners sentenced to more than 1 year but held in local jails or houses of corrections in the Commonwealth of Massachusetts. The 2007 imprisonment rate includes 6,200 sentenced males held in local jails or houses of corrections in the Commonwealth of Massachusetts and an estimated number of sentenced prisoners in Nevada. See *Methodology.*

[b] The 2008 imprisonment rate includes 4,012 male prisoners sentenced to more than 1 year but held in local jails or houses of corrections in the Commonwealth of Massachusetts. The 2007 imprisonment rate includes 6,200 sentenced male prisoners held in local jails or houses of corrections in the Commonwealth of Massachusetts.

[c] Prisons and jails form one integrated system. Data include total jail and prison populations.

[d] Includes some prisoners sentenced to one year or less.

[e] Prison population based on custody counts.

[f] The 2007 imprisonment rate includes an estimated number of sentenced prisoners in Nevada. See *Methodology.*

Appendix Table 11. Number of Sentenced Prisoners Admitted to and Released from State or Federal Jurisdiction, by Jurisdiction, December 31, 2000, 2007 and 2008

Region and jurisdiction	Admissions					Releases				
	2000	2007	2008	Average annual change, 2000-2007	Percent change, 2007-2008	2000	2007	2008	Average annual change, 2000-2007	Percent change, 2007-2008
U.S. total	625,219	742,875	739,132	2.5 %	-0.5 %	604,858	721,161	735,454	2.5 %	2.0 %
Federal	43,732	53,618	53,662	3.0	0.1	35,259	48,764	52,348	4.7	7.3
State	581,487	689,257	685,470	2.5	-0.5	569,599	672,397	683,106	2.4	1.6
Northeast	67,765	73,283	70,665	1.1 %	-3.6 %	70,646	71,509	71,413	0.2 %	-0.1 %
Connecticut	6,185	6,982	6,503	1.7	-6.9	5,918	6,056	6,404	0.3	5.7
Maine	751	1,111	756	5.8	-32.0	677	1,090	720	7.0	-33.9
Massachusetts	2,062	2,670	2,988	3.8	11.9	2,889	2,248	2,667	-3.5	18.6
New Hampshire	1,051	1,290	1,464	3.0	13.5	1,044	1,179	1,507	1.8	27.8
New Jersey	13,653	13,791	12,984	0.1	-5.9	15,362	14,358	13,885	-1.0	-3.3
New York	27,601	26,291	25,302	-0.7	-3.8	28,828	27,009	27,482	-0.9	1.8
Pennsylvania	11,777	17,666	17,493	6.0	-1.0	11,759	16,340	15,618	4.8	-4.4
Rhode Island	3,701	1,120	1,090	:	-2.7	3,223	884	1,086	:	22.9
Vermont	984	2,362	2,273	:	-3.8	946	2,345	2,241	:	-4.4
Midwest	117,776	148,972	146,194	3.4 %	-1.9 %	114,382	149,826	148,780	3.9 %	-0.7 %
Illinois	29,344	35,968	36,125	3.0	0.4	28,876	35,737	35,780	3.1	0.1
Indiana	11,876	17,232	18,363	5.5	6.6	11,053	17,099	18,308	6.4	7.1
Iowa	4,656	5,706	5,592	2.9	-2.0	4,379	5,718	5,557	3.9	-2.8
Kansas	5,002	4,849	4,506	-0.4	-7.1	5,231	4,966	4,655	-0.7	-6.3
Michigan	12,169	13,330	12,101	1.3	-9.2	10,874	14,685	13,621	4.4	-7.2
Minnesota	4,406	7,856	7,555	8.6	-3.8	4,244	7,971	7,936	9.4	-0.4
Missouri	14,454	18,300	18,611	3.4	1.7	13,346	19,323	18,864	5.4	-2.4
Nebraska	1,688	2,076	2,059	3.0	-0.8	1,503	1,952	1,963	3.8	0.6
North Dakota	605	1,028	1,085	7.9	5.5	598	977	1,051	7.3	7.6
Ohio	23,780	30,808	29,510	3.8	-4.2	24,793	29,236	28,552	2.4	-2.3
South Dakota	1,400	3,227	3,116	12.7	-3.4	1,327	3,259	3,102	13.7	-4.8
Wisconsin	8,396	8,592	7,571	0.3	-11.9	8,158	8,903	9,391	1.3	5.5
South	217,950	258,223	260,626	2.5 %	0.9 %	210,777	245,998	257,065	2.2 %	4.5 %
Alabama	6,296	10,708	11,037	7.9	3.1	7,136	11,079	11,556	6.5	4.3
Arkansas	6,941	6,651	7,017	-0.6	5.5	6,308	6,045	6,610	-0.6	9.3
Delaware	2,709	1,899	1,494	-4.9	-21.3	2,260	1,905	1,617	-2.4	-15.1
Florida	35,683	33,552	40,860	-0.9	21.8	33,994	28,705	37,277	-2.4	29.9
Georgia	17,373	21,134	18,625	2.8	-11.9	14,797	18,774	19,463	3.5	3.7
Kentucky	8,116	15,359	14,273	9.5	-7.1	7,733	13,819	15,413	8.6	11.5
Louisiana	15,735	14,548	15,854	-1.1	9.0	14,536	14,984	14,991	0.4	0.0
Maryland	10,327	10,716	10,396	0.5	-3.0	10,004	10,123	10,383	0.2	2.6
Mississippi	5,796	9,749	7,908	7.7	-18.9	4,940	8,455	7,817	8.0	-7.5
North Carolina	9,848	10,834	11,825	1.4	9.1	9,687	10,074	10,615	0.6	5.4
Oklahoma	7,426	8,795	7,935	2.4	-9.8	6,628	8,486	7,915	3.6	-6.7
South Carolina	8,460	9,912	9,650	2.3	-2.6	8,676	9,461	9,506	1.2	0.5
Tennessee	13,675	14,535	14,196	0.9	-2.3	13,893	15,537	15,414	1.6	-0.8
Texas	58,197	72,525	72,804	3.2	0.4	59,776	73,023	72,168	2.9	-1.2
Virginia	9,791	13,973	13,625	5.2	-2.5	9,148	12,559	13,194	4.6	5.1

Appendix Table 11. (Continued)

Region and jurisdiction	Admissions					Releases				
	2000	2007	2008	Average annual change, 2000-2007	Percent change, 2007-2008	2000	2007	2008	Average annual change, 2000-2007	Percent change, 2007-2008
West Virginia	1,577	3,333	3,127	11.3	-6.2	1,261	2,969	3,126	13.0	5.3
West	177,996	208,779	207,985	2.3 %	-0.4 %	173,794	205,064	205,848	2.4%	0.4 %
Alaska	2,427	3,272	3,635	4.4	11.1	2,599	3,286	3,741	3.4	13.8
Arizona	9,560	14,046	14,867	5.7	5.8	9,100	12,560	13,192	4.7	5.0
California	129,640	139,608	140,827	1.1	0.9	129,621	135,920	136,925	0.7	0.7
Colorado	7,036	10,959	11,089	6.5	1.2	5,881	10,604	10,616	8.8	0.1
Hawaii	1,594	1,514	1,731	-0.7	14.3	1,379	1,518	1,795	1.4	18.2
Idaho	3,386	4,055	3,867	2.6	-4.6	2,697	3,850	3,891	5.2	1.1
Montana	1,202	2,055	2,264	8.0	10.2	1,031	2,176	2,117	11.3	-2.7
Nevada*	4,929	6,375	4,610	:	:	4,374	4,904	5,278	:	:
New Mexico	3,161	4,146	4,092	4.0	-1.3	3,383	4,507	4,013	4.2	-11.0
Oregon	4,059	5,331	5,395	4.0	1.2	3,371	5,080	5,055	6.0	-0.5
Utah	3,270	3,466	3,394	0.8	-2.1	2,897	3,393	3,400	2.3	0.2
Washington	7,094	16,478	15,070	12.8	-8.5	6,764	16,488	15,061	13.6	-8.7
Wyoming	638	746	779	2.3	4.4	697	778	764	1.6	-1.8

Note: Totals based on prisoners with a sentence of more than 1 year. Totals exclude escapees, AWOLS, and transfers to and from other jurisdictions. *See Methodology.*

: Not calculated.

*Includes estimates for Nevada for December 31 2007.

Appendix Table 12. Number of Sentenced Prisoners Admitted and Released from State or Federal Jurisdiction, by Type, December 31, 2008

Region and jurisdiction	Admissions			Releases		
	Total	New court commitments	Parole violators	Total	Conditional releases	Unconditional releases
U.S. total	739,132	478,100	252,707	735,454	506,393	216,276
Federal	53,662	49,270	4,390	52,348	1,225	50,708
State	685,470	428,830	248,317	683,106	505,168	165,568
Northeast	70,665	46,338	22,726	71,413	51,129	18,376
Connecticut	6,503	5,335	1,077	6,404	2,972	3,403
Maine	756	379	377	720	365	355
Massachusetts	2,988	2,678	310	2,667	903	1,735
New Hampshire[a]	1,464	/	/	1,507	/	/
New Jersey	12,984	9,715	3,201	13,885	9,068	4,612
New York	25,302	15,178	10,027	27,482	23,856	3,314

Appendix Table 12. (Continued)

Region and jurisdiction	Admissions			Releases		
	Total	New court commitments	Parole violators	Total	Conditional releases	Unconditional releases
Pennsylvania	17,493	10,564	6,099	15,618	10,396	3,923
Rhode Island	1,090	929	161	1,086	514	567
Vermont	2,273	799	1,474	2,241	2,012	227
Midwest	146,194	97,395	45,649	148,780	117,825	28,858
Illinois	36,125	24,266	11,789	35,780	31,370	4,333
Indiana	18,363	11,165	6,977	18,308	17,778	462
Iowa	5,592	3,073	1,285	5,557	2,880	1,410
Kansas	4,506	3,142	1,341	4,655	3,380	1,246
Michigan	12,101	7,677	3,927	13,621	11,557	1,714
Minnesota	7,555	4,919	2,624	7,936	6,672	1,247
Missouri	18,611	9,952	8,646	18,864	16,618	2,152
Nebraska	2,059	1,789	270	1,963	908	1,042
North Dakota	1,085	733	350	1,051	810	233
Ohio	29,510	24,881	4,606	28,552	14,321	14,107
South Dakota	3,116	1,185	888	3,102	2,744	349
Wisconsin	7,571	4,613	2,946	9,391	8,787	563
South	260,626	193,964	63,708	257,065	148,530	103,046
Alabama	11,037	9,627	1,393	11,556	7,280	4,083
Arkansas	7,017	5,286	1,691	6,610	6,254	311
Delaware	1,494	1,175	291	1,617	1,212	266
Florida	40,860	39,997	116	37,277	12,678	24,303
Georgia	18,625	10,731	7,854	19,463	1,893	17,402
Kentucky	14,273	10,624	3,649	15,413	8,760	6,575
Louisiana	15,854	10,587	4,960	14,991	13,709	1,109
Maryland	10,396	6,520	3,875	10,383	9,429	872
Mississippi	7,908	6,858	1,040	7,817	5,160	1,771
North Carolina	11,825	11,377	419	10,615	3,061	7,388
Oklahoma	7,935	5,530	2,319	7,915	4,353	3,372
South Carolina	9,650	6,483	2,990	9,506	4,926	4,348
Tennessee	14,196	8,425	5,771	15,414	10,129	5,222
Texas	72,804	46,285	25,450	72,168	56,343	13,671
Virginia	13,625	13,001	624	13,194	1,689	11,312
West Virginia	3,127	1,458	1,266	3,126	1,654	1,041
West	207,985	91,133	116,234	205,848	187,684	15,288
Alaska[a]	3,635	/	/	3,741	1,709	1,811
Arizona	14,867	12,436	2,377	13,192	10,131	2,181
California	140,827	46,380	94,447	136,925	134,974	1,759

Appendix Table 12. (Continued)

Region and jurisdiction	Admissions			Releases		
	Total	New court commitments	Parole violators	Total	Conditional releases	Unconditional releases
Colorado	11,089	6,355	4,720	10,616	9,021	1,240
Hawaii	1,731	823	908	1,795	658	316
Idaho	3,867	3,584	283	3,891	3,370	500
Montana	2,264	1,920	344	2,117	1,816	284
Nevada[b]	4,610	3,184	1,426	5,278	2,886	2,354
New Mexico	4,092	2,392	1,395	4,013	2,603	1,392
Oregon	5,395	3,703	1,456	5,055	4,796	18
Utah	3,394	1,777	1,617	3,400	2,422	966
Washington	15,070	7,918	7,144	15,061	12,879	2,133
Wyoming	779	661	117	764	419	334

Note: Totals are based on prisoners with a sentence of more than 1 year. Totals exclude transfers, escapes, and AWOLS.

/ Not reported.

[a] New reporting systems prevent the disaggregation of admission and/or release type.

[b] Includes estimates for Nevada for December 31 2007.

Appendix Table 13. Estimated Number of Sentenced Prisoners under State or Federal Jurisdiction, by Gender, Race, Hispanic Origin, and Age, December 31, 2008

Age	Male				Female			
	Total[a]	White[b]	Black[b]	Hispanic	Total[a]	White[b]	Black[b]	Hispanic
Total[c]	1,434,800	477,500	562,800	295,800	105,300	50,700	29,100	17,300
18-19	23,800	6,500	10,400	4,900	1,000	400	300	200
20-24	208,400	59,400	85,000	48,400	11,500	5,400	3,000	2,300
25-29	246,400	66,000	102,800	60,000	16,000	7,300	4,400	3,100
30-34	238,100	70,700	96,800	54,400	18,500	8,900	5,000	3,200
35-39	226,700	75,200	90,500	45,900	20,800	9,900	5,900	3,200
40-44	202,500	75,500	77,400	35,600	17,900	8,700	5,100	2,600
45-49	136,300	53,100	51,300	22,600	10,700	5,200	3,100	1,500
50-54	75,800	31,600	27,000	12,300	5,000	2,500	1,400	700
55-59	39,100	19,000	11,900	6,200	2,100	1,300	500	300
60-64	19,200	10,700	4,700	3,000	1,000	600	200	200
65 or older	15,800	9,300	3,700	2,200	600	400	100	100

Note: Totals based on prisoners with a sentence of more than 1 year. See Methodology for estimation method.

[a] Includes American Indians, Alaska Natives, Asians, Native Hawaiians, other Pacific Islanders, and persons identifying two or more races.

[b] Excludes persons of Hispanic or Latino origin.

[c] Includes persons under age 18.

Appendix Table 14. Estimated Rate of Sentenced Prisoners under State or Federal Jurisdiction Per 100,000 U.S. Residents, by Gender, Race, Hispanic Origin, and Age, December 31, 2008

Age	Male				Female			
	Total[a]	White[b]	Black[b]	Hispanic	Total[a]	White[b]	Black[b]	Hispanic
Total[c]	952	487	3,161	1,200	68	50	149	75
18-19	528	238	1,532	614	23	16	44	25
20-24	1,916	893	5,553	2,474	112	86	202	131
25-29	2,238	1,017	7,130	2,612	153	115	301	167
30-34	2,366	1,217	8,032	2,411	190	155	380	174
35-39	2,159	1,171	7,392	2,263	201	156	434	183
40-44	1,903	1,090	6,282	2,032	169	127	364	170
45-49	1,202	671	4,056	1,523	93	65	211	106
50-54	713	407	2,385	1,085	45	31	106	61
55-59	429	276	1,325	739	22	18	44	30
60-64	259	184	738	502	12	9	25	23
65 or older	95	69	294	186	3	2	6	4

Note: Totals based on prisoners with a sentence of more than 1 year. Rates are per 100,000 U.S. residents in each reference population group. See Methodology for estimation method.
[a] Includes American Indians, Alaska Natives, Asians, Native Hawaiians, other Pacific Islanders, and persons identifying two or more races.
[b] Excludes persons of Hispanic or Latino origin.
[c] Includes persons under age 18.

Appendix Table 15. Estimated Number of Sentenced Prisoners under State Jurisdiction, by Offense, Gender, Race, and Hispanic Origin, Yearend 2006

Offense	All inmates	Male	Female	White[a]	Black[a]	Hispanic
Total	1,331,100	1,238,900	92,200	474,200	508,700	248,900
Violent	667,900	638,100	29,800	217,100	256,400	145,300
Murder[b]	144,500	135,700	8,800	34,700	61,400	36,800
Manslaughter	16,700	14,900	1,800	6,900	6,100	2,400
Rape	54,800	54,400	400	26,600	16,900	7,400
Other sexual assault	105,500	104,100	1,400	56,800	20,600	23,900
Robbery	179,500	172,400	7,100	37,500	91,500	33,900
Assault	136,600	128,800	7,900	42,800	49,800	34,700
Other violent	30,300	27,800	2,400	11,800	10,100	6,100
Property	277,900	251,200	26,700	135,300	96,000	25,000
Burglary	138,000	132,300	5,700	68,700	53,600	2,800
Larceny	51,600	43,800	7,800	23,300	17,600	7,200
Motor vehicle theft	27,100	25,500	1,600	10,900	7,100	7,900
Fraud	34,400	25,000	9,400	19,200	10,000	2,900

Appendix Table 15. (Continued)

Offense	All inmates	Male	Female	White[a]	Black[a]	Hispanic
Other property	26,800	24,700	2,100	13,300	7,600	4,200
Drug offenses	265,800	240,500	25,400	72,100	117,600	55,700
Public-order offenses[c]	112,300	106,100	6,200	48,200	35,400	21,000
Other/unspecified[d]	7,200	2,900	4,300	1,400	3,300	1,900

Note: Totals based on prisoners with a sentence of more than 1 year. Detail may not add to total due to rounding. See *Methodology* for estimation method.

[a] Excludes Hispanics and persons identifying two or more races.
[b] Includes negligent manslaughter.
[c] Includes weapons, drunk driving, court offenses, commercialized vice, morals and decency offenses, liquor law violations, and other public-order offenses.
[d] Includes juvenile offenses and other unspecified offense categories.

Appendix Table 16. Estimated Percent of Sentenced Prisoners under State Jurisdiction, by Offense, Gender, Race, and Hispanic Origin, Yearend 2006

Offense	All inmates	Male	Female	White[a]	Black[a]	Hispanic
Total	100.0%	100.0%	100.0%	100.0%	100.0%	100.0%
Violent	50.2%	51.5%	32.3%	45.8%	50.4%	58.4%
Murder[b]	10.9	11.0	9.5	7.3	12.1	14.8
Manslaughter	1.3	1.2	2.0	1.5	1.2	1.0
Rape	4.1	4.4	0.5	5.6	3.3	3.0
Other sexual assault	7.9	8.4	1.5	12.0	4.1	9.6
Robbery	13.5	13.9	7.7	7.9	18.0	13.6
Assault	10.3	10.4	8.5	9.0	9.8	13.9
Other violent	2.3	2.2	2.6	2.5	2.0	2.5
Property	20.9%	20.3%	28.9%	28.5%	18.9%	10.0%
Burglary	10.4	10.7	6.2	14.5	10.5	1.1
Larceny	3.9	3.5	8.5	4.9	3.5	2.9
Motor vehicle theft	2.0	2.1	1.8	2.3	1.4	3.2
Fraud	2.6	2.0	10.2	4.0	2.0	1.2
Other property	2.0	2.0	2.3	2.8	1.5	1.7
Drug offenses	20.0%	19.4%	27.5%	15.2%	23.1%	22.4%
Public-order offenses[c]	8.4%	8.6%	6.7%	10.2%	7.0%	8.4%
Other/unspecified[d]	0.5%	0.2%	4.6%	0.3%	0.6%	0.8%

Note: Totals based on prisoners with a sentence of more than 1 year. Detail may not add to total due to rounding. See *Methodology* for estimation method.

[a] Excludes Hispanics and persons identifying two or more races.
[b] Includes negligent manslaughter.
[c] Includes weapons, drunk driving, court offenses, commercialized vice, morals and decency offenses, liquor law violations, and other public-order offenses.
[d] Includes juvenile offenses and other unspecified offense categories.

Appendix Table 17. Number of Sentenced Prisoners in Federal Prison, by Most Serious Offense, 2000, 2007 and 2008

Offense	2000	2007	2008	Average annual change, 2000-2007	Percent change, 2007-2008
Total	131,739	179,204	182,333	4.5%	1.7 %
Violent offenses	13,740	15,647	15,483	1.9%	-1.0 %
Homicide[a]	1,363	2,915	2,949	11.5	1.2
Robbery	9,712	8,966	8,718	-1.1	-2.8
Other violent	2,665	3,767	3,817	5.1	1.3
Property offenses	10,135	10,345	11,080	0.3%	7.1%
Burglary	462	504	475	1.3	-5.7
Fraud	7,506	7,834	7,728	0.6	-1.3
Other property	2,167	2,006	2,876	-1.1	43.4
Drug offenses	74,276	95,446	95,079	3.6%	-0.4%
Public-order offenses	32,325	56,273	59,298	8.2%	5.4%
Immigration	13,676	19,528	19,678	5.2	0.8
Weapons	10,822	25,435	26,942	13	5.9
Other	7,827	11,311	12,678	5.4	12.1
Other/unspecified[b]	1,263	1,492	1,394	2.4%	-6.6%

Note: Based on prisoners with a sentence of more than 1 year. All data are for September 30 from the BJS Federal Justice Statistics Program.

[a] Includes murder, negligent and non-negligent manslaughter.

[b] Includes offenses not classified.

Appendix Table 18. Number of State or Federal Prisoners in Private Facilities, December 31, 2000-2008

Year	Number of prisoners			Percent of all prisoners
	Total	Federal	State	
2000	87,369	15,524	71,845	6.3%
2001	91,828	19,251	72,577	5.8
2002	93,912	20,274	73,638	6.5
2003	95,707	21,865	73,842	6.5
2004	98,628	24,768	73,860	6.6
2005	107,940	27,046	80,894	7.1
2006	113,697	27,726	85,971	7.2
2007	123,942	31,310	92,632	7.8
2008	128,524	33,162	95,362	8.0%
Average annual change, 2000-2007	5.1%	10.5%	3.7%	:
Percent change, 2007-2008	3.7	5.9	2.9	:

: Not calculated.

Appendix Table 19. Number of State and Federal Prisoners in Private Facilities, by Jurisdiction, December 31, 2000, 2006-2008

Region and jurisdiction	Number of prisoners			Percent of all prisoners 12/31/2008
	12/31/2000	12/31/2007	12/31/2008	
U.S. total	87,369	123,942	128,524	8.0 %
Federal[a]	15,524	31,310	33,162	16.5
State	71,845	92,632	95,362	6.8
Northeast	2,509	4,268	4,186	2.3 %
Connecticut	0	0	0	0.0
Maine	11	42	0	0.0
Massachusetts	0	0	0	0.0
New Hampshire	0	0	0	0.0
New Jersey[b]	2,498	2,686	2,641	10.2
New York	0	0	0	0.0
Pennsylvania	0	1,022	819	1.6
Rhode Island	0	0	0	0.0
Vermont[b]	0	518	726	34.3
Midwest	7,836	5,048	5,415	2.1 %
Illinois	0	/	/	:
Indiana	991	1,683	2,642	9.3
Iowa	0	0	0	0.0
Kansas	0	0	0	0.0
Michigan	449	0	0	0.0
Minnesota	0	1,183	612	6.5
Missouri	0	0	0	0.0
Nebraska	0	0	0	0.0
North Dakota	96	0	0	0.0
Ohio	1,918	2,138	2,133	4.1
South Dakota	45	21	15	0.4
Wisconsin	4,337	23	13	0.1
South	45,560	56,117	57,888	8.9 %
Alabama	0	355	101	0.3
Arkansas	1,540	0	0	0
Delaware	0	0	0	0.0
District of Columbia	2,342	~	~	:
Florida	3,912	8,769	9,158	8.9
Georgia	3,746	4,974	5,138	9.7
Kentucky	1,268	2,404	2,209	10.2
Louisiana	3,068	3,004	2,928	7.6
Maryland	127	151	186	0.8
Mississippi	3,230	4,794	5,497	24.2
North Carolina	330	213	217	0.5
Oklahoma	6,931	5,917	5,711	22.1

Appendix Table 19. (Continued)

Region and jurisdiction	Number of prisoners			Percent of all prisoners 12/31/2008
	12/31/2000	12/31/2007	12/31/2008	
South Carolina	0	9	12	0.0
Tennessee	3,510	5,121	5,155	18.9
Texas	13,985	18,871	20,041	11.6
Virginia	1,571	1,535	1,535	4.0
West Virginia	0	0	0	0.0
West[a]	15,940	27,199	27,873	8.8%
Alaska	1,383	1,524	1,450	28.9
Arizona	1,430	7,790	8,369	21.1
California	4,547	3,032	3,019	1.7
Colorado	/	4,878	5,274	22.7
Hawaii	1,187	2,129	2,108	35.4
Idaho	1,162	1,969	2,114	29.0
Montana	986	1,324	1,314	36.4
Nevada[c]	508	0	0	0.0
New Mexico	2,155	2,720	2,935	45.8
Oregon	0	0	0	0.0
Utah	208	0	0	0.0
Washington[b]	0	1,203	863	4.8
Wyoming	275	630	427	20.5

: Not calculated.

/ Not reported.

~ Not applicable. After 2001, responsibility for sentenced felons from the District of Columbia was transferred to the Federal Bureau of Prisons.

[a] Includes federal prisoners held in non-secure, privately operated facilities (8,644 at yearend 2008; numbers from other years can be found in earlier publications).

[b] Includes prisoners held in out-of-state private facilities.

[c] Includes estimates for Nevada for December 31, 2007. See *Methodology.*

Appendix Table 20. Number of State or Federal Prisoners in Local Facilities, December 31, 2000-2008

Year	Number of prisoners			Percent of all prisoners
	Total	Federal	State	
2000	63,140	2,438	60,702	4.5%
2001	70,681	2,921	67,760	5.0
2002	72,550	3,377	69,173	5.0
2003	73,440	3,278	70,162	5.0
2004	74,445	1,199	73,246	5.0
2005	73,164	1,044	72,120	4.8
2006	77,912	2,010	75,902	5.0
2007	80,621	2,144	78,477	5.0
2008	83,093	2,738	80,355	5.2
Average annual change, 2000-2007	3.6%	-1.8%	3.7%	:
Percent change, 2007-2008	3.1	27.7	2.4	:

:Not calculated

Appendix Table 21. Number of State and Federal Prisoners in Local Jail Facilities, by Jurisdiction, December 31, 2000, 2006-2008

Region and jurisdiction	Number of prisoners held in local jails			Percent of all prisoners 12/31/2008
	12/31/2000	12/31/2007	12/31/2008	
U.S. total	63,140	80,621	83,093	5.2 %
Federal	2,438	2,144	2,738	1.4
State	60,702	78,477	80,355	5.7
Northeast	3,823	1,686	1,454	0.8 %
Connecticut[a]	~	~	~	:
Maine	24	9	90	4.1
Massachusetts	457	136	185	1.6
New Hampshire	14	52	46	1.6
New Jersey[b]	3,225	1,468	1,122	4.3
New York	45	21	11	0.0
Pennsylvania	58	0	0	0.0
Rhode Island[a]	~	~	~	:
Vermont[a]	~	~	~	:
Midwest	2,103	3,381	3,567	1.4 %
Illinois	0	0	0	0.0
Indiana	1,187	2,002	1,930	6.8
Iowa	0	0	0	0.0
Kansas	0	0	0	0.0
Michigan	286	43	28	0.1
Minnesota	149	518	550	5.8
Missouri	0	0	0	0.0
Nebraska	0	0	0	0.0
North Dakota	38	48	71	4.9
Ohio	0	0	0	0.0
South Dakota	16	55	58	1.7
Wisconsin	427	715	930	4.0
South	49,455	67,071	69,445	10.7 %
Alabama	3,401	1,596	1,790	5.9
Arkansas	728	1,007	1,541	10.5
Delaware[a]	~	~	~	:
District of Columbia	1,329	~	~	:
Florida	0	1,147	1,144	1.1
Georgia	3,888	4,919	4,690	8.9
Kentucky	3,850	7,912	7,363	33.9
Louisiana	15,599	17,079	17,524	45.7
Maryland	118	151	141	0.6
Mississippi	3,700	4,952	4,858	21.4
North Carolina	0	0	0	0.0
Oklahoma	970	1,892	2,148	8.3
South Carolina	433	377	361	1.5
Tennessee	5,204	7,019	7,860	28.9
Texas	6,477	12,774	12,805	7.4

Appendix Table 21. (Continued)

Region and jurisdiction	Number of prisoners held in local jails			Percent of all prisoners 12/31/2008
	12/31/2000	12/31/2007	12/31/2008	
Virginia	2,962	5,097	6,057	15.8
West Virginia	796	1,149	1,163	19.2
West	5,321	6,339	5,889	1.9 %
Alaska[a]	~	~	~	:
Arizona	237	46	47	0.1
California	2,758	3,023	2,736	1.6
Colorado	2,178	175	63	0.3
Hawaii[a]	~	~	~	:
Idaho	450	575	365	5.0
Montana	548	522	642	17.8
Nevada[c]	175	155	199	1.6
New Mexico	0	116	0	0.0
Oregon	7	23	20	0.1
Utah	1,050	1,286	1,341	20.5
Washington	0	362	430	2.4
Wyoming	17	56	46	2.2

~Not applicable. After 2001, responsibility for sentenced felons from the District of Columbia was transferred to the Federal Bureau of Prisons.

/ Not reported.

: Not calculated.

[a] Priso ns and jails form one integrated system.

[b] Includes prisoners held in out-of-state private facilities.

[c] Includes estimates for Nevada for December 31, 2007. See *Methodology.*

Appendix Table 22. Prisoners in Custody of Correctional Authorities in the U.S. Territories and Commonwealths, Yearend 2007 and 2008

Jurisdiction	Total			Sentenced to more than 1 year			
	2007	2008	Percent change, 2007-2008	2007	2008	Percent change, 2007-2008	Incarceration rate, 2008[a]
Total[b]	14,678	13,576	-7.5 %	11,465	10,346	-9.8 %	237
American Samoa	236	132	-44.1	122	48	-60.7	74
Guam[b]	535	578	8.1	320	304	-5.0	173
Commonwealth of the Northern Marina Islands	137	124	-9.5	78	78	0.0	141
Commonwealth of Puerto Rico	13,215	12,130	-8.2	10,553	9,642	-8.6	244
U.S. Virgin Islands	555	612	10.3	392	274	-30.1	249

[a] The number of prisoners with a sentence of more than 1 year per 100,000 persons in the resident population. July 1, 2008 population estimates were provided by the U.S. Census Bureau, International Data Base.

[b] Includes estimates for 2008. Data not available for Guam at time of publication. See *Methodology.*

Appendix Table 23. Prisoners under Military Jurisdiction, by Branch of Service, Yearend 2007 and 2008

Branch of service	Total			Sentenced to more than 1 year		
	2007	2008	Percent change, 2007-2008	2007	2008	Percent change, 2007-2008
Total	1,794	1,651	-8.0 %	1,089	1,005	-7.7 %
To which prisoners belong						
Air Force	280	281	0.4	185	178	-3.8
Army	829	701	-15.4	555	477	-14.1
Marine Corps	396	427	7.8	164	180	9.8
Navy	268	231	-13.8	173	163	-5.8
Coast Guard	21	11	-47.6	12	7	-41.7
Holding prisoners						
Air Force	61	61	0.0	9	9	0.0
Army	912	746	-18.2	721	602	-16.5
Marine Corps	338	351	3.8	97	103	6.2
Navy	483	493	2.1	262	291	11.1

Appendix Table 24. Reported State and Federal Prison Capacities, December 31, 2008

Region and jurisdiction	Type of capacity measure			Custody population as a percent of—	
	Rated	Operational	Design	Highest capacity[a]	Lowest capacity[a]
Federal	122,479	...	...	135 %	135 %
Northeast					
Connecticut[b]	...	...	...	...	...
Maine	1,885	1,885	1,885	109 %	109 %
Massachusetts	...	...	7,959	140	140
New Hampshire	2,145	2,904	2,145	98	133
New Jersey	...	23,022	16,876	96	132
New York	59,830	60,978	57,403	99	105
Pennsylvania	43,298	43,298	43,298	101	101
Rhode Island	4,004	4,004	4,265	88	93
Vermont	1,732	1,470	1,371	80	101
Midwest					
Illinois	34,300	34,300	30,391	133%	150%
Indiana	...	27,084	...	88	88
Iowa	...	...	13,680	64	64
Kansas	9,317	...	...	92	92
Michigan	...	50,462	...	97	97
Minnesota	...	8,361	...	101	101
Missouri	...	31,296	...	96	96
Nebraska	...	3,969	3,175	113	141
North Dakota	1,044	991	1,044	132	139

Appendix Table 24. (Continued)

Region and jurisdiction	Type of capacity measure			Custody population as a percent of—	
	Rated	Operational	Design	Highest capacity[a]	Lowest capacity[a]
Ohio	38,320	...	...	127	127
South Dakota	...	3,451	...	97	97
Wisconsin[c]	...	...	17,773	125	125
South					
Alabama[d]	...	25,686	13,403	98%	188%
Arkansas	13,163	13,812	13,163	95	100
Delaware	5,648	5,250	4,161	123	167
Florida[d]	...	102,625	...	88	88
Georgia[e]	...	56,305	...	103	103
Kentucky	13,708	13,708	14,043	93	95
Louisiana[e]	20,857	20,769	...	114	115
Maryland	...	23,638	...	97	97
Mississippi[e]	...	24,019	24,019	75	75
North Carolina[d]	39,529	40,014	34,364	100	116
Oklahoma[e]	25,312	25,312	25,312	94	94
South Carolina	...	24,126	...	98	98
Tennessee	20,408	19,949	...	70	71
Texas[c]	160,371	160,371	164,388	85	87
Virginia	33,250	...	33,250	93	93
West Virginia	4,135	5,017	4,135	98	118
West					
Alaska	3,058	3,206	...	111%	116 %
Arizona	35,286	39,292	37,328	79	88
California	...	161,530	84,066	106	204
Colorado	...	14,946	13,055	120	137
Hawaii	...	3,487	2,451	96	137
Idaho[e]	6,534	6,207	6,534	108	113
Montana[c]	...	2,539	...	116	116
Nevada	11,894	10,891	8,689	108	148
New Mexico[e]	...	7,024	6,458	48	52
Oregon	...	14,353	14,353	94	94
Utah	...	6,650	6,886	75	77
Washington	13,777	15,502	15,502	111	125
Wyoming	1,713	1,603	1,598	75	80

...Data not available.

[a] Population counts are based on the number of inmates held in facilities operated by the jurisdiction. Excludes inmates held in local jails, in other states, or in private facilities.

[b] Connecticut no longer reports capacity because of a law passed in 1995.

[c] Excludes capacity of county facilities and inmates housed in them.

[d] Capacity definition differs from BJS definition, see NPS jurisdiction notes.

[e] Includes capacity of private and contract facilities and inmates housed in them.

End Notes

[1] New court commitments include felony offenders sentenced to state prison and probation violators entering prison for the first time on a violation of a condition of probation. Parole violators include any conditionally released parolee admitted to prison either for a technical violation of the conditions of supervision or for a new crime.

[2] Unconditional releases include expirations of sentence, commutations, and other unconditional releases.

[3] Conditional releases include releases to probation, supervised mandatory release, and other unspecified conditional releases.

[4] See *Drug Use and Dependence, State and Federal Prisoners, 2004* , BJS Web. 11 Oct. 2006.

Chapter 3

PRISON CONSTRUCTION: CLEAR COMMUNICATION ON THE ACCURACY OF COST ESTIMATES AND PROJECT CHANGES IS NEEDED*

United States Government Accountability Office

WHY GAO DID THIS STUDY

The federal Bureau of Prisons (BOP) is responsible for the custody and care of more than 201,000 federal offenders. To provide housing for the federal prison population, BOP manages the construction and maintenance of its prison facilities and oversees contract facilities. GAO was asked to look into recent increases in estimated costs for Federal Correctional Institution (FCI) construction projects located in Mendota, CA; Berlin, NH; and McDowell, WV, which have led to almost $278 million or 62 percent more being provided in funding than initially estimated. This chapter addresses (1) the reasons for the changes to the estimated costs and (2) the actions BOP has taken—or plans to take—to control future cost increases and delays. GAO reviewed and analyzed BOP's fiscal years 2001 to 2009 budget documents, files for these three projects, and project management guidance. GAO also reviewed government and industry guidance on project management and met with BOP officials.

WHAT GAO RECOMMENDS

GAO recommends that the Attorney General of the United States instruct the Director of BOP to clearly communicate in DOJ's annual congressional budget submission (1) the extent

---

* This is an edited, reformatted and augmented version of a U. S. Government Accountability Office publication dated May 2008.

to which project costs may vary from initial estimates and (2) changes that may impact the functionality of projects. BOP agreed with GAO's recommendations.

WHAT GAO FOUND

For these three projects, delays in starting construction or disruptions in available funding that interrupted construction contributed to increases in cost estimates due to inflation and unexpected increases in construction material costs. According to BOP officials, delays resulted from problems with selecting and approving the sites for the prisons and with the availability of funding. BOP officials stated that they expected costs to increase by the inflation rate during the delay period, but did not anticipate that market forces would cause the construction costs to increase above the inflation rate, as they did. For example, steel prices rose about 60 percent and oil prices rose by almost 170 percent between the time that BOP prepared the initial cost estimates for these projects and when construction was ready to begin. In addition, because BOP estimates initial project costs early in the planning process, generally before an actual prison location is selected, variance from the initial estimates would be expected to some extent, even if the projects are not delayed. BOP, like other agencies, is not required to communicate how much it expects costs may vary from its estimates in its budget documents. Without such information, Congress and other stakeholders do not know the extent to which additional funding may be required to complete the project, even absent any project delays.

BOP eliminated or reduced portions of two projects to remain within the amount that was funded and plans to use its construction management policies and procedures to control further cost increases and schedule delays. When awarding the contract for FCI Mendota in 2007, BOP eliminated a UNICOR facility, which would have provided additional employment and job skills training opportunities for inmates, and the minimum-security prison camp. At FCI Berlin, BOP eliminated the UNICOR facility when it awarded the contract in 2007, but subsequently added a smaller UNICOR facility to the project, which will be paid for by UNICOR. Intended to reduce costs, these changes also reduced the functionality of the two prisons, deviating from what BOP planned and requested funding for. In the subsequent budget submission to Congress and other stakeholders, BOP did not clearly communicate these changes, since BOP does not provide such detailed project information. Now that BOP has awarded the construction contracts for the three projects, BOP officials believe that their construction management policies and procedures will allow them to control cost increases and schedule delays. These policies and procedures reflect current government and industry project management practices to monitor and track projects, and to report on their status. Furthermore, BOP officials said that they plan to continue to avoid making changes that would increase construction costs after construction begins. GAO did not evaluate the effectiveness of BOP's construction policies and procedures in controlling cost increases and schedule delays on these projects because while construction contracts were awarded, little construction had been done.

ABBREVIATIONS

BOP	Bureau of Prisons
CII	Construction Industry Institute
CPC	Capacity Planning Committee
DOJ	Department of Justice
EPA	Environmental Protection Agency
FCI	Federal Correctional Institution
ICIPPI	*Inputs to Construction Industries Producer Price Index*
LRPC	Long-Range Planning Committee
OMB	Office of Management and Budget

May 29, 2008

The Honorable Barbara A. Mikulski
Chairman
The Honorable Richard C. Shelby
Ranking Member
Subcommittee on Commerce, Justice,
Science, and Related Agencies
Committee on Appropriations
United States Senate

The federal Bureau of Prisons (BOP), within the Department of Justice (DOJ), is responsible for the custody and care of more than 201,000 federal offenders. To accommodate the current and future confinement needs of the U.S. federal prison population, BOP manages the construction and maintenance of its prison facilities. BOP also contracts with other facilities to house about 17 percent of the federal offenders. Cost estimates that BOP provided to Congress for BOP's three current prison construction projects that are located in Mendota, California; Berlin, New Hampshire; and McDowell, West Virginia, have increased significantly beyond the initial estimates. For the purposes of this chapter, we refer to these Federal Correctional Institution (FCI) construction projects as FCI Mendota, FCI Berlin, and FCI McDowell. To date, additional funding has been provided for these projects totaling almost $278 million, or 62 percent more than the projects' initial estimates.

To assist the Subcommittee in its oversight role and in making future funding decisions, you requested that we examine the circumstances surrounding the increases in the cost estimates for the three current construction projects. Accordingly, for the three prisons currently under construction, this chapter addresses (1) the reasons for the changes to the estimated costs to date and (2) the actions BOP has taken—or plans to take—to control future cost increases and schedule delays.

To assess the reasons for the changes to the estimated costs related to the three prisons currently under construction, we analyzed DOJ's congressional budget submissions for BOP from the first year that project funding was requested in fiscal years 2001 through 2009, and relevant appropriation laws. We also reviewed and analyzed BOP's cost estimates, project files, and capital planning guidance. We analyzed the Office of Management and Budget's

(OMB) guidance on capital planning and preparing budget submissions. In addition, to identify the rate of inflation and other price indicators that could have affected the cost estimates for the three project schedules, we analyzed the Department of Labor, Bureau of Labor Statistics, pricing indexes for 2003 through 2007, and interviewed BOP officials in Washington, D.C.

To assess the actions taken by BOP—or that BOP plans to take—to control cost increases and schedule delays on the three current construction projects, we analyzed BOP's construction guidance and BOP's project files. Furthermore, we reviewed federal government and construction industry data concerning project cost management and compared them with BOP's guidance. We also interviewed BOP headquarters officials in Washington, D.C. We discuss the scope and methodology of this chapter in more detail in appendix I.

We conducted this performance audit from June 2007 through May 2008, in accordance with generally accepted government auditing standards. Those standards require that we plan and perform the audit to obtain sufficient, appropriate evidence to provide a reasonable basis for our findings and conclusions based on our audit objectives. We believe that the evidence obtained provides a reasonable basis for our findings and conclusions based on our audit objectives.

RESULTS IN BRIEF

Delays in starting project construction or disruptions in available funding that interrupted construction contributed to increases in cost estimates due to inflation and unexpected increases in construction material costs. According to BOP officials, problems with selecting and approving the sites for FCI Mendota, FCI Berlin, and FCI McDowell, along with receiving funding later than assumed in the initial estimates, delayed the three prison projects. BOP officials stated that costs increased by the associated inflation that occurs over time, but BOP could not anticipate construction industry costs that increased at an accelerated rate due to other market factors. For example, steel prices rose by about 60 percent and oil prices rose by almost 170 percent from the time that BOP prepared the initial cost estimates for these projects until the projects were ready to proceed with construction. In addition, because BOP estimates its initial project costs and requests funding early in the planning process—generally, before an actual location for a prison has been selected—variance from the initial estimates would be expected to some extent, even if the projects are not delayed. BOP, like other agencies, is not required to communicate how much it expects costs might vary from its estimates in the budget documents submitted to Congress and other stakeholders. Without such information, however, Congress and other stakeholders do not know the extent to which additional funding may be required to complete the project, even absent any project delays.

BOP eliminated or reduced portions of two projects to remain within the amount funded, and it plans to use its construction management policies and procedures to control further cost increases and schedule delays. When awarding the construction contract for FCI Mendota in 2007, BOP eliminated a Federal Prison Industries facility (UNICOR), which would have provided additional employment and job skills training opportunities for inmates, and the minimum-security prison camp. At FCI Berlin, BOP eliminated the UNICOR facility when it awarded the contract in 2007, but it subsequently added a smaller UNICOR facility to the project, which will be paid for by UNICOR. Although intended to reduce costs, these changes also reduced the functionality of the two prisons and deviated from what BOP planned and requested funding for. In the subsequent budget submission to Congress and other stakeholders, BOP did not clearly communicate these changes, since it does not provide such detailed project information. Now that BOP has awarded contracts to construct these three projects, BOP officials believe that their construction management policies and procedures will allow them to control cost increases and schedule delays. These policies and procedures reflect current government and industry project management practices to monitor and track projects, and to report on their status. In addition, BOP officials told us that their use of the Design-Build project delivery system will help to control cost increases during construction. Under this system, the contractor designs and builds the project and generally has the responsibility for costs associated with design errors, should they occur. Furthermore, BOP officials told us that they plan to continue to carefully consider and approve changes that would increase construction costs after construction begins. We did not evaluate the effectiveness of BOP's construction policies and procedures in controlling cost increases and schedule delays on these three projects because while design and construction contracts were awarded, little construction had been done.

To improve accountability and transparency, we are making two recommendations to the Attorney General of the United States to instruct the Director of BOP to clearly communicate the following to Congress and other stakeholders in DOJ's annual congressional budget submission, in which BOP provides its requests for funding and reports the status of construction projects: (1) the extent to which project costs might vary from initial estimates and (2) the changes that might impact the functionality of projects. BOP concurred with our recommendations.

BACKGROUND

BOP's mission is to protect society by confining offenders in the controlled environments of prisons and community-based facilities that are safe, humane, cost-efficient, and appropriately secure, and that provide work and other self-improvement opportunities to assist offenders in becoming law-abiding citizens. BOP is organized into six regions of the country—Mid-Atlantic, North Central, Northeast, South Central, Southeast, and Western. BOP manages the construction of and operates institutions at five security levels—minimum, low, medium, high, or administrative security—to confine offenders in an appropriate manner. Institutions constructed for a given security level generally have the same design and features. For example, FCIs, which are medium-security institutions, generally have strengthened perimeter fencing, cell-type housing, and a wide variety of work and treatment programs. As such, FCI construction projects typically include a UNICOR facility that employs and provides job skills training to inmates.[1] UNICOR is a government corporation administered by DOJ, with the Director of the Bureau of Prisons as its Chief Executive Officer. FCI construction projects also generally include an adjacent work- and program-oriented minimum- security Federal Prison Camp, where inmates help serve the labor needs of the larger, higher-security FCI.

We have previously reported that BOP follows a centralized, long-term capacity planning process, with the aim of ensuring sufficient institutional capacity while maintaining prison populations at safe-and-secure targeted levels.[2] BOP has two planning committees that are involved in the capital decision-making process to identify new facility prison construction projects: the Capacity Planning Committee (CPC) and the Long-Range Planning Committee (LRPC).[3] According to BOP headquarters officials, CPC proposes new projects by BOP region using the Capacity Plan, which provides projections of inmate population and rates of prison overcrowding. BOP develops initial budget estimates for the projects that CPC proposes, and LRPC ranks the proposed new prison facility construction projects and makes specific funding recommendations to the Director of BOP. The new construction projects are ranked on the basis of agency need, funding, and the speed with which the projects can be constructed.

BOP includes its proposed new construction projects in its annual Federal Prison System budget request made to DOJ. As part of the DOJ annual congressional budget submission, BOP also provides its Federal Prison System Status of Construction report (status report), which provides information on the status of construction for major projects that have received funding. The specific information provided is as follows: each project's descriptive title, with name, type, and location; the amounts funded, by fiscal year; the total project cost estimates; the funds obligated to date; the estimated year of use; and a brief status of the project. However, detailed project information is not provided in this status report. Although BOP provides information to Congress about the specific projects that it plans to support with the funds it requests, funding for BOP construction is provided as a lump sum into its "Buildings and Facilities Account," rather than by the specific project. As a result, BOP can shift funds within this account to fund cost increases on different projects.

In the last 10 years, BOP has completed 30 prison projects at a cost totaling over $3.6 billion. BOP has received about $710 million for the 3 prison projects currently under construction—FCI Mendota, FCI Berlin, and FCI McDowell. BOP has plans for 10 additional prison projects that have received about $363 million in funding to date, as listed in its fiscal year 2009 congressional budget submission.[4]

Developing Initial Project Cost Estimates

To request funding for construction projects such as a prison, an agency must develop an initial project cost estimate several years before it plans to begin construction. Cost estimating requires both science and judgment. Since answers are seldom—if ever—precise, the goal is to find a reasonable "answer. "[5] Cost estimates are based on many assumptions, including the rate of inflation and when construction will begin. Generally, the more information that is known about a project and is used in the development of the estimate, the more accurate the estimate is expected to be.[6] OMB's guidance for preparing budget documents identifies many types and methods of estimating project costs. The expected accuracy of the resulting project cost estimates varies, depending on the estimating method used.

As part of the project planning and budgeting process, BOP officials develop an initial cost estimate when the need is identified for a prison in a particular region of the country. Given that its prisons for a specific security level generally have the same design features,

BOP uses cost and pricing information from a previous project to create a national average cost for construction as the basis for its initial estimate of a new project. To develop an initial cost estimate, BOP adjusts its national average cost by assumptions for various factors, such as the difference in construction costs for different regions of the country, the difficulty of construction, and the expected inflation until construction is planned to begin. For example, in 1999, BOP created a national average construction cost for an FCI on the basis of the average of the 1998 bids for FCI Petersburg, Virginia, the most recently available FCI construction cost information. BOP adjusted FCI Petersburg's pricing information to take into account inflation between 1998 and 1999 and the relative construction costs in Petersburg. To establish the initial estimate for FCI Mid-Atlantic—which became FCI McDowell, located in McDowell County, West Virginia—BOP adjusted the national average to take into account the relative construction costs and difficulty of construction for the Mid-Atlantic region of the country and inflation adjustment to 2001, which is when BOP expected to begin construction. BOP used this estimate as the basis for requesting funding.

BOP's process of using cost information from an earlier project to estimate the cost of a similar proposed project is one of the types of estimates discussed in OMB's guidance. Because this type of cost estimate is based on a single overall project cost, guidance indicates that actual project costs may vary from such an estimate by as much as ± 40 percent.[7] Actual costs may vary by this percentage even if the project begins as assumed in the estimate because detailed project information, such as quantities of particular construction components, was not used in developing the estimate. A BOP official stated that he believes BOP's estimates are more accurate than ± 40 percent because it uses its own historical project information, and the similarities shared by BOP projects.

PROJECT DELAYS CONTRIBUTED TO INCREASED COST ESTIMATES, AND THE IMPRECISE NATURE OF ESTIMATES WAS NOT COMMUNICATED TO CONGRESS AND OTHER STAKEHOLDERS

Delays in starting project construction or disruptions in available funding, which interrupted construction, contributed to increases in cost estimates due to inflation and to unexpected increases in construction material costs. According to BOP officials, problems associated with selecting sites for FCI Mendota, FCI Berlin, and FCI McDowell and with receiving the funding later than planned in the initial estimates contributed to the increase in the cost estimates. During the time that the projects were delayed, construction costs rose at a rate higher than inflation. Also, cost estimates are imprecise and should be expected to vary from the initial estimates, but Congress and other stakeholders were not informed about the extent to which costs might vary from the initial estimates.

Problems with Site Selection and the Availability of Funding Contributed to Project Construction Delays

According to BOP officials, all three projects experienced delays in beginning construction because of problems associated with selecting and approving the sites for the prisons as well as with the availability of funding. FCI Mendota also experienced disruptions in available funding that led to an interruption in construction. See appendix II for project estimates, budget requests, and funding for the three projects.

FCI Mendota

In fiscal years 2001 and 2002, about $150 million was appropriated for a high-security United States Penitentiary in California as requested in the President's budget. Funding was reduced in fiscal year 2002 when BOP applied a rescission of about $5.7 million to the project. When BOP initially estimated the cost for this project, it expected the contract to be awarded in fiscal year 2001 and the construction to begin in fiscal year 2002. However, BOP did not award the contract to design and construct the prison until fiscal year 2004. Mendota was selected as the prison site in fiscal year 2002, at which time BOP changed the project to a medium- security FCI.[8] Subsequent environment impact studies and approvals, which included review and approval by the Environmental Protection Agency (EPA), were completed in fiscal year 2004. In addition, the continued availability of funding for this project came into question in fiscal year 2004, when Congress rescinded almost $52 million of funding.[9] Furthermore, in fiscal year 2005 an amendment to the President's Budget proposed canceling $55 million from the unobligated balances in the Buildings and Facilities Account previously provided for the FCI Mendota project.

Despite this disruption in the available funding, BOP continued with the FCI Mendota project because it expected that the rescinded funds would be restored the following year. Partly as a result of the rescission, BOP officials separated the work for this project into several pieces. This decision enabled BOP to award a single contract for the project's design and construction in September 2004. The contract was structured for the contractor to begin with design and allowed BOP to decide when and what pieces of the construction would be done on the basis of the availability of funding. In December 2004, with the funding it had, BOP directed the contractor to construct the central utility plant, water tower, and general housing units. The contract required BOP to award the remaining pieces necessary to complete the facility—such as the support structures, UNICOR factory, and Federal Prison Camp—no later than 2006 or the option to do this work under the contract would expire. BOP did not exercise the contract option because it had not received additional funds. As a result, when the contractor completed its work, BOP could not house prisoners at FCI Mendota. Figure 1 shows a comparison of the uncompleted FCI Mendota in California to the completed FCI Forest City in Arkansas.

Before BOP could solicit for construction bidders to complete the required work at FCI Mendota, it had to contract for additional engineering services to prepare construction documents. This was necessary to inform bidders about what work had been done and what work remained to be completed. In September 2007 after it received additional funding, BOP awarded the contract to complete FCI Mendota.

Source: BOP.
Incomplete: FCI Mendota, CA

Source: United States Geological Survey.
Complete: FCI Forest City, AR

Figure 1. FCI Mendota in California and FCI Forest City in Arkansas

We have previously raised concerns about this type of construction management. For example, we have reported that nonconcurrent construction—that is where different phases of a project are constructed at different times—increases the overall cost to the government because it requires additional and expensive mobilization of contractor staff and equipment, security, work to procure building materials, and construction management oversight.[10] We also have raised concerns in prior work about starting capital projects without all of the funding necessary to complete the project or, if the project is divisible into stages, to complete a standalone stage that would result in a useable asset.[11] While BOP had funding for the pieces for which it awarded a contract, the pieces did not result in a usable asset because it did not have enough of the pieces of the project completed to house prisoners safely and securely. Although BOP shifted some funds to help pay for the Mendota project, according to BOP officials, sufficient funds were not available to fully fund the Mendota project without delaying or canceling other projects that BOP had told Congress it planned to begin.

To date, the total funding for FCI Mendota has exceeded the initial fiscal year 2001 estimate by about $72 million, or almost 45 percent. However, the latest project estimate is over $6 million, or 2.8 percent, more than the current funding. BOP officials have told us that they do not plan to request any more funding for this project, and that BOP will shift funds within its Buildings and Facilities Account as necessary to complete FCI Mendota.

FCI Berlin and FCI McDowell

In fiscal year 2004, about $154 million was appropriated for FCI Berlin, and about $40 million was appropriated for an FCI in the Mid-Atlantic region.[12] When BOP initially estimated the costs for these projects, it expected to receive funding for design and construction of these facilities in fiscal years 2004 and 2002, respectively. BOP did not award contracts for the design and construction of these projects until fiscal years 2007 and 2006, respectively. According to BOP, both projects experienced delays in selecting the locations for the prisons and the environment impact studies. For FCI Berlin, the property was acquired and EPA completed its approval process in fiscal year 2007. For FCI McDowell, these events occurred in fiscal years 2006 and 2005. In addition, BOP officials stated that they were reluctant to proceed with construction because of OMB's moratorium on new construction for fiscal years 2005 through 2007. Also, the President's Budget included proposed cancellations of unobligated funds from BOP's Buildings and Facilities Account for fiscal years 2004, 2006, and 2007.[13]

To date, the total funding for FCI Berlin and FCI McDowell has exceeded the initial estimates by about $93.5 million and $112.3 million, or 56 percent and 89 percent, respectively. However, the latest project estimates are more than $11 million and $9 million, or 4.2 percent and 3.7 percent, more than the current funding for FCI Berlin and FCI McDowell, respectively. BOP officials told us that they do not plan to request any more funding for these projects, and that BOP will shift funds within its Buildings and Facilities Account as necessary to complete them.

Construction Costs Increased at a Rate Higher Than the Rate of Inflation

BOP factors into its estimates the project's expected start date and duration, on the basis of when BOP expects to receive funding. Generally, if a project does not start as assumed in the cost estimate, the estimated cost of the project should be expected to change at least by the rate of inflation that occurs during the time that elapses between the expected start date and the actual start date. BOP officials stated that during the time that these projects were delayed, construction industry costs increased at a rate greater than inflation. Costs for materials used in construction, such as concrete, steel, copper, and oil, rose substantially. For example, steel prices rose by about 60 percent and oil prices rose by almost 150 percent between 2003 and 2007—a time between when the initial cost estimates were prepared and when the projects were ready to proceed with construction.[14]

We analyzed national data on construction material costs from 2003 through 2007 to provide some context on increases to construction prices. Specifically, to identify nationwide trends in the costs of many of the materials used in construction—from concrete to electrical equipment— we analyzed the Department of Labor, Bureau of Labor Statistics' *Inputs to Construction Industries Producer Price Index* (ICIPPI).[15] As shown in table 1, from 2003 through 2007, the ICIPPI increased more than the consumer price index, indicating that construction costs increased at a higher rate than other costs.[16]

Cost Estimates Are Imprecise, and Congress and Other Stakeholders Were Not Informed of the Extent to Which They Might Vary

Because BOP estimates its initial project costs and requests funding early in the planning process, generally before the specific location for the prison has been selected, actual project costs can be expected to vary from the initial estimates to some extent. This variance would be in addition to any cost implications of a change in the project, such as a delay in beginning construction. As we have previously noted in this chapter, the extent to which one might expect actual costs to vary from estimates typically depends on the type of estimating process used.

In developing its initial estimate prior to the selection of a site for the prison, BOP relies on the cost of a previous prison as the foundation of its estimate. However, BOP has more detailed information available than just the cost of a previous prison, which, if used, would likely result in a more accurate estimate. For example, BOP could analyze the design documents or itemized costs that contractors on previous projects included in their bills. In addition, when the project sites have been selected, actual local market pricing for labor and material costs could be used.[17] More BOP resources would be needed to develop such an analysis.

According to government guidance, BOP's method of using total cost information from a prior project as the basis for its estimate may result in actual project costs varying from the estimate by as much as ± 40 percent. A BOP official stated that BOP's estimating method results in more precise estimates than ± 40 percent, but an analysis of the accuracy of BOP's estimating method has not been done.

Table 1. Bureau of Labor Statistics' Indexes

Fiscal year	Consumer Price Index-All Urban Consumers		Producer Price Index-Inputs to Construction Industries	
	CPI	Percentage increase	ICIPPI	Percentage increase
2003	185.0	2.0%	142.4	3.2%
2004	190.9	3.2	156.6	10.0
2005	199.2	4.3	170.1	8.6
2006	201.8	1.3	175.6	3.2
2007	208.9	3.5	182.4	3.9
Total[a]		12.9%		28.1%

Source: GAO analysis of Department of Labor, Bureau of Labor Statistics, data.
[a]To align with the federal government fiscal year, we compared October data.

Regardless of the estimating method used, Congress relies on information provided by agencies when making funding decisions. Although BOP, like other agencies, is not required to communicate the extent to which actual costs may be expected to vary from its estimates in budget documents or reports on project status, we have recently identified providing such information as a best practice.[18] BOP has not provided this information to Congress and other stakeholders. Thus, BOP has not alerted them of the risks that BOP might require additional funding to complete the projects as originally planned. OMB guidance points out that estimating inaccuracy—both overestimating and underestimating—can adversely affect other projects. With overestimating, an agency may request and be provided with more resources than it will actually need for the project, thereby resulting in less resources being available for other projects or programs. Underestimating projects can lead an agency to request less resources than it will actually need to complete the project, potentially leading to a significant reduction in the project scope, termination of the project, or the shifting of funds from other projects. Inaccurate estimates also reduce confidence in the accuracy of future estimates provided by an agency. Consequently, BOP's ability to inform Congress and other stakeholders about the extent to which costs may vary from its initial project cost is important as it plans additional prison projects and submits subsequent funding requests.

BOP HAS ELIMINATED OR REDUCED PORTIONS OF TWO PROJECTS, AND PLANS TO USE ITS CONSTRUCTION MANAGEMENT POLICIES AND PROCEDURES TO CONTROL COST AND SCHEDULE CHANGES

BOP eliminated or reduced portions of two projects, but did not clearly communicate these changes to Congress and other stakeholders. BOP also plans to use its construction management policies and procedures to control cost increases and schedule delays during construction.

BOP Has Eliminated or Reduced Facilities at FCI Berlin and FCI Mendota, but Did Not Clearly Communicate These Changes to Congress and Other Stakeholders

Congress appropriated funds for fiscal year 2007 that BOP indicated in its status report were required to complete the three prison projects. However, BOP eliminated portions of the FCI Berlin and FCI Mendota projects when it awarded contracts in May and September 2007, respectively, to keep the projects within the estimated costs provided to Congress. According to BOP officials, the contractors' bids for FCI Berlin and FCI Mendota were higher than expected. In response, at FCI Berlin, BOP chose to eliminate the UNICOR facility where inmates were to be employed and provided with job skills training. Subsequently, UNICOR has agreed to pay for the cost of constructing a smaller than originally planned facility, which has now been added back to the project. At FCI Mendota, BOP eliminated both the UNICOR facility and the minimum security Federal Prison Camp. Eliminating or reducing the UNICOR facilities affects BOP's mission to provide work and other self-improvement opportunities for inmates. As a result, these two projects are no longer the same as those for which BOP initially sought and received appropriated funds.

While eliminating or reducing portions of two projects enabled BOP to award contracts, the resulting facilities will not provide the same range of services as originally planned. As part of its annual congressional budget submission, BOP reports on the status of projects that have received funding in the past. This status report includes the following information: each project's descriptive title, with name, type, and location; the amounts funded, by fiscal year; the total project cost estimates; the funds obligated to date; the estimated year of use; and a brief status of the project. However, detailed project information is not provided in this status report. In reviewing the BOP Status of Construction report in DOJ fiscal year 2009 budget documents, we found that the report does not discuss the elimination of the UNICOR facility at FCI Mendota.[19] Furthermore, BOP did not mention that the Federal Prison Camp had been eliminated from FCI Mendota. The only indication of this change is that the project title no longer includes the words "with camp." While BOP receives a lump-sum appropriation for prison construction, Congress makes its appropriation on the basis of, among other things, the project information provided by BOP in its annual congressional budget submission. For FCI Berlin and FCI Mendota, BOP did not clearly communicate to Congress or other stakeholders that the facilities being constructed differed from those for which funds were requested and appropriated.[20] In addition, if BOP should decide to construct these omitted facilities in the future and fulfill these projects' initial designs, it would likely cost more than if the facilities had been constructed as one project. We have previously reported that nonconcurrent construction of a project increases the overall cost to the government because such construction requires additional and expensive (1) mobilization of contractor staff and equipment, (2) security, (3) work to procure building materials, and (4) construction management oversight.

BOP Plans to Use Its Policies and Procedures to Control Cost Increases and Schedule Delays during Construction

BOP officials told us that they will have more ability to control project costs because they have awarded design and construction contracts for the three projects. These officials believe that using their construction management policies and procedures will allow them to control cost increases and schedule delays. Controlling schedule delays is critical because such delays can lead to cost increases. BOP officials said they will use their *Design and Construction Procedures* and *Construction Management Guidelines* to manage the construction of prison projects. Within BOP, the Design and Construction Branch is responsible for the oversight and management of prison construction, and each project has a BOP project manager.

BOP's *Design and Construction Procedures* outlines the specific tasks that the Design and Construction Branch must complete to manage the coordination, execution, oversight, and monitoring of the activities required to construct the projects. For example, this guidance states that the project manager must monitor and report on the contractor's performance during construction and review changes or a modification to the contract to evaluate the extent to which BOP can hold the contractor reasonably liable and, therefore, responsible for the resulting costs.[21] To accomplish these tasks, BOP's *Construction Management Guidelines* provides additional guidance, which identifies the processes that BOP staff must follow to monitor the requirements and implementation of BOP construction projects. For example, this guidance requires BOP officials and the contractor to hold numerous design and construction meetings throughout the duration of the project's schedule to ensure good communication and effective management of the project.

In addition, the *Construction Management Guidelines* requires specific reports—including weekly status reports, monthly project progress reports, performance evaluations of the contractor's team members, and other reports—to facilitate oversight and monitoring of the projects within BOP. For example, this guidance requires the use of critical path method scheduling that breaks a project down into a sequence of necessary activities, which are placed into a project schedule that the project manager can closely monitor. With this management tool, BOP has the ability to monitor and track a project's current progression of work in relation to its initial schedule. This tool also gives the project manager the ability to evaluate proposed construction changes or modifications to the project and to understand their resulting impacts on the project's schedule. This evaluation step remains crucial because once BOP awards the contract, any construction changes that impact the project schedule may also lead to cost changes.

BOP's guidance establishes clear lines of responsibility and documentation requirements. The bureau's *Construction Management Guidelines* also outlines a detailed process that BOP must follow to manage and approve any changes or contract modifications to the project. For example, this guidance states that BOP's project manager should review any proposed changes or modifications to the project and determine if the changes or modifications need further review by BOP's Design and Construction Branch chief. If further review is warranted, sufficient background information supporting the changes or modifications should be provided to the branch chief, along with the proposal. In addition, this guidance states that all change or modification proposals should be discussed at regularly scheduled—or specially scheduled—progress meetings with the contractor. If the changes or modifications will affect the work, more detailed information should be provided to justify them, and the project management team must also evaluate them to ensure they are in compliance with BOP's contract requirements. Furthermore, to document the process, the guidance requires that detailed files be created and maintained for all changes or modifications.

We found that BOP's construction guidance—specifically, its *Design and Construction Procedures* and *Construction Management Guidelines*— generally conform to government and industry management practices. We compared BOP's existing construction management policies and procedures with existing guidance from OMB,[22] the General Services Administration's *Construction Excellence Features*, the Department of Energy's *Project Management for the Acquisition of Capital Assets*, and the Construction Industry Institute's (CII) *Guidelines for Implementation of CII Concepts: Best Practices for the Construction Industry*.[23] Our review showed that BOP's construction management policies and procedures required systems for monitoring, tracking, analyzing, forecasting, and reporting the status of a project. For example, we found that BOP has procedures for reporting important project information—such as cost and schedule, and their deviations from trends—to the appropriate personnel, including management. Furthermore, BOP has procedures for corrective actions when deviations in cost and schedule occur as well as procedures for controlling project changes or modifications.

In addition to the guidance, BOP officials said that the use of the Design- Build delivery system for two of these projects will help to reduce the risk of additional costs being incurred during construction.[24] This type of project delivery system places the project design and construction under one contract. This can reduce the risk of design errors being identified during construction and leading to project delays or cost increases. To provide some context to the extent that Design-Build contracting is effective in managing construction, we reviewed the National Institute of Standards and Technology and the CII study of the performance of the Design-Build delivery method versus the traditional Design-Bid-Build delivery system.[25] The study found that for maintaining the project's schedule, as well as for managing any changes or rework needed during the project's construction, when the project was managed by its owner the Design-Build system performed better than the Design-Bid-Build system.

BOP officials stated that they have more ability to control costs while the project is under construction, and that for the FCI Mendota, FCI Berlin, and FCI McDowell prison projects, they plan to continue to carefully consider and approve changes after construction has begun to stay within its budget. Since construction of the projects has just begun, it is too early to evaluate the effectiveness of BOP's construction policies and procedures in controlling cost increases and schedule delays.

CONCLUSIONS

When BOP asks Congress or other stakeholders to fund or support projects, it is important for them to be aware of the extent to which actual project costs may vary from the initial estimate. Given the continual competition for limited funds, understanding that a proposed project may need an additional 30 percent in funding as opposed to an additional 10 percent may influence their approval and funding decisions. In addition, BOP is developing its estimates and requests funding on the basis of the various facilities it intends to include in each project. If elements of a proposed and funded project that can affect its functionality are eliminated, the project may not fulfill decision makers' expectations. In addition, later construction of the omitted facilities would likely cost more than if they had been constructed as one project. As the need for prison space continues to grow, BOP's ability to complete projects within budget and with the elements initially anticipated will be important to demonstrating BOP's ability to manage its construction program. By providing information on the accuracy of its cost estimates and clearly communicating changes that could impact the projects functionality, BOP would establish more accountability and transparency to its stakeholders.

RECOMMENDATIONS FOR EXECUTIVE ACTION

To improve accountability and transparency, we are making two recommendations to the Attorney General of the United States to instruct the Director of BOP to clearly communicate to Congress and other stakeholders in DOJ's annual congressional budget submission, in which BOP provides its requests for funding and reports on the status of construction projects:

- the extent to which project costs may vary from initial estimates and
- changes that may impact the functionality of projects.

APPENDIX I. OBJECTIVES, SCOPE, AND METHODOLOGY

To assess the extent to which costs changed for the three prisons currently under construction and the reasons for those changes, we obtained and analyzed the President's budgets, the Department of Justice's budget justifications for the federal Bureau of Prisons (BOP) for fiscal years 2001 through 2009, and appropriation laws for fiscal years 2001 through 2008. We obtained and analyzed BOP's project files for three Federal Correctional Institution (FCI) construction projects in Mendota, California; Berlin, New Hampshire; and McDowell, West Virginia. To determine the rate of inflation and other price indicators for the duration of the three projects' schedules, we obtained and analyzed the following Department of Labor, Bureau of Labor Statistics' data: (1) *Producer Price Index-Commodities, Metals and metal products, Steel mill products*; (2) P*roducer Price Index-Commodities, Fuels and related products and power, Crude petroleum (domestic production)*; (3) *Producer Price Index Industry Data, Inputs to construction industries*; and (4) *Consumer Price Index-All Urban Consumers*. We obtained and analyzed (1) BOP's initial cost estimates for FCI Mendota, FCI Berlin, and FCI McDowell and (2) information on prison projects completed from 1998 to 2007—10 years prior to our review—to learn about BOP historical costs. We reviewed BOP's capital planning guidance. We obtained and analyzed the Office of Management and Budget's (OMB) guidance for Capital Planning and Budget Submission. We interviewed BOP construction, budget, and financial officials in Washington, D.C.

To assess the actions BOP has taken—or plans to take—to control cost increases and schedule delays on the three current construction projects, we obtained and analyzed BOP's construction guidance and BOP's project files for FCI Mendota, FCI Berlin, and FCI McDowell. We obtained and analyzed government and construction industry data concerning project cost management and guidance from OMB's Circular A-11, the General Services Administration's *Construction Excellence Features*, the Department of Energy's *Project Management for the Acquisition of Capital Assets*, and the Construction Industry Institute's (CII) *Best Practices for the Construction Industry*. We obtained and analyzed government and construction industry data concerning the performance of the Design-Build delivery method versus the traditional Design-Bid-Build delivery system from the National Institute of Standards and Technology and the CII study. We interviewed BOP construction, budget, and financial officials in Washington, D.C. We did not evaluate the effectiveness of BOP's construction policies and procedures in controlling cost increases and schedule delays on these projects because although design and construction contracts were awarded, little construction had been done.

We conducted this performance audit from June 2007 through May 2008, in accordance with generally accepted government auditing standards. Those standards require that we plan and perform the audit to obtain sufficient, appropriate evidence to provide a reasonable basis for our findings and conclusions based on our audit objectives. We believe that the evidence obtained provides a reasonable basis for our findings and conclusions based on our audit objectives.

APPENDIX II. FCI MENDOTA, FCI BERLIN, AND FCI MCDOWELL: PROJECT ESTIMATES, BUDGET REQUESTS, AND FUNDING FOR FISCAL YEARS 200 1–2009

Dollars in thousands			
Fiscal year/Project information category	Prison construction project		
	FCI Mendota	FCI Berlin	FCI McDowell
2001			
Estimate	$1 58,930[a]	N/A	$1 26,430[a]
Request	11,930	N/A	5,430
Funded	8,930	N/A	2,430
2002			
Estimate	158,930	$1 66,000[a]	126,430
Request	147,000	9,963	91,047
Funded	141,256[b]	5,000	94,047
2003			
Estimate	158,930	173,039	131,314
Request	0[c]	0[c]	0[c]
Funded	0[c]	20,000	0c
2004			
Estimate	150,186	179,500	136,777
Request	0[c]	Cancellation[d]	Cancellation[d]
Funded	(48,895)[e]	154,500	40,300
2005			
Estimate	150,186	179,500	136,777
Request	(55,000)	0[c]	0[c]
Funded	1,900	0[c]	0[c]
2006			
Estimate	165,291	179,500	136,777
Request	0[c]	Cancellation[d]	Cancellation[d]
Funded	4,000	0[c]	0[c]
2007			
Estimate	196,291	179,500	136,777
Request	0[c]	Cancellation[d]	Cancellation[d]
Funded	122,050	80,000	102,000
2008			
Estimate	225,000 to 235,000	250,000 to 275,000	225,000 to 235,000
Request	115,000	0[c]	0[c]
Funded	2,000	0[c]	0[c]
2009			
Estimate	238,000	271,000	248,000
Request	0[c]	0[c]	0[c]
Funded	f	f	f
Total funding	$231,241	$259,500	$238,777
Minus initial estimate	158,903	166,000	126,430
Dollar increase	$72,311	$93,500	$112,347
Percentage increase	45%	56%	89%

Source: GAO analysis of Department of Justice, Bureau of Prisons, data.

Note: In the President's fiscal year 2005 budget, a moratorium on new prison construction was announced. This moratorium was in place for fiscal years 2005, 2006, and 2007.

[a]Initial estimate of project costs.

[b]Includes a rescission to the Buildings and Facilities Account of $5.744 million, which was applied by BOP.

[c]The use of "zeros" indicates either no budget requests or no project funding.

[d]The term "cancellation" refers to a proposal by the President to reduce budget resources.

[e]The Appropriation Conference Report named the project, which became FCI Mendota, to apply the rescission to the Buildings and Facilities Account. In fiscal year 2004, BOP shifted $3 million to this project.

[f]Fiscal year 2009 funds have not been determined.

APPENDIX III: COMMENTS FROM THE DEPARTMENT OF JUSTICE, FEDERAL BUREAU OF PRISONS

U.S. Department of Justice

Federal Bureau of Prisons

Office of the Director   _Washington, DC 20534_

May 16, 2008

Terrell Dorn, Director
Physical Infrastructure Issues
Government Accountability Office
Washington, DC   20548

Dear Mr. Dorn:

The Bureau of Prisons (Bureau) appreciates the opportunity to
formally respond to the Government Accountability Office's
(GAO's) draft report entitled <u>Prison Construction: Clear
Communication on the Accuracy of Cost Estimates and Project
Changes Needed</u>.

The purpose of this report is to explain (1) the reasons for the
changes to the estimated costs for federal correctional
institution construction projects located in Mendota, California;
Berlin, New Hampshire; and McDowell, West Virginia; and (2) the
actions the Bureau has taken - or plans to take - to control
future costs and schedule changes.

The Bureau has the following specific comments:

- Summary Page - The GAO Report should note the Status of
  Construction Exhibit (in the Bureau's budget) does not
  normally discuss specific details regarding various program
  areas of each prison project - such as UNICOR work areas.

- Page 3, 2nd paragraph and thereafter - We suggest the
  following wording change be included: "Inmates are employed
  in many areas of BOP institutions (food service, commissary,
  facility maintenance, landscaping/grounds work, barber shop,
  cleaning, etc.) not just UNICOR." The GAO's current
  statement might lead the reader to believe there will be no
  work opportunities for inmates at these locations without a
  UNICOR operation. In fact, all sentenced general population
  BOP inmates at all locations are required to work and are
  given a job if they are medically able.

- Page 4, 9th line beginning with, "Furthermore,..." - We suggest the sentence should read, "Furthermore, BOP officials told us they will continue to carefully consider and analyze before approving changes that would increase construction costs after construction begins."

- Page 5, 6th line from the top beginning with, "UNICOR is a..." - We suggest the sentence read, "The Director of the Federal Prison System, Chief Executive Officer, and a board of six Directors, appointed by the President, reviews and approves the policy of the Corporation."

- Page 6, footnote #3: Add the underlined words to the footnote "One of the ten, a _secure female_ FCI to be built in Aliceville, AL,..."

- Page 8, Title - _Project Delays Contributed to Increased Cost Estimates and Imprecise Nature of Estimates Not Communicated to Stakeholders_, we suggest replacing "Project Delays" with "Delays Related to Funding".

- Middle of Page 8, Title - _Problems with site selection and receiving funding later then planned contributed to project construction delays_ we suggest replacing then with than.

- Page 8, 2nd paragraph beginning with, "FCI Mendota also experienced..." Change to make more accurate/precise, "FCI Mendota also experienced a number of disruptions in available funding including proposals for and actual rescissions of funds that led to delays and an interruption in construction."

- Page 8, end of 2nd paragraph, please add, "For example, the Administration offered a FY 2005 Budget Amendment to rescind $55 million from the Mendota project, which was eventually denied in Congressional action (Attachment 4).

- Page 9, top of page where the 2004 rescission is referenced, please include the FY 2002 rescission amount of $5.744 million which was applied to the Mendota project.

- Page 11, 1st paragraph, 8th line, containing "...EPA completed its approval process ..." Instead of EPA, we suggest... "the environmental review and approval process was completed..."

- Page 11 and Appendix II beginning with, "Also, the President's Budget..." The OMB did call these rescissions in the budget documents and only clarified, after submission of the FY 2007 President's Budget, that they were proposed cancellations (Attachment 1).

- Page 16, Line 8, "For FCIs Berlin and Mendota, BOP did not clearly communicate..." Changes are included in the Status of Construction Report which shows any planned satellite camp right after the name of the project. The Bureau did clearly change this on the Status report (Attachment 3) that went to all shareholders after award of the construction contract that did not include the camp.

- Page 23, table should be updated to reflect FY 2002 rescission of $5.744 million applied to the Mendota project. Further, budget documents (Attachment 2) clearly state "rescinds" not "cancel" for projects prior to FY 2007. The table should be updated to reflect this issue. In addition, as agreed upon in George Depaoli's May 6, 2008, e-mail, please correct the FY 2005 Request Line entry and identify the $55 million Mendota rescission proposal in the Administration's budget amendment (Attachment 4).

In addition to the above concerns, our response to the Recommendations for Executive Action is as follows:

Recommendations: To improve accountability and transparency, we are making two recommendations to the Attorney General to instruct the Director of the BOP to clearly communicate to Congress and other stakeholders in DOJ's annual congressional budget submission, in which BOP provides its requests for funding and reports on the status of construction projects:

- the extent to which project costs may vary from initial estimates; and
- changes that may impact the functionality of projects.

Response: The Bureau concurs with these recommendations and will incorporate these elements into the next required DOJ annual congressional budget submission.

If you have any questions regarding this response, please contact VaNessa P. Adams, Senior Deputy Assistant Director, Program Review Division, at (202) 616-2099.

Sincerely,

Thomas R. Kane

for Harley G. Lappin
Director

Attachments

cc: Richard Theis, Assistant Director
     Audit Liaison Group, JMD

End Notes

[1] BOP provides job opportunities for inmates in many areas of the institutions, including food service, commissary, facility maintenance, landscaping/grounds work, barber shop, and cleaning. The general population BOP inmates are required to work and are given a job, if they are medically able.

[2] GAO, *Budget Issues: Agency Implementation of Capital Planning Principles Is Mixed*, GAO-04-138 (Washington, D.C.: Jan. 16, 2004).

[3] CPC consists of senior-executive-level staff of several BOP divisions and subject matter experts from the Administration Division. LRPC consists of members of the Administration Division who are senior-executive-level staff, senior managers, and branch chiefs.

[4] One of these 10 planned prison projects, a secure female FCI to be built in Aliceville, Alabama, received funding for construction in fiscal year 2008. We did not include this FCI in our review because it had not received construction funding at the time that we started our work in June 2007.

[5] GAO, *Cost Assessment Guide: Best Practices for Estimating and Managing Program Costs, Exposure Draft*, GAO-07-1134SP (Washington, D.C.: July 2007).

[6] Office of Management and Budget, *Planning, Budgeting, Acquisition, and Management of Capital Assets*, OMB Circular A-11, Part 7, Section 300, "Planning, Budgeting, Acquisition, and Management of Capital Assets," Supplement to Part 7, "Capital Programming Guide" (Washington, D.C.: June 2006); and GAO-07-1134SP.

[7] OMB Circular A-11, Part 7, refers to the Department of Energy's "Cost Estimating Guide," DOE G 4301.1-1 (Washington, D.C.: Mar. 28, 1997).

[8] BOP identified Mendota, California, as the site for this prison in its budget documents in fiscal year 2006.

[9] In fiscal year 2004, Congress rescinded $51,895,000 of the unobligated balances available for Federal Prison System, Buildings and Facilities. The conference report indicated that the rescission was to apply from prior year unobligated balances originally made available for the FCI California prison construction project. H.R. Conf. Rep. No. 108-401, at 646 (2003) accompanying Pub. L. No. 108-199, 118 STAT. 3, 106 (2004).

[10] GAO, *Embassy Construction: Achieving Concurrent Construction Would Help Reduce Costs and Meet Security Goals*, GAO-04-952 (Washington, D.C.: Sept. 24, 2004).

[11] GAO, *Budget Issues: Alternative Approaches to Finance Federal Capital*, GAO-03-1011 (Washington, D.C.: Aug. 21, 2003).

[12] McDowell, West Virginia, was selected by BOP in fiscal year 2005 and was identified in BOP's budget documents as FCI McDowell beginning in fiscal year 2007.

[13] GAO, *Status of Funds Proposed for Cancellation in the President's Fiscal Year 2007 Budget*, GAO-B-308011 (Washington, D.C.: Aug. 4, 2006).

[14] Department of Labor, Bureau of Labor Statistics, *Producer Price Index-Commodities, Metals and metal products, Steel mill products*, Series ID WPU1017 (Washington, D.C.: Nov. 15, 2007); and *Producer Price Index-Commodities, Fuels and related products and power, Crude petroleum (domestic production)*, Series ID WPU056 (Washington, D.C.: Nov. 15, 2007).

[15] Department of Labor, Bureau of Labor Statistics, *Producer Price Index Industry Data, Inputs to construction industries*, Series ID PCUBCON—BCON (Washington, D.C.: Nov. 15, 2007).

[16] Department of Labor, Bureau of Labor Statistics, *Consumer Price Index-All Urban Consumers*, Series ID CUUR0000SA0 (Washington, D.C.: Nov. 15, 2007).

[17] Office of Management and Budget, *Planning, Budgeting, Acquisition, and Management of Capital Assets*, OMB Circular A-11, Part 7, Section 300, "Planning, Budgeting, Acquisition, and Management of Capital Assets," Supplement to Part 7, "Capital Programming Guide" (Washington, D.C.: June 2006); and GAO-07-1134SP.

[18] GAO-07-1134SP.

[19] This is the first report submitted after the construction contracts were awarded in 2007 for FCI Berlin and FCI Mendota, and after the decision to eliminate portions of the projects was made.

[20] According to a BOP official, stakeholders within BOP, DOJ, and OMB are advised by BOP staff of significant changes and receive a monthly updated copy of the status report.

[21] For the technical discussion of change orders and modifications, see the Federal Acquisition Regulation, Part 43, Contract Modifications.

[22] Office of Management and Budget, *Planning, Budgeting, Acquisition, and Management of Capital Assets*, OMB Circular A-11, Part 7, Section 300, "Planning, Budgeting, Acquisition, and Management of Capital Assets," Supplement to Part 7, "Capital Programming Guide" (Washington, D.C.: June 2006).

[23] Construction Industry Institute, *Guidelines for Implementation of CII Concepts: Best Practices for the Construction Industry*, Special Publication 42-2 (Austin, TX: September 1995).

[24] The Design-Build delivery system was not used for the current FCI Mendota construction phase.

[25] United States Department of Commerce, Technology Administration, National Institute of Standards and Technology, Office of Applied Economics, Building and Fire Research Laboratory, *Measuring the Impacts of the Delivery System on Project Performance— Design-Build and Design-Bid-Build* (Gaithersburg, MD: November 2002).

In: Prison Growth and Economic Impact
Editor: Lewis C. Sawyer

ISBN: 978-1-61728-864-7
© 2010 Nova Science Publishers, Inc.

Chapter 4

COST OF PRISONS: BUREAU OF PRISONS NEEDS BETTER DATA TO ASSESS ALTERNATIVES FOR ACQUIRING LOW AND MINIMUM SECURITY FACILITIES[*]

United States Government Accountability Office

WHY GAO DID THIS STUDY

Over the last 10 years, the cost to confine federal Bureau of Prison (BOP) inmates in non-BOP facilities has nearly tripled from about $250 million in fiscal year 1996 to about $700 million in fiscal year 2006. Proponents of using contractors to operate prisons claim it can save money; others question whether contracting is a cost-effective alternative. In response to Conference Report 109-272, accompanying Pub. L. No. 109-108 (2005), this chapter discusses the feasibility and implications of comparing the costs for confining federal inmates in low and minimum security BOP facilities with those managed by private firms for BOP. GAO reviewed available data on a selection of 34 low and minimum security facilities; related laws, regulations, and documents; and interviewed BOP and contract officials.

WHAT GAO RECOMMENDS

GAO recommends that BOP develop a cost-effective way to collect comparable data across low and minimum security facilities and conduct analyses that compare the cost of confining federal inmates in these facilities, consistent with OMB requirements. BOP disagreed with GAO's recommendation and said it did not see the value of developing a

---

[*] This is an edited, reformatted and augmented version of a U. S. Government Accountability Office publication dated October 2007.

methodology to compare facilities. GAO believes this comparison puts BOP in the best position to weigh alternatives for confining inmates to help ensure it is using the most cost-effective alternative. OMB did not comment on this chapter.

To view the full product, including the scope and methodology, click on GAO-08-6. For more information, contact Eileen Larence at (202) 512-6510 or larencee@gao.gov.

WHAT GAO FOUND

A methodologically sound cost comparison analysis of BOP and private low and minimum security facilities is not currently feasible because BOP does not gather data from private facilities that are comparable to the data collected on BOP facilities. GAO's past work has shown that generally accepted evaluation criteria for comparing private and public prisons calls for the comparison to be based on a variety of factors, including selection of facilities with similar characteristics (i.e., staffing levels and educational programs offered) and quality of service (i.e., levels of safety and security for staff, inmates, and the general public). However, according to BOP officials, BOP and private facilities differ in characteristics and quality of service, and BOP does not collect or maintain sufficient data on private facilities to account or adjust for these differences in a cost comparison. According to private contractors, some characteristics data are maintained for their own purposes, but at present the data are not in a format that would enable a methodologically sound cost comparison. BOP officials stated that there are two reasons why they do not require such data of contractors. First, federal regulations do not require these data as a means for selecting among competing contractors. Second, BOP believes collecting comparable data from contractors could increase the cost of the contracts, but BOP officials did not provide support to substantiate these concerns.

Without comparable data, BOP is not able to evaluate and justify whether confining inmates in private facilities is more cost-effective than other confinement alternatives such as building new BOP facilities. The Office of Management and Budget (OMB) requires agencies to consider and weigh various alternatives using analyses that help determine the benefits and costs of making decisions about the acquisition of assets, such as prisons. According to OMB requirements, selecting alternatives to meet capacity needs without adequate analysis by federal agencies has resulted in higher costs than expected. OMB provides guidance to help federal agencies analyze and weigh the costs and benefits of alternatives, which is important for BOP because BOP officials stated that the population for low and minimum security facilities continues to grow. OMB staff also added that they need more and better cost comparison information on the various alternatives for BOP's low and minimum security facilities to help them better understand the long-term costs and benefits of owning versus the short-term costs and benefits of privatization. Without analyses consistent with OMB requirements, it is difficult to know whether BOP is deciding on the most cost-effective alternative for acquiring low and minimum security facilities to confine inmates, including whether to contract, build, or expand.

ABBREVIATIONS

BOP   Federal Bureau of Prisons
FAR   Federal Acquisition Regulation
IGA   intergovernmental agreement
NIJ   National Institute of Justice
OMB   Office of Management and Budget

October 5, 2007

The Honorable Barbara A. Mikulski
Chair
The Honorable Richard C. Shelby
Ranking Member
Subcommittee on Commerce, Justice, Science, and Related Agencies
Committee on Appropriations
United States Senate

The Honorable Alan B. Mollohan
Chairman
The Honorable Rodney Frelinghuysen
Ranking Member
Subcommittee on Commerce, Justice, Science, and Related Agencies
Committee on Appropriations
House of Representatives

At the end of fiscal year 2006, approximately 83,000 federal, adult male inmates within the Department of Justice's Federal Bureau of Prisons (BOP) were housed or confined in low or minimum security facilities, and in recent years BOP has relied on means other than building and operating its own facilities to confine many of these inmates, such as contracts with private sector firms. BOP's operating budget nearly doubled over the last decade from approximately $2.6 billion in fiscal year 1996 to just under $5 billion in fiscal year 2006. In fiscal year 1996, BOP received approximately $250 million of its $2.6 billion for contract confinement, including confining inmates in facilities owned and operated by private contractors and by state and local governments under intergovernmental agreements (IGA) with BOP.[1] By fiscal year 2006, the amount for contract confinement, including the cost of confining about 19,000 inmates housed in private and IGA facilities, had nearly tripled to $700 million of BOP's $5 billion operating budget.

There has been an ongoing debate over the privatization of prisons, that is, contracting for the management of prisons by private firms, whether the prisons are owned by the private sector or by the government. In particular, proponents of privatization claim it can save money without reducing the levels or quality of service such as safety and security (i.e., levels of safety and security for staff, inmates, and the general public), whereas others have questioned whether privatization is a cost-effective alternative to publicly run facilities. Federal guidance from the Office of Management and Budget (OMB) requires that economic and cost comparison analyses be conducted to demonstrate the benefits of privatization, including how it would reduce the government's long-term costs. BOP's use of contracting to meet inmate bed space needs at low and minimum security facilities, in particular, has generated significant interest in the comparative costs of confining federal inmates in BOP, private, and IGA facilities. Conference Report 109-272, accompanying the Science, State, Justice, Commerce, and Related Agencies Appropriations Act of 2006,[2] directed GAO to compare the costs of confining federal inmates in BOP, private, and IGA low and minimum security facilities.

Regarding IGA facilities, BOP has used IGAs for a number of years to confine low and minimum security inmates on a short term basis—less than 45 days—for the purposes of transferring them between facilities or as halfway houses when inmates are released from prison. These IGAs are in hundreds of locations throughout the country. However, according to BOP officials, over time four of the IGAs—located in western Texas, in the cities of Big Spring and Eden, Texas, and Garza County and Reeves County, Texas—evolved into facilities confining inmates on a long-term basis, similar to BOP-owned and -operated low and minimum security facilities. BOP officials told us that these four facilities confined approximately 83 percent of BOP's total IGA inmate population. During the course of our review, BOP did not renew the four Texas IGAs. Instead, BOP awarded five contracts to confine inmates in facilities with approximately 10,000 beds, which are about 3,000 more beds than the capacity provided under the four IGAs.[3] According to BOP officials, BOP chose to compete the bed space associated with these former agreements partly because the four Texas facilities outgrew their original purpose of confining small populations for short periods of time. BOP officials also stated that acquiring bed space via contracts rather than IGAs enhances their ability to oversee operations at the facilities. Because BOP no longer plans to use IGAs to confine inmates on a long-term basis, we shifted the focus of our review to BOP and private facilities only. Also, we did not include the five new contracts in the scope of our review because no federal inmates were housed under the new contract arrangements during fiscal years 2002 through 2006, the period covered by our review.

This chapter discusses the feasibility of comparing the cost of confining inmates in low and minimum security facilities owned and operated by BOP with the cost of confining these inmates in private facilities and the implications this has for making decisions on low and minimum security confinement.

To address this objective, we reviewed applicable laws, regulations, and studies on BOP programs, prison management, and contracting requirements.[4] We also examined available BOP and private facility documents on the management of low and minimum security facilities. In addition, we met with BOP officials and worked with them to identify potential BOP and private facilities that could be compared considering basic criteria, including inmate gender (male or female inmates, assuming that costs for programs and services might be different depending on gender) and whether cost data might be available on the individual facility level for a 5-year period covering fiscal years 2002 through 2006.[5] Our discussions with BOP officials resulted in the selection of 34 low and minimum security facilities managed by BOP and private operators that confined federally sentenced male inmates on a long-term basis over the 5-year period. Specifically, we focused on (1) 27 BOP-owned and -operated low and minimum security facilities that are not on the same campus as medium and high security prisons (BOP does not isolate the costs of operating individual low and minimum security facilities located on the same campus with high and medium security facilities), and (2) 7 facilities operated by private firms under contract to BOP.

Once we selected facilities, we interviewed BOP officials in Washington, D.C. and private contractors at their corporate headquarters to determine what data on prison costs and characteristics would be available. Where possible, we gathered and analyzed available data on the facilities and examined whether the data would lend themselves to a comparison based, in part, on key factors—such as similar facility characteristics and levels of service—needed to do a methodologically sound comparison as outlined in our 1996 report that provides lessons learned for comparisons of private and public correctional facilities.[6] In addition, we examined BOP efforts within the context of OMB requirements for capital planning and space acquisition. We also met with OMB staff responsible for BOP budget review and preparation to discuss BOP's efforts to acquire space to confine inmates in low and minimum security facilities in order to determine what information BOP provides OMB on capital investments, how this information is used to inform decisions, and what additional information OMB needs to make informed decisions. In addition, we met with officials from the Department of Justice's National Institute of Justice (NIJ) to discuss NIJ's current and past work on prison privatization and we met with experts from Florida State University College of Criminology and Criminal Justice and from the JFA Institute—a nonprofit agency conducting justice and corrections research for effective policy making— to further our understanding about prisons and the complexities of comparing the cost of operating private and public prisons. Appendix I contains more detailed information on our scope and methodology.

We conducted our work from May 2006 through August 2007 in accordance with generally accepted government auditing standards.

RESULTS IN BRIEF

It is not currently feasible to conduct a methodologically sound cost comparison of BOP and private low and minimum security facilities because these facilities differ in several characteristics and BOP does not collect comparable data to determine the impact of these differences on cost. Our past work has shown that generally accepted evaluation criteria for any comparative study of private and public prisons call for the comparison to be based not just on operational costs, but on a variety of factors including selection of facilities with similar characteristics (i.e., staffing levels and programs offered) and quality of service. This is to ensure that cost comparison analyses either compare similar facilities or can account for differences in order to address whether facilities operating at lower costs can provide the same or better levels of service as those operating at higher costs. However, according to BOP officials and private contractors, facilities differed in characteristics and in quality of service. Although BOP collects and maintains characteristic data on its own low and minimum security facilities, BOP does not gather data on private contract facilities that would enable us or them to account or adjust for any differences. While private contractors told us that they maintain some data for their records, these officials said that the data are not readily available or in a format that would enable a methodologically sound cost comparison at this time. According to BOP officials and private contractors,

- In terms of facility characteristics, BOP facilities generally confine U.S. citizens, and programs are designed to teach inmates skills that they can use when they are released so as to avoid returning to prison. By contrast, private facilities primarily confine criminal aliens—non-U.S. citizens or foreign nationals who are serving time for a U.S. federal conviction. Programs that focus on preventing returns to prison are not required of private facilities because criminal aliens are released for removal from the country and are not expected to return to U.S. communities or BOP custody.

- BOP does not require private facility data comparable to what it maintains for its own facilities with regard to safety and security issues and, consequently, a facility's quality of service. These include data on the number of inmates attended to by health care professionals due to misconduct, staff turnover rates, and the experience level of the staff.

BOP does not collect comparable data on private facilities needed to conduct a methodologically sound cost comparison with BOP low and minimum security facilities because (1) federal regulations do not require BOP to do so when selecting among competing contractors, and (2) according to BOP officials, collecting additional facility characteristic and quality of service data could add costs to contracts. Regarding the latter, BOP's Senior Deputy Assistant Director stated that private contractors might charge higher contract prices as a result of having to collect and provide this information but that BOP has not determined what these additional costs would be. BOP officials told us they are committed to contracting to confine inmates in low and minimum security facilities. They said that their construction priority is medium and high security facilities because inmates in medium and high security facilities are at higher risk in terms of their behavior (i.e., rates of misconduct, assaults, and history of violence) and private contractors have yet to demonstrate the ability to handle these higher security populations. According to BOP officials, because of its commitment to contracting, BOP has not recently considered, nor does it plan to evaluate contracting in relation to other alternatives for inmates confined in low and minimum security facilities. These alternatives can include constructing new BOP low and minimum security facilities, acquiring and using excess military properties, or expanding or renovating existing BOP facilities.

While BOP does not need to collect comparable data for selecting among contractors, the purpose of analyzing these data is to evaluate and justify whether confining inmates in private facilities is more cost-effective than these other confinement alternatives. In fact, OMB requires agencies to consider and weigh various alternatives using analyses, such as benefit-cost or cost-effectiveness analyses, when making decisions about the acquisition of capital assets, such as office buildings, hospitals, schools, and prisons.[7] According to OMB, selecting alternatives to meet space requirements without adequate analysis by federal agencies has resulted in higher costs than anticipated. Additionally, OMB staff stated that they need more and better cost comparison information on the various alternatives for BOP's low and minimum security facilities to help better understand the long-term costs and benefits of owning versus the short- term costs and benefits of privatization. These analyses are especially important because BOP officials stated that the population for these facilities continues to grow. Without such analyses, it is difficult to know whether BOP is deciding on the most cost-effective alternative for acquiring low and minimum security facilities to confine inmates, including whether to contract, build, or expand.

Recognizing that there is a cost associated with gathering and analyzing additional data needed to compare costs across BOP and private facilities, we are making one recommendation designed to help BOP evaluate alternatives for confining inmates in low and minimum security facilities. We are recommending that the Attorney General direct the Director of BOP to develop a cost-effective way to collect comparable data across BOP and private low and minimum security facilities confining inmates under BOP's custody, and design and conduct methodologically sound analyses that compare the cost of confining inmates in these facilities in order to consider contracting among other alternatives for low and minimum security confinement, consistent with OMB requirements.

BOP disagreed with our recommendation and stated that it does not own or operate facilities to house solely criminal aliens. BOP also said it does not expect to receive funding to construct such low security facilities. Therefore, BOP does not believe there is value in developing data collection methods to compare costs of confining these inmates in private facilities with other alternatives for confining inmates. BOP further commented that, through open competition, it has been able to determine a fair and reasonable price for its existing contracts and said that requiring contractors to provide specific comparable data would have the potential to increase current contract costs at a time when BOP is facing budget constraints. BOP also noted that it believes a 2005 study conducted for BOP by a private contractor has already met the intent of our recommendation because the study compares the cost of operating a government-owned, contractor-operated facility in Taft, California, with other low security BOP facilities.[8]

We agree that full and open competition can establish fair and reasonable costs for services provided by contractors. However, our recommendation is about selecting the most cost-effective alternative for confining inmates, not about selecting among contractors as the only alternative. We believe that developing data collection methods to determine the costs of confining inmates in low and minimum security facilities—regardless of whether those facilities are owned and operated by BOP or a contractor and regardless of whether the facility confines criminal aliens, U.S. citizens, or both—is critical to BOP's ability to evaluate the cost- effectiveness of contracting compared to other alternatives for confining inmates, such as constructing a new facility or modifying existing facilities. Absent this evaluation, key decision makers, including BOP managers, OMB, and Congress, are not positioned to have the information needed to make the most cost-effective investment decisions. We agree that requiring contractors to provide data so that BOP can conduct a comparison has the potential of increasing contract costs, but BOP has not assessed what the costs of collecting the data would be or whether the costs would outweigh the benefit of being able to determine the most cost- effective alternative for confining inmates in low and minimum security facilities. Finally, we disagree that BOP has met the intent of our recommendation via the study referenced by BOP because it does not compare the costs of various alternatives for confining inmates in low and minimum security facilities, as we recommended.

BACKGROUND

BOP was established in 1930 to provide progressive and humane care for federal inmates in the 11 federal prisons in operation at the time. Since then, BOP's mission has evolved into protecting society by controlling offenders in the controlled environments of prisons and community-based facilities that are safe, humane, cost-efficient, and appropriately secure and that provide work and other self-improvement opportunities to assist offenders in becoming law-abiding citizens.

At the end of fiscal year 2006, there were over 114 federal prison facilities located throughout the country at four primary security levels—minimum, low, medium, and high. BOP facilities are given a security designation based on the level of security and staff supervision the facility is able to provide. According to BOP, minimum security facilities, also known as Federal Prison Camps, have dormitory housing and limited or no perimeter fencing; low security Federal Correctional Institutions have double-fenced perimeters and mostly dormitory or cubicle housing; medium security Federal Correctional Institutions have strengthened perimeters (often double fences with electronic detection systems) where inmates are mostly confined to prison cells; and high security institutions, also known as United States Penitentiaries, have highly secured perimeters (featuring walls or reinforced fences) and multiple- and single- occupant cell housing. BOP also maintains administrative facilities, which are institutions with special missions, such as the detention of pretrial offenders;[9] the treatment of inmates with serious or chronic medical problems; or the containment of extremely dangerous, violent, or escape- prone inmates. Administrative facilities are capable of holding inmates at all security levels.

According to BOP population data, at the end of fiscal year 2006, BOP's total inmate population was approximately 193,000 inmates, of which about 43 percent, or 83,000, were long-term, adult male inmates confined in BOP, private, or IGA low and minimum security facilities. About 52,000 (27 percent) of the total inmates were confined in medium security facilities, and approximately 18,000 (about 9 percent) were in high security facilities. Additionally, approximately 21 percent of the 193,000 total inmates, or 40,000 inmates, were females, juveniles, inmates in halfway houses, inmates in home confinement, or inmates confined in BOP's administrative facilities. See figure 1 for a breakout of these populations.

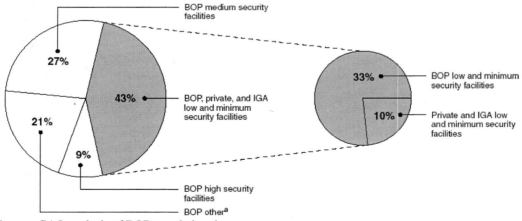

Source: GAO analysis of BOP population data.

[a]BOP other includes females, juveniles, inmates in halfway houses, inmates in home confinement, or inmates confined in BOP's administrative facilities (i.e., medical facilities or detention facilities).

Figure 1. BOP Inmate Population at the End of Fiscal Year 2006

BOP LACKS DATA NEEDED TO PERFORM A METHODOLOGICALLY SOUND COST COMPARISON AND IS NOT POSITIONED TO EVALUATE ALTERNATIVES FOR CONFINING INMATES IN LOW AND MINIMUM SECURITY FACILITIES

A methodologically sound cost comparison analysis of BOP and private low and minimum security facilities is not currently feasible because BOP does not gather data from private facilities that are comparable to the data collected on BOP facilities. BOP is not required under federal contracting regulations to gather data that would enable a comparison, and although BOP has not evaluated the cost of collecting additional information, BOP officials maintain that it could increase the price contractors charge BOP for contract services. However, without comparable data, BOP is not able to analyze and justify whether confining inmates in private facilities would be more cost-effective than other confinement alternatives such as constructing new BOP facilities or renovating existing BOP facilities. Such an analysis would be consistent with OMB requirements, which call for agencies to identify and evaluate various alternatives when making decisions about the acquisition of capital assets (e.g., office buildings, hospitals, schools, and prisons).

A Cost Comparison Is Not Currently Feasible because BOP Lacks Data Needed to Perform a Methodologically Sound Comparison

We determined that it is not currently feasible to compare the cost of confining male federal inmates in low and minimum security BOP and private facilities because data needed for a methodologically sound comparison are not currently available. Our review of BOP documentation showed that BOP collects basic cost data on a per inmate basis across BOP and private facilities. For BOP-owned and -operated facilities, BOP maintains per inmate costs that include salaries, employee benefits, equipment, and utilities. For private facilities, BOP maintains the negotiated per inmate contract price, award fees, and deductions made as a result of the performance-based contract terms. However, these cost data are not sufficient for doing a methodologically sound cost comparison. As we reported in 1996, any comparative study of private and public prisons should not only be based on operational costs but also on an analysis of similar facilities—including the design, capacity, security level, and types of inmates and quality of service—and on sufficient statistical controls to measure and account for any differences among facilities.[10] Otherwise, any comparative analysis of operational costs could be skewed. For example, one study we reviewed as part of our 1996 report did not assess quality of service as part of the cost comparison between private and public facilities and, as a result, could not conclude whether the levels of service affected the differences in costs.

According to BOP officials and private contractors, BOP and private facilities have different characteristics and provide different levels of service. Thus, statistical methods would need to be used to account for these differences once cost data were collected to determine the impact they have on the operating cost of the facilities. Using guidelines established in our previous work, we sought to compare facilities with similar characteristics to ensure results of a comparison would not be skewed. However, we were unable to do so because the data needed to do the comparison were not available. BOP and private contracting officials reported that there are numerous differences among BOP and private facilities, including inmate population, program requirements, and economic differences within the different geographic locations of the facilities. According to BOP officials, private contractor facilities have fewer contractual requirements for programming, such as vocational training and release preparation courses, than BOP facilities, in part, because of the different types of inmates confined in the facilities. In general, BOP facilities confine U.S. citizens and programs are designed to teach inmates skills that they can use when they are released, such as job training skills, so as to help avoid their return to prison. By contrast, private facilities primarily confine criminal aliens—non-U.S. citizens or foreign nationals, who are serving time for a U.S. federal conviction. Programs that focus on preventing returns to prison are not required of private facilities because criminal aliens are released for removal from the country and are not expected to return to U.S. communities or BOP custody.

Given the differences with regard to facility characteristics, statistical techniques such as analyzing the extent to which characteristics— including program differences—vary among facilities, would have to be applied to strengthen conclusions of a cost comparison analysis. For example, if BOP facilities provide more programs for inmates than contractors do, then comparable data on the number and types of programs across all facilities would be needed to adjust for this difference in order to conclude how the difference in programs affect operating costs. BOP maintains data on its own low and minimum security facilities and collects some similar facility data on private facilities, including the age of the facility, the citizenship status of inmates, and inmate population. However, BOP does not maintain comparable data on various aspects of private facilities, such as inmate-to-staff ratios, size of the facility, specific programs available to inmates, and whether inmates in private facilities are completing those programs. Because BOP does not maintain comparable data for private facilities on the differing facility characteristics that could affect costs, we could not determine the extent to which these facilities differed nor use statistical methods to determine the impact of these differences on costs. Since we could not control or adjust for such differences, the results of a cost comparison analysis conducted at this time would be skewed.

With regard to quality of service, BOP also lacks sufficient data on measurements of safety and security for inmates, staff, and the general public for a methodologically sound cost comparison of BOP and private facilities. As we reported in 1996, a cost comparison analysis should include not just operational costs but also an assessment of quality to ensure that if a contractor is operating at lower costs than BOP, it is providing the same or a better level of service. We attempted to review numerous quality of service data—such as data that measure safety and security—so that differences could be accounted for by comparing data on what is achieved by these services. However, according to officials in BOP's Office of Research and Evaluation, BOP does not maintain data on private facilities that we could use to compare quality of service across the different facilities. This includes the number of grievances submitted by inmates, the number of inmates attended to by health care professionals due to misconduct,[11] staff turnover rates, and the experience level of the staff. As a result, we could not assess the trade-offs between the levels of services being offered and the costs of operating the facilities.

While the contract requirements for the private facilities direct contractors to maintain some data on inmates in BOP's central database system called SENTRY,[12] according to BOP officials, the data private contractors enter are not necessarily consistent with those data collected on BOP facilities, and BOP officials stated that they cannot attest to the reliability or validity of the private contractor data. For example, BOP officials and private contractors we spoke with stated that although private contractors are required to report incidences of misconduct to BOP, neither could confirm if the private contractor system for categorizing or tracking incidences of misconduct is consistent with BOP's misconduct categories.[13] BOP further reported that program data were not comparable. For example, according to BOP officials, private contractors reported that inmates completed the U.S. General Educational Development program, when the program actually completed by the inmates was a Mexican equivalent of the program. Additionally, private contractors we spoke with told us that they maintain some facility characteristic and quality of service data, but the data are not maintained in the same format as BOP facility data and are not readily available because they are only maintained in hard copies at some of the facilities contractors manage.

BOP officials provided two reasons why they do not collect or require contractors to collect comparable data that would facilitate a comparison of the cost of confining inmates in low and minimum security BOP and private facilities: (1) federal regulations do not require such data as a means for selecting among competing contractors, and (2) BOP believes collecting comparable data from contractors could add costs. However, BOP officials had not evaluated the probable amount of added costs.

When choosing among private contractors, federal regulations do not require BOP to collect comparable facility characteristic or quality of service information from private facilities. According to BOP officials, all BOP private contracts in our review are firm-fixed price and, under federal regulations for competing contracts, BOP does not need this information for technical evaluations of the proposals.[14] BOP officials added that during the acquisition process, BOP maintains data needed to evaluate proposed contract prices, such as the price to manage and operate each facility and the government's estimate of the price, in accordance with the Federal Acquisition Regulation (FAR). The FAR requires the contracting official to determine if proposed prices are fair and reasonable and further states that the performance of a cost analysis is not needed if there is adequate price competition.[15] In general, adequate price competition is established when two or more responsible parties independently submit prices for the solicitation that meet the government's requirements. The award is made to the party whose proposal represents the best value and there is no finding that the price of the other parties is unreasonable. In addition to price, the FAR recommends agencies evaluate one or more nonprice criteria, such as past performance and prior experience. However, agencies have broad discretion in the selection criteria and in determining the relative importance of each criterion. Consequently, the regulation does not require BOP to collect comparable data on various facility characteristics and quality of service measures needed to conduct a methodologically sound cost comparison.

Additionally, while BOP is concerned that the cost of contracts could increase if it were to require comparable data from private contractors because it would be beyond the scope of existing contract requirements, it has not evaluated the costs or benefits of acquiring the additional data. BOP's Senior Deputy Assistant Director and other BOP officials said they suspect that it is likely that private contractors would charge BOP a higher contract price if it required private contractors to meet additional requirements, such as providing data similar to those collected by BOP for its facilities. However, because BOP has not requested such data during the contract process or estimated the incremental costs and benefits of requiring comparable data from private facilities, BOP officials could not speak to the extent of the potential cost increase.

Although in the Department of Justice Fiscal Year 2003-2008 Strategic Plan BOP identified several alternatives for space acquisition, such as expanding or renovating existing facilities, acquiring military properties for prison use, contracting with private companies, and constructing new facilities, BOP officials stated that they do not consider all of these alternatives for confining inmates in low and minimum security facilities because they are committed to contracting with nonfederal entities for low and minimum security bed space.

Our past work has shown that over the long term, it is usually more cost- effective for an agency to own a facility than to lease one.[16] For example, we previously reported that for nine major operating lease acquisitions proposed by the General Services Administration—the central leasing agent for most federal agencies—construction would have been the least expensive option in eight cases and would have saved an estimated $126 million compared to two leasing options that spread payments out over time.[17] However, when funds for ownership are not available, leases become a more attractive option from the agency's budget perspective because they add much less to a single year's appropriation total than other alternatives. According to BOP officials, they consider alternatives for space acquisition only for medium and high security facilities, because medium and high security facilities are BOP's priority based on capacity needs. In addition to capacity needs, from BOP's perspective, inmates in medium and high security facilities are at higher risk in terms of their behavior (i.e., rates of misconduct, assaults, and history of violence) and private contractors have yet to demonstrate the ability to handle these higher security populations, so BOP has chosen to continue to confine the higher security inmates in BOP-owned and -operated facilities. As a result, BOP officials stated that they have not considered nor do they plan to consider alternatives besides contracting for low and minimum security facilities.

BOP Cannot Evaluate whether Privately Contracted Facilities Provide Better or Worse Value than Other Low and Minimum Security Confinement Alternatives

Because BOP is not able to compare the cost of BOP and private facilities in a methodologically sound manner, it cannot determine if confining inmates in private facilities is more or less cost-effective than other confinement alternatives such as constructing and operating new BOP facilities, acquiring and using excess properties (i.e., former military bases), or expanding or renovating existing BOP facilities. OMB requires agencies to follow capital planning principles set forth in its *Capital Programming Guide*.[18] OMB's guide identifies the need for effective planning and management of investments. Among other things, this guide articulates key principles agencies should follow when making decisions about the acquisition of capital assets such as prisons. The *Capital Programming Guide* requires that agencies consider as many alternatives as possible because, according to the guide, whenever the government lacks viable alternatives, it may lack a realistic basis to manage contract costs. Once a list of alternatives is established, the guide requires that agencies then compare those alternatives based on a systematic analysis of expected benefits and costs. The fundamental method for formal economic analysis is a benefit-cost analysis.

OMB guidance on benefit-cost analyses can be found in OMB Circular A-94—a circular that helps agencies conduct a study on the benefits and costs of whether to acquire a new capital asset, undertake a major modification to an existing asset, or use some other method such as contracting for services.[19] More specifically, the goal of the circular is to promote efficient resource allocation through well-informed decision making by the federal government. The circular provides general guidance for conducting benefit-cost and cost-effectiveness analyses, and serves as a checklist of whether an agency has considered and properly dealt with all elements of a sound analysis.

OMB's *Capital Programming Guide* reports that credible cost and benefit analyses, such as those described in OMB Circular No. A-94, are the basis of sound management decision making, enabling agencies to determine the best investment option for meeting their goals and making them better equipped to evaluate alternatives. OMB's guide states that data are the most important piece of such analyses, including various procurement or contract data. Consequently, to do the analyses described in OMB Circular No. A-94, BOP would have to first collect and maintain comparable BOP and private facility data. BOP senior officials acknowledged that they have not done any such analyses to assess alternatives for confining inmates in low and minimum security facilities, and they were unable to explain why such analyses have not been done. Nonetheless, according to the OMB guide, selecting alternatives to meet space requirements without adequate analysis by federal agencies has resulted in higher costs than anticipated. Consequently, without such an analysis, it is difficult to know whether BOP is deciding on the most cost-effective alternative for acquiring low and minimum security facilities to confine inmates, including whether to contract, build, or expand.

The results of any analysis conducted by BOP consistent with OMB requirements would be important because BOP officials expect inmate populations in low and minimum security facilities to rise. Inmates in low and minimum security facilities made up approximately 43 percent of BOP's total population in fiscal year 2006, and according to BOP officials, this population will continue to grow. As a result, there would be an increase of inmates requiring confinement in low and minimum security facilities. BOP also projects about a one-third increase in its long-term criminal alien population,[20] or approximately 5,700 more criminal alien inmates between fiscal years 2005 and 2008, which could further strain BOP resources as these inmates are confined primarily in low security facilities. While the private sector has additional capacity to accommodate at least some of this expected growth in inmate populations, BOP cannot determine whether private contracting is or would be the most cost-effective alternative because of the data limitations discussed above.

While there are costs associated with gathering data needed to compare costs across BOP and private facilities, without the data to conduct benefit-cost or cost-effectiveness analyses, BOP is not able to compare alternatives for confining inmates in a methodologically sound manner. Additionally, the absence of data also has potential long-term costs because BOP managers, OMB staff, and congressional decision makers do not have the information needed to weigh alternatives and make the best investment decisions. Although OMB staff told us that BOP provides several documents in accordance with the *Capital Programming Guide,* such as information about facilities in BOP's inventory and weekly reports about inmate population, OMB staff stated that it would be useful to have more and better comparison information on the cost of confining inmates in BOP and private low and minimum security facilities. They said that without such data, it is difficult to understand how BOP is making decisions on the most cost-effective way to manage and confine future inmates sentenced to low and minimum security facilities. OMB staff added that they consider contracting a viable option because it gives BOP the flexibility to immediately deal with population changes. However, according to OMB staff, they would not expect contracting to always be cheaper because owning a facility may be more cost-effective in the long run. As a result, comparative analyses would be beneficial to help them better understand the long-term costs and benefits of owning versus the short-term costs and benefits of privatization.

CONCLUSIONS

Because of projections of future growth of inmate populations, BOP will need to continue to acquire additional capacity. However, deciding what to do in response to this need will be difficult because BOP does not have the data necessary to do a methodologically sound cost comparison of its various alternatives for confining inmates in low and minimum security facilities. Because contracting regulations do not require BOP to collect private facility data comparable to BOP facility data, BOP has not gathered or maintained data needed to conduct a methodologically sound cost comparison. Additionally, BOP is concerned with increased contract costs. However, BOP has not assessed the cost of collecting the data or whether the estimated costs would outweigh the benefits of having it. As a result, BOP is not in a position to meet OMB's capital planning requirements and evaluate whether contracting is more cost-effective than other alternatives, such as building new low and minimum security facilities, buying existing facilities that may be available, or expanding facilities already operated by BOP. Without such data, BOP cannot determine whether procuring prison confinement and services from private firms costs the government more or less than other confinement alternatives, as required by OMB.

RECOMMENDATION FOR EXECUTIVE ACTION

To help BOP evaluate alternatives for confining inmates in low and minimum security facilities, and recognizing that there is a cost associated with gathering and analyzing data needed to compare costs across BOP and private facilities, we recommend that the Attorney General direct the Director of BOP to develop a cost-effective way to collect comparative data on low and minimum security facilities confining inmates under BOP's custody and design and conduct methodologically sound analyses that compare the costs of confining inmates in these facilities in order to consider contracting among other alternatives for low and minimum security confinement, consistent with OMB requirements.

AGENCY COMMENTS AND OUR EVALUATION

We requested comments on a draft of this chapter from the Director of the Office of Management and Budget and from the Attorney General. While OMB did not provide comments, in a September 17, 2007, letter, BOP provided written comments, which are summarized below and included in their entirety in appendix II.

BOP disagreed with our recommendation and stated that it does not own or operate facilities to house solely criminal aliens. BOP also said it does not expect to receive funding to construct such low security facilities. Therefore, BOP does not believe there is value in developing data collection methods to compare costs of confining these inmates in private facilities versus other alternatives for confining inmates. BOP stated that, through open competition, it has been able to determine a fair and reasonable price for its contracts. In a related comment, BOP stated that our report does not reference that Congress has provided funds to contract out for inmate bed space but has not provided funding for new construction of low and minimum security facilities. BOP also noted that it does not currently have the capacity to confine low security criminal aliens and is dependent on private contractors to fill the gap, and, if construction funds were available for low and minimum security facilities, it would take several years before the bed space would become available. In addition, BOP noted that it is committed to contracting, in part, because OMB has directed BOP to take greater advantage of state and local governments and the private sector to meet its space requirements to confine inmates in low and minimum security facilities. With regard to the recommendation, BOP also stated that gathering data from contractors to aid in a cost comparison would have the potential to increase current contract costs at a time when BOP is facing budget constraints. Finally, BOP pointed out that an independent review conducted in 2005 which compared the operational cost of a BOP-owned, contractor-operated facility in Taft, California, with other low security BOP facilities meets the intent of our recommendation.[21]

We agree that full and open competition can establish fair and reasonable costs for services provided by contractors. However, our recommendation is about selecting the most cost-effective alternative for confining inmates, not about selecting among contractors as the only alternative. We believe that developing data collection methods to determine the costs of confining inmates in low and minimum security facilities—regardless of whether those facilities are owned and operated by BOP or a contractor and regardless of whether the facility confines criminal aliens, U.S. citizens, or both—is critical to BOP's ability to evaluate the cost-effectiveness of contracting compared to other alternatives for confining inmates, such as constructing a new facility, modifying an existing facility, or acquiring military properties for prison use. OMB's *Capital Programming Guide* requires agencies to undertake the kind of comparison we are recommending in order to consider alternatives when making decisions about the acquisition of capital assets, such as prisons. Adhering to OMB requirements better ensures that key decision makers, including OMB and Congress, have the information needed to make the most cost-effective investment decisions.

We recognize that BOP has not received funding to construct new low and minimum security facilities, but this does not mean that funds will not be appropriated in the future, especially if data demonstrate that this option is more cost-effective. Without these data, BOP is not in a position to justify funding for new construction or other alternatives because BOP cannot do a methodologically sound comparison among low and minimum security facilities. With regard to BOP's comment that it currently does not have the capacity to confine criminal aliens and must rely on contracting to address capacity issues, our report noted that, according to OMB staff, contracting may be a viable option because it provides BOP the flexibility to immediately deal with population changes. Nonetheless, OMB staff also said that they need more and better cost comparison information to help them understand the long-term costs and benefits of owning versus the short-term costs and benefits of privatization. OMB staff also stated that they would not always expect contracting to be cheaper because owning a facility may be more cost-effective over the long run, which is consistent with our past work.[22]

With regard to BOP's concern that requiring comparable data from contractors could raise the cost of current contracts, our report recognized that there is a cost associated with gathering and analyzing additional data needed to compare costs across BOP and private facilities. However, BOP has not determined the cost of collecting the data or whether the estimated costs would outweigh the benefits of knowing the most cost-effective alternative for confining inmates. Without a cost- effective way to collect comparable data, BOP cannot conduct a methodologically sound cost comparison analysis that takes into account factors, such as facility characteristics and quality of service, which can differ from facility to facility. Collecting and analyzing these data would provide key decision makers the information needed to make the most cost-effective investment decisions.

We disagree with BOP's assertion that it has met the intent of our recommendation via the 2005 study by the Center for Naval Analysis. In citing this study, BOP failed to recognize that this study does not compare the costs of various alternatives for confining inmates in low and minimum security facilities. Rather, it compares BOP-owned and -operated facilities with one BOP-owned and contractor-operated facility in Taft, California.

In addition, BOP stated it had provided detailed cost information and that it believed we would obtain comparable data from the private sector in order to conduct a methodologically sound cost comparison. As discussed throughout our report, the cost data BOP provided were not sufficient to conduct a methodologically sound cost comparison. As our report states, any comparative study of private and public prisons should not only be based on operational costs, but should also account for facility characteristics and the quality of services provided. We requested this information from the private sector. As our report notes, private contractors do not maintain similar data, because BOP does not require them to report or collect the data it requires of its own facilities.

BOP also provided technical comments, which we considered, and we have amended our report to incorporate these clarifications, where appropriate.

APPENDIX I. OBJECTIVES, SCOPE, AND METHODOLOGY

Our work focused on the comparative cost of confining federal inmates in low and minimum security facilities owned by the Federal Bureau of Prisons (BOP) and privately managed facilities under contract to BOP. Specifically, our objective was to assess the feasibility of comparing the costs for confining inmates in low and minimum security facilities owned and operated by BOP with the cost to confine these inmates in private facilities and the implications this has for making decisions on low and minimum security confinement. Our work was initially designed to address Conference Report 109-272, accompanying the Science, State, Justice, Commerce, and Related Agencies Appropriations Act of 2006,[23] which directed GAO to compare the costs of confining federal inmates in low and minimum security facilities owned by BOP, privately managed facilities under contract to

BOP, and local facilities or jails via intergovernmental agreements (IGA) with BOP.[24] However, during the course of our review, BOP did not renew IGAs for four facilities in Western Texas—in the cities of Big Spring and Eden, Texas, and Garza County and Reeves County, Texas—that confined 83 percent of federal inmates in IGA facilities. Although BOP has, over time, used hundreds of IGAs across the country to confine inmates on a short term basis—45 days or less—the four Texas facilities had evolved into facilities confining inmates on a long-term basis, similar to BOP-owned and -operated low and minimum security facilities. In January 2007, BOP awarded five contracts to confine inmates in facilities with approximately 10,000 beds, which are about 3,000 more beds than the capacity provided under the four IGAs.[25] According to BOP officials, BOP chose to compete the bed space associated with these agreements partly because the four Texas facilities outgrew their original purpose of confining small populations for short periods of time. BOP officials also stated that acquiring bed space via contracts rather than IGAs enhances their ability to oversee operations at the facilities. Because BOP no longer plans to use IGAs to confine inmates on a long-term basis, we shifted the focus of our review to BOP and private facilities only.

We did our work at BOP headquarters and the Office of Management and Budget (OMB) in Washington, D.C. We reviewed applicable laws, regulations, and studies on BOP programs, prison management, and contracting requirements.[26] We also examined available BOP and private contractor documents on the management of low and minimum security facilities. In addition, we met with BOP officials and worked with them to identify potential BOP and private facilities that could be compared considering basic criteria including inmate gender (male or female inmates, assuming that costs for programs and services might be different depending on gender) and whether cost data might be available on the individual facility level for a 5-year period covering fiscal years 2002 through 2006. In selecting low and minimum security facilities, we met with BOP officials to identify potential BOP and private facilities that could be compared over a 5-year period covering fiscal years 2002 through 2006. Our discussions with BOP officials resulted in the identification of 34 low and minimum security facilities operated by BOP and private contractors that confined federally sentenced male inmates over the 5-year period. Specifically, we focused on (1) 27 BOP-owned and -operated low and minimum security facilities, and (2) 7 facilities operated by private firms under contract to BOP. Table 1 lists the 34 facilities we selected.

Table 1. List of Low and Minimum Security Facilities within our Scope

BOP low and minimum security facilities[a]	Location	Security level	Security level of adjacent facility (if applicable)
Allenwood	Pennsylvania	Low	Minimum
Ashland	Kentucky	Low	Minimum
Bastrop	Texas	Low	Minimum
Beaumont	Texas	Low	Minimum
Big Spring	Texas	Low	Minimum
Butner	North Carolina	Low	
Coleman	Florida	Low	
Elkton	Ohio	Low	Minimum
Forrest City	Arkansas	Low	Minimum
Fort Dix	New Jersey	Low	Minimum

Fort Worth	Texas	Low	
La Tuna	Texas	Low	Minimum
Lompoc	California	Low	
Loretto	Pennsylvania	Low	Minimum
Milan	Michigan	Low	
Petersburg	Virginia	Low	Minimum
Safford	Arizona	Low	
Sandstone	Minnesota	Low	
Seagoville	Texas	Low	Minimum
Texarkana	Texas	Low	Minimum
Waseca	Minnesota	Low	
Yazoo City	Mississippi	Low	Minimum
Duluth	Minnesota	Minimum	
Montgomery	Alabama	Minimum	
Morgantown	West Virginia	Minimum	
Pensacola	Florida	Minimum	
Yankton	South Dakota	Minimum	
California City	California	Low	
Cibola	Arizona	Low	
Northeast Ohio	Ohio	Low	
McRae	Georgia	Low	
Moshannon Valley	Pennsylvania	Low	
Rivers	North Carolina	Low	
Taft	California	Low	Minimum

Source: BOP.

Note: The facilities included in this table confined federal inmates for fiscal years 2002 through 2006.

[a]During the early stages of our work, BOP identified the 27 BOP low and minimum security facilities listed above as those that had individual facility costs for fiscal years 2002 through 2006. However, in the later stages of our work, BOP officials clarified that 8 of the 27 facilities— Allenwood, Beaumont, Butner, Coleman, Forrest City, Lompoc, Petersburg, and Yazoo City— were part of complexes which included medium or high security facilities during some or all of this time period. Therefore, the individual costs for the low and minimum security facilities within these 8 complexes could not be isolated for fiscal years 2002 through 2006.

Several facilities were excluded from our scope because of issues with the availability of cost data for fiscal years 2002 through 2006. We excluded from our analysis those BOP low and minimum security facilities that are co-located with other facilities in a prison complex, since BOP does not isolate the costs of operating individual low and minimum security facilities located on the same campus with high and medium security facilities. Additionally, the Federal Correctional Institutions Miami, Oakdale, and Terminal Island are excluded from the list, as between November 2004 and June 2005 they were converted from medium to low security facilities so they do not have a comparable low security cost history. We did not include the competitive, private contract Reeves County Detention Center III in our study because the facility did not begin receiving federal inmates until 2007 and consequently did not have cost data associated with confining federal inmates. We also excluded the privately operated facility in Eloy, Arizona, as BOP chose to not exercise its option to continue contracting with the private operator at this facility in February 2006 and it became an

Immigration and Customs Enforcement detention facility exclusively. In addition, because the private facilities do not confine female inmates or juveniles, we excluded all female and juvenile BOP facilities from our analysis, assuming that costs might be different depending on these inmate characteristics.

Once we selected facilities, we interviewed BOP procurement officials; budget officials; and officials from the Office of Research and Evaluation, Office of Policy Development and Planning, and Office of Design and Construction. We interviewed accounting, contracting, and operations officials as well as general counsel representing the seven individual prisons of the private firms. Over the course of our review, we used numerous studies as well as data from the Bureau of Justice Statistics to put together a list of variables that might affect a cost comparison analysis. We coordinated with BOP officials from the Office of Research and Evaluation to generate a list of comparable variables for BOP and private facilities. Later, we were told by BOP officials that data for many variables needed for a cost comparison analysis are not collected or maintained for private facilities. Given the current status, we focused our efforts on whether a methodologically sound cost comparison was feasible. Where possible, we gathered and reviewed available data on the facilities and examined whether the data would be suitable for a comparison based, in part, on key factors—such as similar facility characteristics and levels of service—needed to do a methodologically sound comparison as outlined in our 1996 report and Office of Management and Budget (OMB) Circular No. A-76: *Performance of Commercial Activities.*[27] Some studies in our 1996 report, for instance, used a variety of quality measures or outcomes such as safety, incident data, and the extent of programs available to inmates.[28]

In order to determine if the selected BOP and private facilities were sufficiently similar to allow a methodologically sound comparison, we attempted to analyze facility characteristics data. In addition, we analyzed the historical costs to the government including direct (i.e., salaries, supplies, and cost of services) and indirect costs, such as support costs and operating and maintenance costs for buildings, equipment, and utilities and cost-related data between fiscal years 2002 and 2006 associated with operating low and minimum security BOP and private facilities. Additionally, we met with prison experts from Florida State University College of Criminology and Criminal Justice and from the JFA Institute—a nonprofit agency conducting justice and corrections research for effective policy making—to further our understanding about prisons and the complexities of comparing the costs of operating private and public prisons. We reviewed documentation on how BOP evaluates and assesses contract proposals to determine what data are used to make contracting decisions. In addition, we reviewed the Federal Acquisition Regulation to determine what requirements were applicable to BOP with respect to cost data and cost comparisons. Finally, we examined studies done to compare the cost of operating one BOP facility in Taft, California, that is owned by BOP but operated by a private contractor, as well as a study conducted by the National Academy for Public Administration on the feasibility of using low and minimum security BOP facilities to confine federal medium and high security inmates.

To assess the implications a cost comparison has for making decisions on low and minimum security facilities, we met with BOP officials and reviewed BOP population data, population projection data, and data on short-term and long-term facility planning. We also examined BOP documents within the context of OMB requirements on capital planning and space acquisition.[29] In addition, we met with OMB staff responsible for BOP budget review and preparation to discuss BOP efforts to acquire space to confine inmates in low and minimum security facilities in order to determine the information BOP provides OMB on capital investments and how this information is used to inform decisions. We also met with officials from the National Institute of Justice (NIJ) to discuss NIJ's current and past work on prison privatization and NIJ's role within the Department of Justice.

We conducted our work from May 2006 through August 2007 in accordance with generally accepted government auditing standards.

APPENDIX II. COMMENTS FROM THE FEDERAL BUREAU OF PRISONS

U.S. Department of Justice

Federal Bureau of Prisons

Office of the Director   _Washington, DC 20534_

September 17, 2007

Eileen Regan Larence, Director
Homeland Security and Justice Issues
Government Accountability Office
Washington, DC   20548

Dear Ms. Larence:

The Bureau of Prisons (Bureau) appreciates the opportunity to
formally respond to the Government Accountability Office's
(GAO's) draft report entitled <u>Bureau of Prisons Needs Better Data
to Assess Alternatives for Acquiring Low</u> and Minimum Security
Facilities.

The purpose of the report was for the GAO to compare the costs
incurred by the Bureau in operating stand-alone minimum and low
security institutions to what it costs to operate private
facilities or intergovernmental agreement facilities for the same
type of operation. Over the course of this review, the Bureau
provided GAO with considerable amounts of detailed cost
comparison data for Fiscal Years 2002-2006. If the GAO staff
believed that more detailed information from the private sector
was needed, it was our understanding they would obtain the cost
data and its basis from the private sector companies involved.

The current contracts the Bureau has in place were awarded after
full and open competitions were conducted. Given the market, we
believe the agency is paying a fair and reasonable cost for the
services provided by the contractors.

In addition to the above general comments, we have the following
specific comments:

- Page 2, paragraph 2, line 12 - Change the following wording
  from: "Instead, BOP awarded 5 contracts to confine..."
  to "Instead, the BOP conducted a full and open competition
  which resulted in 5 contract awards to confine inmates..."

- Page 5, paragraph 1 - The Bureau does maintain and collect sufficient data on real property owned by the Bureau. However, data is not collected on private contract facilities because the contracts are service contracts with a firm fixed rate for the care of inmates.

- Page 5, paragraph 4 - The Bureau does not collect facility data from private providers because, as stated above, the private providers have service contracts with a firm fixed rate. When private providers submit proposals, the rate includes all the costs to operate a facility. The report does not acknowledge the type of contracts involved (i.e., firm fixed price) and instead infers the Bureau does not collect this data only because it is not required.

- Page 5, paragraph 4 - The Bureau is committed to contracting out the confinement of inmates in low and minimum security facilities, as mandated by Office of Management and Budget (OMB). OMB has repeated the following direction regarding BOP "...take greater advantage of state and local and private sector bedspace to meet its space requirements..." in the FY 2006 and FY 2007 PART updates to the FY 2003 PART Improvement Plan. These updates are based on OMB's PART assessment of BOP's S&E budget. OMB has directed contracting out despite the cost evidence we have provided.

- Page 7, paragraph 1 - The Bureau's mission statement referenced should be reflected as follows:

  The BOP's mission has evolved into protecting society by controlling offenders in the controlled environments of prisons and community-based facilities that are safe, humane, cost-efficient, and appropriately secure and that provide work and other self improvement opportunities to assist offenders in becoming law-abiding citizens.

- There is no reference in the draft report indicating congressional appropriators have been committed to having the Bureau contract out (to the greatest extent possible) for bed space for minimum and low security inmates. This commitment is evidenced by the increases provided in enacted budgets for Contract Confinement, while no funding has been provided for New Prison Construction (for low and minimum security inmates) for over 14 years. Due to the continued increases in the inmate population and lack of bed space, crowding in Bureau facilities remains at high levels. The Bureau has become more and more dependent on the use of private contractors to house certain low and minimum security inmates (criminal aliens in particular).

- The Bureau does not currently have the capacity to house this particular group of inmates (low security criminal aliens) in any Bureau facility, or in the near future (2 to 5 years out). We are clearly dependent on private contractors. If funding were received to construct a low or minimum security facility, it would take at least 3 years before the bed space would become available. Meanwhile, private contractors anticipate the growing inmate populations (federal, state, local) and are continually prepared to expand their operations.

In addition to the above concerns, our response to the recommendation is as follows:

Recommendation: BOP develop a cost-effective way to collect comparative data on low and minimum security facilities confining inmates under Bureau custody and design and conduct methodologically sound analyses that compare the cost of confining inmates in these facilities in order to consider contracting among other alternatives for low and minimum security confinement, consistent with the OMB requirements.

Response: We disagree with this recommendation. The Bureau does not own or operate facilities to house solely criminal aliens and will not be receiving funding to construct such low security facilities. Accordingly, there is no value in developing data collection methods in an attempt to determine the costs of housing this particular group of inmates in a Bureau facility.

The Bureau has been able to determine what it actually costs to contract out this particular population to private contractors via open competition. In addition, we are able to determine what is fair and reasonable with regard to pricing through the use of firm fixed price contracts.

We do not see the value of requiring existing private contractors to provide specific comparable data to aid in a cost comparison. This requirement would have the potential to increase current contract costs at a time when the Bureau is facing serious budget constraints.

We believe the independent review by the Center for Naval Analysis, which compared the operational cost of the contractor-operated facility in Taft, California, with other low security BOP facilities, meets the intent of the recommendation.

If you have any questions regarding this response, please contact VaNessa P. Adams, Senior Deputy Assistant Director, Program Review Division, at (202) 616-2099.

Sincerely,

Harley G. Lappin
Director

cc: Richard Theis, Assistant Director
      Audit Liaison Group, JMD

End Notes

[1] IGAs are agreements between BOP and state and local governments to confine BOP inmates in state and local prison facilities.

[2] Pub. L. No. 109-108, 119 Stat. 2290 (2005).

[3] BOP awarded these five contracts on January 17, 2007.

[4] According to BOP, prison programs include services and classes that provide productive use-of-time activities and facilitate the successful reintegration of inmates into society, consistent with community expectations and standards.

[5] Because the private facilities we selected for our review do not confine female inmates or juveniles, we excluded all female and juvenile BOP facilities from our analysis.

[6] GAO, *Private and Public Prisons: Studies Comparing Operational Costs and/or Quality of Service,* GAO/GGD-96-158 (Washington, D.C.: Aug. 16, 1996).

[7] Office of Management and Budget, Executive Office of the President, OMB Circular No. A-11, Part 7, *Capital Programming Guide* (2006). A benefit-cost analysis is a systematic quantitative method of weighing the costs associated with implementing or operating an alternative against any benefits expected from the alternative. A cost-effectiveness analysis is a systematic quantitative method for comparing the cost of alternatives when such alternatives achieve the same benefits. According to OMB, it is a less comprehensive technique than a benefit-cost analysis, but can be appropriate for ranking alternatives when the benefits of competing alternatives are the same. An alternative is considered cost-effective when it is determined to have the lowest cost for a given amount of benefit.

[8] Nelson, Julianne, *Competition in Corrections: Comparing Public and Private Sector Operations*, the Center for Naval Analysis Corporation (Virginia: December 2005).

[9] According to BOP, a pretrial inmate is a person who is legally detained but for whom BOP has not received notification of conviction. Thus, pretrial inmates include persons awaiting trial, being tried, or awaiting a verdict.

[10] GAO/GGD-96-158. While exploring how we would conduct a comparison for this chapter, we took into account factors outlined in our 1996 report on studies that compared the cost of private and public prisons to ensure that our comparison would be methodologically sound and generalizeable to federal low and minimum security facilities nationwide regardless of the operator. In addition to the factors mentioned above, our 1996 report stated that a variety of other factors could affect a cost comparison of prison facilities such as cost-of-living and economic differences among the nation's geographic regions.

[11] Studies we reviewed identified misconduct incidences as inmate-on-inmate assaults, staffon-inmate assaults, inmate-on-staff assaults, drug and contraband violations, sexual assaults, homicides, suicides, and escapes from the facility.

[12] SENTRY is BOP's online, real-time database system, used primarily for maintaining information about federal inmates including sentencing, work assignments, admission/release status, and other special assignments for monitoring inmate status. According to contracting requirements, each private contractor is required to provide and maintain hardware and software to access SENTRY.

[13] Although we reviewed the available data maintained by BOP, for the purposes of this chapter, we did not assess the contractor's compliance with BOP's data entry requirements to confirm whether the private sector data

were consistent with BOP's misconduct categories because BOP's monitoring and oversight of its contracts was beyond the scope of our review.

[14] Firm-fixed price contracts provide for a price that is not subject to any adjustment on the basis of the contractor's cost experience in performing the contract. This contract type places upon the contractor maximum risk and full responsibility for all costs and resulting profit or loss.

[15] Federal Acquisition Regulation, 48 C.F.R. §§ 15.305(a)(1), 15.403-1(c) (2006).

[16] GAO, *Federal Real Property: Reliance on Costly Leasing to Meet New Space Needs Is an Ongoing Problem*, GAO-06-136T (Washington, D.C.: Oct. 6, 2005), 5-8.

[17] The cost of construction was compared to the options of (1) lease-purchases in which payments are spread out over time and ownership of the asset is eventually transferred to the government, and (2) operating leases in which periodic lease payments are made over the specified length of the lease.

[18] Office of Management and Budget, Executive Office of the President, OMB Circular No. A-11, Part 7, *Capital Programming Guide* (2006).

[19] Office of Management and Budget, Executive Office of the President, OMB Circular No. A-94, *Guidelines and Discount Rates for Benefit-Cost Analysis of Federal Programs* (1992).

[20] According to BOP, long-term criminal aliens are those criminal aliens confined in low and minimum security facilities for more than 45 days.

[21] Nelson (2005).

[22] GAO-06-136T.

[23] Pub. L. No. 109-108, 119 Stat. 2290 (2005).

[24] IGAs are agreements between BOP and state and local governments to confine BOP inmates in state and local prison facilities.

[25] Three of the five contracts were awarded to the private firms that operated the former IGA facilities for the local governments. The fourth contract was awarded directly to the local government that owns the facility, Reeves County. BOP also awarded a fifth contract to a new contractor in Pine Prairie, Louisiana.

[26] According to BOP, prison programs include services and classes that provide productive use-of-time activities and facilitate the successful reintegration of inmates into society, consistent with community expectations and standards.

[27] GAO/GGD-96-158 and Office of Management and Budget, Executive Office of the President, OMB Circular No. A-76, *Performance of Commercial Activities* (2003).

[28] While we attempted to collect data to compare the level of service provided, we did not attempt to assess BOP's monitoring and oversight of its contracts as they relate to the contractor's performance and quality of service because doing so was beyond the scope of our review.

[29] Office of Management and Budget, Executive Office of the President, OMB Circular No. A-11, Part 7, *Capital Programming Guide* (2006).

In: Prison Growth and Economic Impact
Editor: Lewis C. Sawyer

ISBN: 978-1-61728-864-7
© 2010 Nova Science Publishers, Inc.

Chapter 5

COST, PERFORMANCE STUDIES LOOK AT PRISON PRIVATIZATION[*]

Gerry Gaes

Seven percent of the 1.5 million prisoners in the United States are held in privately operated prisons, according to the most recent survey of prisons published by the Bureau of Justice Statistics.[1] At midyear 2006, there were 84,867 State inmates and 27,108 Federal inmates in privately operated prisons—a 10-percent increase over the previous year.

The overall percentage of adults in private prisons is relatively small, but the actual impact for some States may be much greater. An article in *The New Mexican,* for example, suggested that New Mexico was overpaying millions of dollars to private providers that were housing more than 40 percent of the State's inmate population.[2]

Thus, it is vital that policymakers have the best possible cost and quality information when they are making decisions regarding privatizing prisons in their jurisdiction. But what criteria should prison administrators and policymakers use when making cost and quality evaluations?

To help answer these questions, the National Institute of Justice (NIJ) assembled researchers, prison officials, private service providers, and proponents and opponents of prison privatization on March 28, 2007, to discuss this complicated and often controversial issue. At the core of the meeting was a rare occurrence: two cost and performance analyses of the same four prisons— one privately operated and three publicly operated—with different findings. The two reports are referred to in this article as the "Taft studies."[3]

One of the Taft studies was conducted by Doug McDonald, Ph.D., principal associate with Abt Associates Inc. (referred to as the "Abt report").[4] The other study, funded by the Bureau of Prisons (BOP), had two components: a performance or quality analysis conducted by Scott Camp, Ph.D., a senior research analyst in BOP's Office of Research and Evaluation,[5]

---

[*] This is an edited, reformatted and augmented version of a National Institute of Justice publication dated March 2008.

and a cost analysis conducted by Julianne Nelson, Ph.D., an economist with the Center for Naval Analyses (referred to collectively as the "BOP report").[6]

The Taft studies offer the research and public policy communities a rare opportunity to consider the different approaches that were used, why the results were different, and how this can inform not only the prison privatization debate, but in many ways, the government outsourcing, or privatization, issue in general.

MAKING PRISON PRIVATIZATION DECISIONS

Although every jurisdiction has its own economic and managerial idiosyncrasies, lessons learned from the Taft studies and the NIJ meeting may help administrators and public policy analysts avoid mistakes that could lead to higher taxpayer costs and possible dire consequences of poor performance. These lessons include:

- Cost comparisons are deceivingly complex, and great care should be taken when comparing the costs of privately and publicly operated prisons.
- Special care should be given to an analysis of overhead costs.
- A uniform method of comparing publicly and privately operated prisons on the basis of audits should be developed.
- Quantitative measures of prison performance, such as serious misconduct and drug use, should be incorporated in any analysis.
- Future analytical methods could allow simultaneous cost and quality comparisons.

One key lesson learned from the Taft privatization studies is that cost comparisons are not as simple as might be presumed.

Someone not familiar with the literature on prison privatization might assume that cost comparisons are accomplished without controversy or ambiguity. One key lesson learned from the Taft privatization studies is that comparisons are not as simple as might be presumed.

Consider, for example, per diem (or daily) costs. The chart below lists the per diem costs, in dollars, as analyzed by the Abt and BOP researchers for the three publicly operated prisons and Taft, the privately operated facility, for fiscal years 1999–2002.

According to the Abt analysis, the Taft facility was cheaper to run, every year, than the three publicly operated facilities. In 2002, for example, Abt reports that the average cost of the three public facilities was 14.8 percent higher than Taft.

The BOP analysis, however, presented a much different picture. According to the BOP researchers, the average cost of the public facilities in 2002 was only 2.2 percent higher than Taft.

Why were the Abt and BOP cost analyses so dramatically different? And, importantly, what policy implications does this have?

There are two primary reasons why the cost analyses were different: (1) the way inmate population sizes were treated, and (2) what was included in overhead costs.

With respect to inmate populations, Taft had on average approximately 300 more inmates each year than the three publicly operated prisons throughout the study period. Therefore, the private service provider for Taft benefited from economies of scale that reduced average costs. To adjust for such economies of scale, the BOP researchers made adjustments to the expenditures.

Average Per Diem Costs Per Inmate (in Dollars) for FY 1999–2002

	FY 1999		FY 2000		FY 2001		FY 2002	
	Abt	BOP	Abt	BOP	Abt	BOP	Abt	BOP
Publicly operated prison								
Elkton	$39.72	$35.24	$39.77	$34.84	$44.75	$36.79	$46.38	$40.71
Forrest City	39.46	35.29	39.84	35.28	41.65	37.36	43.61	38.87
Yazoo City	41.46	36.84	40.05	34.92	43.65	37.29	42.15	38.87
Privately operated prison								
Taft	33.82	34.42	33.25	33.21	36.88	37.04	38.37	38.62

HOW DID WE GET THE BENEFIT OF TWO STUDIES?

Due to the sheer expense of conducting evaluation studies, it is a rare occurrence to have competing research analyses like those discussed in this article. To understand how this happened, some historical perspective is in order.

In 1996, the U.S. House of Representatives directed the U.S. Bureau of Prisons (BOP) to perform a 5-year prison privatization demonstration project of the low- and minimum-security prisons in Taft, California. BOP awarded a 10-year contract to the Geo Group (formerly Wackenhut Corrections Corporation), which operated the facilities from 1997 to 2007. The contract was then recompeted, and a new contract to run the Taft prisons was awarded to Management and Training Corporation.

Although the U.S. Congress did not request a formal evaluation of the Taft facilities, BOP leadership decided that an evaluation of cost and quality would help them make better decisions regarding privatization. BOP funded the National Institute of Justice to secure proposals for an evaluation of Taft and similar BOP facilities. Abt Associates won that competition and conducted the study. BOP's Office of Research conducted its own independent study in order to understand how to conduct this new type of research.

Abt, in its analysis, however, did not consider economies of scale, choosing, instead, to use the actual average per diem amount that BOP paid the Taft contractor. In other words, BOP estimated what expenditures would have existed for identically sized prisons, and Abt based its analysis on actual expenditures.

McDonald, the researcher who performed the Abt analysis, argues that his approach—using actual costs that BOP paid to have a private contractor operate Taft—yields a more telling comparison. Although the BOP researchers disagree, this leads to one of the primary points of this article, which is to remind policymakers and others interested in the prison privatization issue that making cost comparisons is not a simple matter of arithmetic.

WHAT SHOULD BE INCLUDED IN OVERHEAD COSTS?

Prison costs comprise:

- Direct operations costs, such as staff salaries, inmate food, medical care, and other services.
- Indirect (overhead) costs, such as regional and central office supervision, computer services, planning, and budget development.

With respect to overhead costs, different approaches by the two research groups led to different findings. Basing its analysis on the extent to which the government actually provided resources to support the Taft operation, Abt concluded that only a bare minimum of support was provided. Therefore, the Abt analysis reported a 100-percent savings of indirect, overhead costs for Taft during the time period in the study. BOP, on the other hand, assumed that most overhead costs (planning, auditing, and other central and regional operations) could continue to be incurred by the government, even if a private company was operating the prison. Therefore, the BOP researchers applied a 10–12 percent overhead rate (the average for BOP prisons during the 1998–2002 Taft study period), calculating privatization savings of 35 percent of overhead for that 5-year period. Here again, BOP estimated the costs that the government would have incurred by central administration, and Abt presented only what was reported.

One can anticipate that underlying assumptions regarding overhead costs will have significant implications for bottom-line estimations of costs and savings. As previously discussed, the assumptions made by Abt led to a finding of much less overhead for the Taft private provider, suggesting that the government could save a great deal of money by privatizing prisons. The assumptions underlying the BOP analysis were different, however, and led to a less sanguine conclusion. Unless policymakers are mindful of these subtleties in basic assumptions, they are not likely to delve so deeply—or even be presented with this level of detail—when considering taxpayer benefits of prison privatization.

At the March 2007 NIJ meeting, Mark Cohen, Ph.D., an economist at Vanderbilt University, presented data showing that privately operated (and sometimes privately financed) prison systems have lower costs over time than publicly operated prison systems. Although this may be true as an overall average, it is not necessarily true for a particular jurisdiction. Any prison administrator or other policymaker considering privatization would be well advised to consider the specific analytic assumptions underlying the studies.

PERFORMANCE: CONTRACT COMPLIANCE VS. AUDITING

Performance is a vital part of any prison privatization discussion. In many jurisdictions, a truly accurate comparison of privately versus publicly operated prisons is hampered by different performance yardsticks. A privately operated prison, such as Taft, has a contract; performance, therefore, can be measured by compliance with specific contract terms (which, of course, can vary from contract to contract). BOP-operated prisons, on the other hand, measure performance through an auditing procedure called program review.

There are two primary reasons why the cost analyses were different: (1) the way inmate population sizes were treated, and (2) what was included in overhead costs.

Because no method existed for measuring publicly and privately operated prisons on many dimensions for performance, both of the Taft studies have limitations. Until a common yardstick exists, any analysis will not be as rich as it could be. Nonetheless, it is important to make whatever performance analyses are possible—in areas such as safety, medical care, programming, and rehabilitation services—when considering prison privatization.

In the Taft comparison studies, the Abt researchers first looked at 19 functional areas—including food services, health care, safety, and security—that were specified in the Taft private-service provider contract. The contract had a scoring system, upon which possible bonuses and possible deductions would be based:

- Unsatisfactory = 0
- Marginal = 1
- Fair = 2
- Good = 3
- Excellent = 4
- Outstanding = 5

Over the first 5 years of its contract (1997– 2001), the Taft private provider received a rating of 2.5; during the 2002–2004 contract period, the average rating was 2.8, which resulted in a possible award fee of nearly 50 percent of the amount allocated.

In their performance analyses, both the BOP and the Abt researchers also looked at misconduct, comparing assaults at the Taft facility to assaults at 20 publicly operated low-security prisons. Both reports found that the Taft assault rate was lower than the average of the 20 prisons; with respect to the four facilities in the Taft studies, Elkton had an assault rate similar to what would have been expected based on its inmate composition; Forrest City, Yazoo City, and Taft had lower than expected assault rates (Yazoo City was the lowest).[7]

The researchers also considered drug use, escapes, inmate grievances, and access to medical care in their performance analyses. During the study period, Taft had a very high drug-use rate compared to the 20 BOP-operated low-security prisons. Abt noted two escapes at Taft and only two in the BOP prisons; the BOP researchers reported the same two Taft escapes, but also noted a disturbance at Taft that involved 1,000 inmates who refused to return to their cells for the 10 p.m. count.

With respect to access to medical care, the researchers found that the Taft inmates were more likely to see a physician than inmates in the 20 BOP-operated prisons.

DESPITE DIFFERENCES, LESSONS LEARNED

Despite differences in the approaches and assumptions used by Abt and BOP in the Taft studies, these reports represent two of the best prison privatization analyses performed so far. Administrators, policy analysts, and researchers looking at prison privatization and the larger public policy issue of government outsourcing would benefit from a closer consideration of the full reports.

ABOUT THE AUTHOR

Gerry Gaes has 27 years of criminal justice experience. From 1988 to 2002, he served as director of research at the Bureau of Prisons (BOP); during that time, he worked on an interim BOP report concerning the Taft privatization study that is discussed in this article. Gaes was a visiting scientist with the National Institute of Justice from 2002 to 2007. His other research interests include the simulation of criminal justice processes, the criminogenic effect of prisons, and inmate gangs.

End Notes

[1] Sabol, W.B., T.D. Minton, and P.M. Harrison, *Prison and Jail Inmates at Midyear 2006,* Bureau of Justice Statistics, U.S. Department of Justice, 2007, available at www.ojp.usdoj. gov/bjs/pub/pdf/pjim06.pdf.

[2] Terrell, S. "Audit: N.M. Private-Prison Costs Soar," *New Mexican,* May 24, 2007, available at www.freenewmexican.com/news/61780. html (accessed January 15, 2008).

[3] The four prisons in the Taft studies are low- and minimum-security facilities constructed by BOP during the same period. The prison operated by the private company (through a contract with BOP) is in Taft, California. The three publicly operated prisons are in Elkton, Ohio; Forrest City, Arkansas; and Yazoo City, Mississippi.

[4] McDonald, D.C., and K. Carlson, *Contracting for Imprisonment in the Federal Prison System: Cost and Performance of the Privately Operated Taft Correctional Institution,* final report submitted to the National Institute of Justice, November 2005 (NCJ 211990), available at www.ncjrs. gov/pdffiles1/nij/grants 1 990.pdf.

[5] Camp, S.D., and D.M. Daggett, *Evaluation of the Taft Demonstration Project: Performance of a Private-Sector Prison and the BOP,* Washington, DC: Federal Bureau of Prisons, October 2005, available at www.bop.gov/ news/research_projects/published_reports/ pub_vs_priv/orelappin2005. pdf.

[6] Nelson, J., *Competition in Corrections: Comparing Public and Private Sector Operations,* Alexandria, VA: The CNA Corporation, December 2005, available at www.bop.gov/news/research_projects/ published_reports/pub_vs_priv/cnanelson .pdf.

[7] In any analysis of prison misconduct, it is important to account for the composition of the inmate population (with respect to risk of misconduct) in addition to the security level of the prisons. An expected level of misconduct takes this into account; an average (actual) level does not take inmate composition into account.

INDEX

A

academics, 5
accountability, 89, 99
accounting, 9, 16, 36, 55, 125
acquisitions, 118
adjustment, 91, 131
administrators, ix, 15, 17, 25, 133, 134
advertisements, 10
age, 5, 7, 20, 52, 74, 75, 116
alcohol, 19, 30
alternatives, 15, 26, 108, 112, 113, 115, 118, 119, 120, 121, 122, 130
ambiguity, 134
annual rate, 36
architects, 15, 47, 53
arithmetic, 52, 135
arrest, vii, 1
assault, 75, 76, 137
assessment, 116
assets, 32, 108, 112, 115, 118, 121
assumptions, 24, 90, 91, 136, 137
asthma, 20
Attorney General, 25, 31, 85, 89, 99, 113, 120
auditing, 88, 100, 111, 126, 136
authority, vii, viii, 2, 7, 14, 24, 35, 50, 51, 53, 57
availability, 86, 92, 124
average costs, 135

B

background, 3, 27, 98
background information, 98
bargaining, 10
behavior, 112, 118
bipolar disorder, 20
bonds, 5, 13, 14, 24
budget cuts, 13

C

candidates, 22
capital punishment, 5
carrier, 25
cell, 56, 89, 114
children, 5
citizenship, 116
classes, 130, 131
cleaning, 106
clusters, 11
cocaine, 43
collective bargaining, viii, 2, 3, 10
college students, 15
communication, 98
Communications Act of 1934, 25
community, 12, 14, 15, 18, 20, 25, 29, 30, 36, 46, 54, 55, 89, 114, 130, 131
comparative costs, 110
compensation, 10
competition, 15, 99, 113, 117, 121, 135
competitors, 20
compliance, 98, 130, 136
components, ix, 91, 133
composition, 137, 138
concentration, 11
concrete, 94, 95
confidence, 96
confinement, 5, 13, 27, 51, 53, 54, 56, 87, 108, 109, 110, 112, 113, 114, 115, 118, 119, 120, 122
conflict, 15
congressional budget, 85, 87, 89, 90, 97, 99
consensus, 18
consulting, 17
consumer price index, 95
contingency, 32
control, viii, 85, 86, 87, 88, 96, 97, 99, 100, 116
conversion, 56

conviction, vii, 1, 51, 112, 116, 130
copper, 94
corporations, 4, 11
cost saving, 4, 17
counsel, 125
counseling, 14, 19, 20
country of origin, 49
covering, 23, 110, 123
CPC, 87, 90, 106
credit, 9, 11, 14, 22
credit rating, 14
crime, 2, 5, 6, 7, 24, 84
criminal justice system, vii, 1, 3
criminals, 7
criticism, 11
crowding out, 2
customers, 18

D

data collection, 50, 54, 113, 121
data set, 12
database, 56, 116, 130
death, 6
deaths, 15
debt, 13, 14, 18, 24
decision makers, 99, 113, 119, 121, 122
decision making, 119
decision-making process, 90
decisions, ix, 19, 26, 87, 96, 99, 108, 110, 111, 112,
    113, 115, 118, 119, 121, 122, 125, 133, 135
definition, 54, 83
delivery, 89, 99, 100, 106
demographics, 12
Department of Agriculture, 30
Department of Commerce, 106
Department of Defense, 22, 50
Department of Energy, 98, 100, 106
depression, 20
designers, 15
detainees, 4, 22, 48, 49
detection, 114
detention, 5, 8, 19, 20, 27, 53, 114, 125
diabetes, 20
diminishing returns, 2, 5
discipline, 5
disclosure, 3
discrimination, 5
distribution, viii, 2
draft, 120
drug offense, 7, 41, 42, 43
drug treatment, 24, 30
drug use, 134, 137

drugs, 20, 43
duration, 94, 98, 100

E

earnings, 5, 12, 16, 18, 19, 22, 23, 32, 33, 34
economic change, 22
economic development, 12, 21, 22, 23, 24
economic downturn, 18
economies of scale, 135
educational programs, 6, 108
efficient resource allocation, 119
elephants, 5
employees, 9, 10, 11, 18, 20, 21, 23, 29
employment, 13, 21, 22, 23, 29, 86, 88
energy, 23
entrepreneurs, 5
environment, 92, 94
EPA, 87, 92, 94
estimating, 90, 95, 96
ethics, 18
execution, 5, 97
exercise, 11, 92, 124
expenditures, 135

F

farms, 30, 50, 53, 54
FCC, 25
Federal Communications Commission, 21, 25
federal courts, 7
federal funds, 3
federal role, 2
feet, 56
female prisoners, 47, 61, 62, 66, 67, 68
females, 37, 114
fencing, 89, 114
finance, 13, 14, 21, 27
financial distress, 4
financing, 4, 13, 14, 21, 24, 26
firms, 4, 5, 12, 14, 15, 16, 18, 20, 30, 109
flexibility, 120, 121
floating, 5
focusing, 43
food, vii, 1, 15, 20, 22, 106, 136, 137
forecasting, 98
foreign nationals, 112, 116
funding, viii, 2, 3, 5, 13, 14, 26, 85, 86, 87, 88, 89,
    90, 91, 92, 93, 94, 95, 96, 97, 99, 101, 102, 106,
    113, 121
funds, 8, 15, 90, 92, 93, 94, 96, 97, 99, 102, 118, 121
furniture, 21

G

gangs, 138
gender, 43, 51, 52, 110, 123
goals, 119
government budget, 18
grants, 6, 25, 138
groups, 10, 15, 48, 52, 55, 136
growth rate, 8, 30, 36, 48
guidance, viii, 85, 87, 88, 90, 91, 95, 96, 97, 98, 99, 100, 108, 109, 119
guidelines, 115

H

health, vii, 1, 3, 4, 7, 10, 14, 18, 19, 20, 22, 26, 112, 116, 137
health care, vii, 1, 3, 4, 7, 10, 14, 18, 20, 112, 116, 137
health care professionals, 112, 116
health problems, 7
health services, 19, 20
heat, 11
height, 12
high school, 9
higher education, viii, 2, 3, 13, 22
hiring, 4, 22
hospitals, 30, 50, 54, 112, 115
host, 23
housing, viii, ix, 3, 7, 12, 13, 15, 19, 23, 24, 27, 30, 85, 89, 92, 114, 133

I

ICC, 56
identification, 123
illegal aliens, 7
immigrants, 5, 8, 13, 15, 17, 19
immigration, 11, 30, 51
implementation, 98
imprisonment, 3, 4, 5, 7, 8, 28, 36, 41, 44, 46, 47, 52, 70
incarceration, vii, viii, 1, 2, 3, 5, 7, 11, 15, 24, 26, 28, 31, 45, 53, 54
incentives, 5, 21
income, viii, 2, 18
income inequality, viii, 2
indication, 12, 97
indicators, 12, 22, 88, 100
industry, vii, viii, 1, 4, 9, 10, 13, 15, 16, 17, 18, 21, 29, 85, 86, 88, 89, 94, 98, 100
inflation, 7, 17, 27, 86, 88, 90, 91, 94, 100
infrastructure, 21, 56

INS, 48
instability, 5
institutions, vii, 1, 3, 4, 5, 6, 11, 12, 13, 16, 17, 18, 19, 20, 21, 30, 47, 54, 55, 56, 89, 106, 114
instruments, 50
interview, 34
investment, 17, 18, 22, 113, 119, 121, 122
investors, 4, 14, 16, 19

J

job skills, 86, 88, 89, 96
job training, 24, 116
jobs, vii, 1, 5, 22, 23, 29
judgment, 90
judiciary, 25
Judiciary Committee, 3, 24, 25
justice, 5, 15, 20, 24, 27, 29, 31, 32, 111, 125, 138
juvenile justice, 14
juveniles, 14, 17, 30, 53, 114, 125, 130

L

labor, 6, 9, 10, 15, 17, 89, 95
labor force, 9, 10
landscape, 5
law enforcement, 6, 25, 53
laws, vii, viii, 1, 2, 3, 4, 7, 13, 24, 26, 87, 100, 107, 110, 123
layoffs, 25
leadership, 135
lease payments, 131
legislation, viii, 2, 3, 10
lifetime, 5
line, 136
links, 20
local government, 2, 6, 9, 13, 14, 15, 20, 25, 54, 109, 121, 130, 131
logging, 6

M

maintenance, viii, 85, 87, 106, 125
males, 37, 44, 56, 70
management, viii, 5, 14, 17, 20, 85, 86, 88, 93, 96, 97, 98, 100, 109, 110, 118, 119, 123
manslaughter, 76, 77
manufacturing, vii, 1, 9
mapping, 30
market, 19, 20, 21, 86, 88, 95
marketing, 20
meals, 20
measures, 11, 19, 31, 47, 53, 117, 125, 134

media, 28
median, 9
medical care, 7, 20, 136, 137
men, 7, 36, 41, 47
mental health, 19
mental illness, 20, 24
military, 20, 22, 24, 30, 45, 46, 50, 112, 118, 121
mining, 6
minorities, 10
missions, 114
momentum, 17
money, viii, 17, 24, 107, 109, 136
moratorium, 94, 102
mortality, 6
mortality rate, 6
movement, 6, 15, 56
murder, 77
music, 21

N

nation, 3, 5, 7, 10, 12, 18, 20, 21, 31, 130
national security, 23
natural resources, 7
needy, 3

O

objectives, 88, 100
obligation, 13
offenders, viii, 2, 5, 6, 7, 13, 20, 22, 24, 25, 36, 37,
    38, 41, 42, 43, 54, 55, 56, 84, 85, 87, 89, 114
Office of Management and Budget, 87, 100, 106,
    108, 109, 120, 123, 125, 130, 131
oil, 86, 88, 94
operator, 54, 124, 130
order, 43, 76, 77, 111, 113, 116, 120, 121, 122, 125,
    126, 135
outsourcing, ix, 134, 138
oversight, 3, 17, 18, 87, 93, 97, 98, 131
overtime, 9
ownership, 118, 131

P

parents, 5
parole, vii, 1, 2, 6, 7, 9, 10, 20, 25, 26, 30, 37, 40, 57
peers, 5, 10
penalties, 5, 14
per capita income, 23
permit, 25
planning, 86, 87, 88, 90, 95, 100, 111, 118, 120, 125,
    136

police, 23
policy making, 111, 125
poor, 22, 134
poor performance, 134
population group, 38, 42, 75
population size, 134, 137
poverty, viii, 2, 5, 22, 23
power, 14, 100, 106
president, 18, 33
prevention, 24
price competition, 117
prices, 86, 88, 94, 112, 117
private firms, viii, 2, 3, 4, 17, 18, 26, 32, 107, 109,
    111, 120, 123, 125, 131
private sector, 14, 17, 18, 20, 21, 109, 119, 121, 122,
    130
privatization, ix, 15, 17, 108, 109, 111, 112, 120,
    122, 126, 133, 134, 135, 136, 137, 138
probability, 13
probation officers, 9
profit, 4, 131
profits, 4, 15
program, 3, 13, 21, 25, 50, 89, 99, 116, 117, 136
programming, 56, 116, 137
progress reports, 98
property taxes, 23
public investment, vii, 2
public policy, ix, 134, 138
public safety, 3, 10, 11, 21, 25
public sector, viii, 2, 10
punishment, 5, 6, 9, 57

Q

quality of service, 108, 109, 111, 112, 115, 116, 117,
    122, 131
questioning, 5

R

race, 43, 51, 52, 55
radio, 30
range, 5, 19, 24, 97
RDP, 30
real estate, 19, 32
reason, 12
recession, vii, viii, 1, 2, 3, 21, 22
recidivism, vii, viii, 1, 2, 3, 8, 13, 25, 26, 27
recidivism rate, 8
recruiting, 10
reforms, 17
region, 90, 94
regulation, 25, 117

rehabilitation, vii, 1, 5, 9, 19, 137
reliability, 117
resources, 27, 29, 95, 96, 102, 119, 136
retirement, 9
retribution, 5
returns, 112, 116
revenue, 5, 13, 14, 24, 31
risk, 18, 26, 99, 112, 118, 131, 138
rural areas, vii, 1, 11, 12, 22, 30
rural development, viii, 2
rural population, 12, 30

S

safety, 108, 109, 112, 116, 125, 137
sanctions, 57
savings, 17, 136
scaling, 13
scheduling, 98
schizophrenia, 20
school, 13, 15, 112, 115
search, 4
selecting, 86, 88, 91, 94, 108, 112, 113, 117, 119, 121, 123
self-improvement, 89, 96, 114
sentencing, vii, 1, 2, 3, 6, 7, 25, 26, 130
service provider, ix, 20, 25, 133, 135, 137
sexual assaults, 130
shortage, 10
simulation, 138
skills, 112, 116
social change, 5
spectrum, 2
speech, 11, 24
speed, 90
staffing, 8, 14, 23, 108, 111
stakeholders, 86, 88, 89, 91, 96, 97, 99, 106
standards, 18, 88, 100, 111, 126, 130, 131
state laws, 27
state oversight, 17
statistics, 29, 50
steel, 86, 88, 94
stigma, 22, 23
strain, 119
strategies, 25
stress, viii, 2
substance abuse, 13, 57
supervision, 25, 36, 84, 114, 136
supervisors, vii, 1, 9
supply, 27
support services, 56
surveillance, 20

T

team members, 98
telephone, 21, 24, 25
temporary jobs, 22
tension, 24
territory, 51
terrorism, 33
theft, 75, 76
torture, 6
total revenue, 18
tracking, 22, 98, 117
tracks, 8
trade, 10, 116
trade-off, 116
training, 6, 9, 50, 54, 86, 88, 89, 96
transparency, 89, 99
transport, 5
transportation, 4, 14
trial, 55, 130
tribes, 25
turnover, 10, 112, 116

U

uncertainty, 18
unemployment, 13, 22, 23
unemployment rate, 22
uniform, 25, 134
unions, 9, 10, 11, 15
urban areas, 3, 12, 15

V

variables, 125
variance, 86, 88, 95
violence, 112, 118
violent crime, 5, 9, 14, 25
vocational training, 13, 116
voters, 7, 13, 14

W

wages, 9, 23
war, 30
warrants, 23
weapons, 76
women, 10, 36, 37, 47
workers, vii, viii, 1, 2, 3, 9, 10, 17, 21, 22, 29
worry, 15